Edexcel GCE History

From Kaiser to Führer: Germany, 1900–45

Martin Collier

Series editors: Martin Collier   Rosemary Rees

Unit 3 Student Book

A PEARSON COMPANY

Published by Pearson Education Limited, a company incorporated in England and Wales, having its registered office at Edinburgh Gate,
Harlow, Essex, CM20 2JE. Registered company number: 872828
www.pearsonschoolsandfecolleges.co.uk

Edexcel is a registered trade mark of Edexcel Limited

Text © Pearson Education Limited 2009

First published 2009

12 11 10 09
10 9 8 7 6 5 4 3 2

British Library Cataloguing in Publication Data
A catalogue record for this book is available from the British Library

ISBN 978 0 435308 05 6

Edited by Florence Production Ltd, Stoodleigh, Devon
Designed by Florence Production Ltd, Stoodleigh, Devon
Typeset by Florence Production Ltd, Stoodleigh, Devon
Produced by Florence Production Ltd, Stoodleigh, Devon
Original illustrations © Pearson Education Limited 2009
Illustrated by Florence Production Ltd, Stoodleigh, Devon
Cover illustration: German helmet © Alamy/Stockbyte;
    German flag © Getty Images/Photo Disc
Printed in China (SWTC/02)

Dedication
To Alli

Disclaimer
This material has been published on behalf of Edexcel and offers high-quality support for the delivery of Edexcel qualifications.
This does not mean that the material is essential to achieve any Edexcel qualification, nor does it mean that it is the only suitable material available to support any Edexcel qualification. Edexcel material will not be used verbatim in setting any Edexcel examination or assessment. Any resource lists produced by Edexcel shall include this and other appropriate resources.
Copies of official specifications for all Edexcel qualifications may be found on the Edexcel website: www.edexcel.com

Contents

Acknowledgements

The author and publisher would like to thank the following individuals and organisations for permission to reproduce the following material:

Photographs

Alamy Images/INTERFOTO, pp. 115, 136; Alamy Images/Mary Evans Picture Library, pp. 2, 51; Alamy/Stockbyte, cover; The Bridgeman Art Library/Galerie Neue Meister, Dresden, Germany/© DACS/© Staatliche Kunstsammlungen Dresden, p. 50; Getty Images/Hulton Archive, pp. 94, 106; Getty Images/PhotoDisc, cover; Randall Bytwerk/http://www.calvin.edu/cas/gpa/, pp. 79, 114, 199; Staatsarchiv, Munich, p. 155.

Written sources

p. 27, Source A and p. 38, Source F: Fritz Fischer, *Germany's Aims In The First World War*. Copyright © 1961 by Droste Verlag and Druckerei GmbH, Dusseldorf. English Translation copyright © 1967 by W.W. Norton and Company, Inc. Used by permission of W.W. Norton and Company, Inc.; p. 35, Source B, p. 38, Source G and p. 229, Source 1: Niall Ferguson, *The Pity of War*, 1998, London: Penguin Books Ltd, copyright © Niall Ferguson, 1998. Reproduced by permission of Penguin Books Ltd; p. 35, Source C, p. 43, Source P and p. 229, Source 2: James Joll, *The Origins of the First World War* (Origins of Modern War) Longman, 10 Sept 1984. Used by permission of Pearson Education; p. 39, Source H and p. 47, Source W: David Blackbourn, *The Blackwell Classic Histories of Europe History of Germany 1780-1918: The Long Nineteenth Century* (Second edition), 2003, Blackwell Press; p. 39, Source I and p. 43, Source O: John Röhl, 'Germany', in Keith Wilson (ed.) *Decisions for War*, Palgrave Macmillan, May 1995; p. 40, Source J: Originally published by Geschichte in Wissenschaft und Unterrich, 1964; p. 40, Source K: William Young, *German Diplomatic Relations 1871–1945: The Wilhelmstrasse and the Formulation of Foreign Policy*, iUniverse, Inc., 4 September 2006; p. 41, Source L: Michael Brock, *The Coming of the First World War* (Clarendon Paperbacks) edited by R.J. Evans and Hartmut Pogge von Strandmann, Clarendon Press, New edition 27 Sept 1990. Used by permission of Oxford University Press; p. 42, Source M: John Röhl, *The Kaiser and his Court: Wilhelm II and the Government of Germany*, Cambridge University Press, Illustrated edition, 10 Nov 1994; p. 42, Source N: Hew Strachan, *The First World War: To Arms*, OUP, 2001. Used by permission of Oxford University Press; p. 44, Source Q: Volker Berghahn, *Germany and the Approach of War in 1914 (The Making of the Twentieth Century)*, Palgrave Macmillan, Dec 1973; p. 44, Source R: Norman Stone, *Europe Transformed, 1878–1919* (Fontana History of Europe), Fontana Press, 24 Feb 1983; p. 45, Source T: Samuel Williamson, *Austria-Hungary and the Origins of the First World War* (Making of the Twentieth Century), Palgrave Macmillan, 1990; p. 45, Source U: Fritz Fellner, 'Austria' in Keith Wilson (ed.) *Decisions for War*, Palgrave Macmillan, May 1995; p. 47, Source V: Volker Berghahn, *Modern Germany: Society, Economy and Politics in the Twentieth Century*, Cambridge University Press, Second revised edition, 27 Nov 1987; p. 136, Source B and p. 137, Source D: J. Noakes and G. Pridham (Eds) *Nazism 1919–1945, Volume 2: State, Economy and Society 1933–39: A Documentary Reader*, New edition, 2000, University of Exeter Press; p. 137, Source C:

Originally published by Piper, 1985; p. 138, Source E and p. 186, Source R: Ian Kershaw, *Hitler, 1889–1936: Hubris*, 1998, Allen Lane, The Penguin Press Ltd, copyright © Ian Kershaw, 1998. Reproduced by permission of Penguin Books Ltd; p. 146, Source H, p. 165, Source AA, p. 169, Source B and p. 175, Source I: Richard Evans, *The Third Reich in Power*, 2005, Penguin Books, copyright © Richard Evans, 2005. Reproduced by permission of Penguin Books Ltd; p. 147, Source J: Robert Gellately, *The Gestapo and German Society: Enforcing Racial Policy, 1933–45*, Clarendon Press, Sept 1990. Used by permission of Oxford University Press; p. 147, Source K, p. 156, Source R and p. 196, Source V: Michael Burleigh, *The Third Reich: A New History*, Macmillan, First edition, 8 Sept 2000; p. 148, Source L: Originally published by Oldenbourg, 1981; p. 149, Source M: Originally published by Munich, 1981; p. 149, Source N: Originally published in *Zeitschrift für Geschichtswissenschaft*, 1993; p. 156, Source P and p. 183, Source N: Ian Kershaw, *The 'Hitler Myth': Image and Reality in the Third Reich*, Oxford Paperbacks, Reissue edition, 27 Sept 2001. Used by permission of Oxford University Press; p. 157, Source T: Stephen Lee, *Hitler and Nazi Germany (Questions and Analysis in History)*, Routledge, First edition, 18 Jun 1998; p. 159, Source U, p. 183, Source O and p. 188, Source U: Ian Kershaw, *Hitler, 1936–1945: Nemesis*, 2000, Allen Lane, The Penguin Press, copyright © Ian Kershaw, 2000. Reproduced by permission of Penguin Books Ltd; p. 163, Source V: Jost Dülffer, *Nazi Germany 1933–1945: Faith and Annihilation*, Hodder Arnold, 22 Dec 1995; p. 164, Source W: Frank McDonough, *Opposition and Resistance in Nazi Germany (Cambridge Perspectives in History)*, Cambridge University Press, 6 Sept 2001; p. 165, Source Y: Originally published by Carl Hanser Verlag, 1981; p. 165, Source Z: Joachim Fest, *The Face of the Third Reich*, 1972, First published in 1963, Penguin Books; p. 169, Source C: Reproduced with permission of Curtis Brown Group Ltd, London on behalf of the estate of Alan Bullock Copyright © Alan Bullock 1952; p. 170, Source F: Sebastian Haffner, *The Meaning of Hitler*, Macmillan, Dec 1979; p. 172, Source G: Martin Broszat, *The Hitler State: The Foundation and Development of the Internal Structure of the Third Reich* (Longman Paperback), Longman, 26 May 1981; p. 172, Source H: Hans Mommsen (Ed.) *Beamtentum im Dritten Reich. Mit ausgewählten Quellen zur nationalsozialistischen Beamtenpolitik* © 1966 Deutsche Verlags-Anstalt, Munich, 1984, Oldenbourg Wissenschaftsverlag, Munich, and Institut für Zeitgeschichte, Munich-Berlin, p. 31; p. 176, Source J: Tim Mason, *Nazism, Fascism and the Working Class*, Cambridge University Press, 9 Mar 1995; p. 183, Source L: Anita J. Prazmowska, 'Hitler and the Origins of World War II', in Gordon Martel (Ed.) *A Companion to Europe 1900–45*, Blackwell, 2005; p. 186, Source Q: Hans Mommsen, 'Cumulative Radicalisation and Progressive Self-destruction as Structural Determinants of the Nazi Dictatorship', in Ian Kershaw and Moshe Lewin *Stalin and Nazism*, Cambridge University Press, 28 April 1997; p. 196, Source W: William Carr, *Hitler: A Study in Personality and Politics*, Palgrave Macmillan, April 1979.

Introduction

The story told in this book is one of the most extraordinary told in history. It is a story of peace and war, of triumph and defeat, of tragedy and destruction. The book begins some 30 years after the unification of Germany in 1871. It describes the development of Germany's political system, shaped by a many people but most obviously by Chancellor Otto von Bismarck. By 1900 Bismarck was long gone, sacked in 1890 by the young Kaiser (Emperor) Wilhelm II.

The book describes Germany in the period between 1900 to 1914. A succession of Chancellors followed Bismarck in grappling with the impact of a dynamic and flourishing economy. The established conservative parties were threatened by the rise of mass politics and, most significantly, socialism. In foreign affairs, Germany challenged the other great powers for her 'place in the sun'; whilst Britain and France had great Empires, Germany did not. In 1914 Germany and her Austro-Hungarian allies went to war against Russia, France and Britain. The question of why Germany went to war in 1914 is still strongly debated amongst historians. Even more controversial is the question of the extent to which Germany was responsible for that war.

The First World War had a huge impact on Germany. The initial euphoria at the outbreak of war was soon tempered by lengthy casualty lists and shortages on the Home Front. One cannot underestimate the significance of the impact on Germany of the cataclysmic defeat in 1918. All political developments which followed can be traced back to the extraordinary trauma of the collapse of the home front, the defeat of German armies and the abdication of the Kaiser.

The new state that emerged out of the ashes of defeat was threatened by communist revolution and by those within the political establishment who despised democracy. The Weimar Republic, as this new state was known, was also threatened by the crushing impact of the Treaty of Versailles. Punished and humiliated, Germany lapsed from political crisis to near economic collapse. From 1924 to 1929 it experienced a period of relative stability but this was not to last; the Great Depression that swept the world in the wake of the Wall Street Crash of October 1929 was to have a disastrous effect on Germany. The following years saw the occurrence of mass unemployment, political polarisation and the collapse of German democracy. Extremist parties including the National Socialist German

Workers' Party (otherwise known as the Nazis) saw their votes increase as many Germans turned to the political extremes for answers. The German establishment, led by President von Hindenburg, misused the constitution to undermine the German parliament, the Reichstag. In January 1933, von Hindenburg made one of the most significant appointments in the history of Germany and the world when he asked the leader of the Nazis, Adolf Hitler, to become German Chancellor.

During 1933 the Nazis removed many of the obstacles to the creation of a dictatorship. Over the course of the next six years the regime consolidated power. There is little debate over the fact that there was considerable support for the Nazi regime in the years running up to the Second World War. However, there is controversy about the reasons for support: why did so many Germans actively and willingly go along with the Nazi State? It is also important to try and understand the nature and extent of opposition before the war.

At the heart of Hitler's world view was a desire to build a new Germany based on racial lines. At the top of the racial pile, according to Nazi theory, were the Aryans. At the bottom of the pile were the Jews. Hitler also promised to destroy the Treaty of Versailles as part of his wider aim to create living space, *Lebensraum*, for Germany in the east. This aim very much fitted in with his hatred of communism and his determination to destroy Bolshevism in the Soviet Union. From 1934 the Nazi regime followed a foreign policy which challenged Versailles. By 1939, the leaders of Britain and France had come to the conclusion that war was the only way to contain German expansionism.

The Second World War was to change Germany fundamentally. Despite initial success, the war was to place an increasing burden on the German people. As the levels of bombing increased and the course of the war turned against Germany, so many Germans became more critical of the Nazi regime. But the home front and German economy stood up well until close to the bitter end in April 1945.

Perhaps the most important question posed in this book is how the government of Germany, which is one of the most civilised and cultured countries in the world, could be responsible for the systematic murder of six million Jews and millions of others who were considered 'undesirable'. The 'Final Solution', as it became known, was the darkest moment in German – and in European – history.

1 What were the main issues in the Second Reich 1900–14?

What is this unit about?

This unit focuses on the **Second Reich** in Germany from 1900 to 1914. It explains the unique nature of the constitution and the relative powers of the Kaiser, the Chancellor and the Reichstag. It explores the tensions in the relationship between these institutions in the run-up to war. The unit looks at the different political parties in Germany and what they stood for. It considers economic growth and social change and the impact that these had on the political landscape. The unit considers important events during the period, notably the Zabern Affair in 1913.

You will:
• consider the structures of the German state in the period 1900–14
• discuss the strengths and weaknesses of the political system in the run-up to war.

Key questions

• What were the relative powers of the Kaiser, the Chancellor and the Reichstag and how did the Second Reich operate between 1900 and 1914?
• How did the economic and social changes impact on the political system?

Timeline

1900	June	Second German Naval Law introduced
	October	Count Bernhard von Bülow becomes Chancellor
1902	December	Tariff Law introduced
1903		Sickness Insurance Law gives greater help to sick workers
1904		Herero uprising begins in German South West Africa
1906	December	Parliamentary crisis leads to election
1907	January	Reichstag elections see Socialist SPD lose votes
1908	December	Law passed restricting hours of factory work
1909	July	Bülow resigns; Dr von Bethmann-Hollweg becomes Chancellor
1911	May	Reform of Alsace Lorraine constitution
1912	January	Reichstag elections; SPD become largest party
1913	June	Reichstag passes Army and Finance Bills increasing size of the armed forces
	December	The Zabern Affair

Definition

Second Reich

Reich is German for the word state. The First Reich was the Holy Roman Empire. The Second Reich was established in 1871 and lasted until 1918.

Study this picture closely. What impression does it give you of the founding of the new German state?

Before 1871, Germany was not a unified country. What does this map tell you about the process of German unification?

1.1 The German Empire is proclaimed, Versailles, 18 January 1871

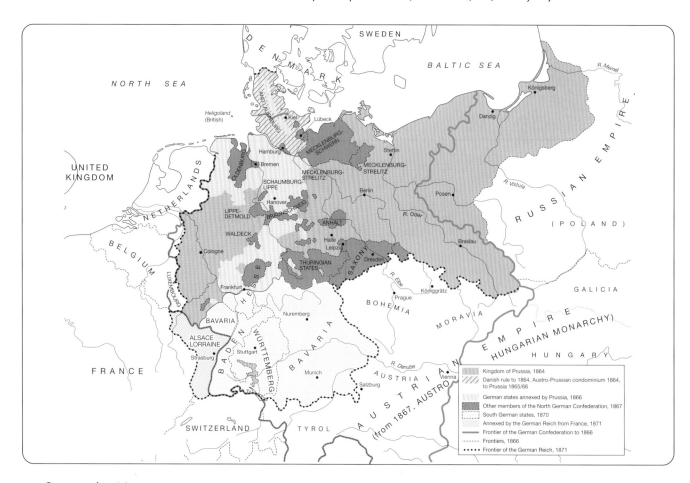

1.2 Germany in 1861–71

Kingdom of Prussia, 1864

Danish rule to 1864, Austro-Prussian condominium 1864, to Prussia 1865/66

German states annexed by Prussia, 1866

Other members of the North German Confederation, 1867

South German states, 1870

Annexed by the German Reich from France, 1871

Frontier of the German Confederation to 1866

Frontiers, 1866

Frontier of the German Reich, 1871

The constitution

As you have seen in the picture, Wilhelm I was proclaimed Emperor or Kaiser of a new German state in the Hall of Mirrors in the Palace of Versailles outside Paris. This new empire was born out of victory on the battlefield over a period of years but most recently over the French army at the Battle of Sedan in September 1870. War against France had been fought by a number of German states in alliance including the states of Prussia and Bavaria. The Prussians had led the army of the North German Confederation, which had been formed in 1867. The North German Confederation was defined by a **constitution** in which the component states kept their own governments but military matters were controlled by the King of Prussia. Under this constitution, there was to be a central law-making body with limited powers. Victory against France in 1871 led to the unification of the states of the North German Confederation with southern kingdoms, including Bavaria and Württemberg. The unification, however, was on Prussia's terms and the constitution adopted was a refinement of the constitution of the North German Confederation. The main aim of the author of the constitution and Germany's first Chancellor, Otto von Bismarck, was to preserve the power of the élite.

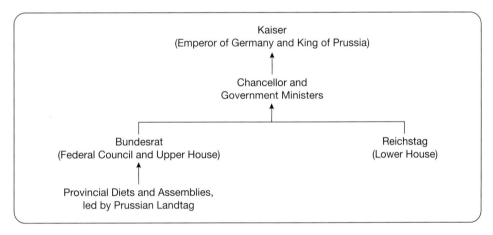

1.3 The constitution of the German Second Reich

Main features of the constitution

A federal state

The new German Reich included 25 states – four kingdoms (Prussia, Bavaria, Saxony and Württemberg), six grand duchies, 12 duchies and principalities, three free cities (Hamburg, Bremen and Lübeck) – plus the territory of Alsace-Lorraine, which had been seized from France in 1871 and was to be ruled by a governor on behalf of all of the German states.

- The states retained their own governments and had different constitutions. Some allowed universal suffrage; others, such as the grand duchies Schwerin and Strelitz, retained seventeenth century style constitutions with near absolutist rulers.

Definition

Constitution

The set of rules by which a country is run. It is, at least in theory, supposed to reflect the values and traditions of that country. Sometimes a constitution is written; sometimes it is a collection of accepted traditions that are not written down.

Biography

Otto von Bismarck

Bismarck was Minister-President of Prussia from 1862 to 1890 and Chancellor of Germany from 1871 to 1890. He was fiercely conservative and had little regard for any form of parliamentary democracy.

Definition

Federal state

A state that is made up of individual states that have control over certain aspects of internal affairs but are also part of a central state.

- The constitution granted the states fairly wide-ranging powers, which included responsibility for education, police, justice and health care. Therefore, much of what one might consider 'domestic affairs' were in the hands of the state governments rather than the federal government.

The Kaiser

By the terms of the constitution the Kaiser held considerable powers, which made the personality of the Kaiser of paramount importance.

- The Kaiser was always to be the Prussian king, which reinforced Prussia's dominant position in the new state.
- The Kaiser held full control over foreign and diplomatic policy. He therefore had the power to make alliances, sign treaties, wage war and sue for peace. In times of war, he was commander in chief of the armed forces of all of Germany's states.
- The Kaiser's influence over the government of the country was considerable. He appointed and dismissed the Chancellor and had the power to dissolve the Reichstag.
- It was the Kaiser's responsibility to publish and oversee the implementation of federal law (law made by the central parliament).
- Last, but by no means least, the Kaiser was the guardian of the constitution.

Kaiser Wilhelm II

These were considerable powers to place in the hands of even the most sensible and competent of rulers. Wilhelm I, who had become King of Prussia in 1861 and had ruled as Kaiser from 1871 until his death in 1888, was such a ruler. He was succeeded as Kaiser by his son Frederick and then his grandson Wilhelm II. Wilhelm came to the throne aged 29. His childhood had been unhappy, in part because his left arm and an ear had been damaged at birth. Wilhelm II believed that it was the Kaiser's responsibility to rule rather than share power with the Reichstag. In May 1891 he stated: 'There is only one man in charge of the Reich and I will not tolerate another.' The problem was that Wilhelm was a poor decision maker, his attention span was short and he did not work hard. Wilhelm was happiest when surrounded by members of the military, and it was to them that he turned for advice. He had a poor opinion of democracy and the Reichstag.

The Chancellor

- The Chancellor was directly responsible to the Kaiser as chief minister of the Reich. He was also in charge of the appointment and dismissal of the state secretaries who oversaw the running of the government ministries.
- As well as being Chancellor of the **federal state**, he was Minister-President of Prussia.
- The Chancellor could ignore the resolutions passed by the Reichstag.

Bismarck gave the position of Chancellor considerable powers to manipulate both the Kaiser and the Reichstag. However, the success of the Chancellor in part depended on his political ability, the character of the Kaiser and the composition of the Reichstag. Even though the Chancellor could ignore Reichstag resolutions, he needed to be able to negotiate legislation through the Reichstag. This meant that he had to be able to strike deals and effectively manage leading politicians. The constitution and the role of Chancellor worked well for Bismarck because he had the necessary political skills; he worked well with Wilhelm I, and for a fair amount of his time in office, the Reichstag was docile and obedient. His successors were not to be so lucky. Both Caprivi and Hohenlohe found it very difficult to make headway with policy because they each had a difficult working relationship with the Kaiser.

Table 1.1 German Chancellors 1871–1917

1871 to 18 March 1890	Prince Otto von Bismarck
1890 to 26 October 1894	General Georg Leo von Caprivi
1894 to 16 October 1900	Prince Chlodwig zu Hohenlohe-Schillingsfürst
1900 to 13 July 1909	Prince Bernhard von Bülow
1909 to 14 July 1917	Dr Theobald von Bethmann-Hollweg

The Bundesrat

- The Bundesrat was the upper house of the federal parliament.
- It consisted of 58 members nominated by the states' assemblies. It was part of the law-making process and was, in theory, able to change the constitution.
- It was created by Bismarck to act as a possible barrier to radical legislation. The Bundesrat could veto legislation if 14 or more of its members voted against a bill.

The dominance of Prussia was assured by the fact that it held 17 of the 58 seats in the Bundesrat, thereby ensuring that no legislation could be passed without the consent of the Prussian Chamber of Deputies. The catch in this arrangement was that the electorate for the Prussian Chamber of Deputies was divided by what was known as a 'three class franchise':

- Voters were categorised into one of three bands.
- The votes of those who paid more tax counted for more than the votes of those who paid less.
- The lowest group of voters was made up of around 92 per cent of the electorate.

As a result, the Prussian Chamber of Deputies was always dominated by Conservatives (see page 8); in the 1908 election in Prussia, 418,000 voters translated into 212 Conservative seats whereas 600,000 votes (mostly from the third tier) were rewarded with six Social Democrat (Socialist) seats.

Definition

Legislative power

The power to make laws.

The Reichstag

- The lower house of the federal parliament, the Reichstag, held joint **legislative power** with the Bundesrat. In that capacity it had influence over such areas as financial affairs and the banking system.

- The most significant power held by the Reichstag was its control over the defence budget. This was to become by far and away the most significant federal government expenditure. In the early 1870s the annual defence budget stood at 100 million marks; by 1913 it stood at 2,405 million marks. However, Bismarck recognised the potential political lever that this might give the Reichstag, and in 1874 he persuaded them to vote through the Septennial Act, with the result that the Reichstag voted on the military budget only once every seven years. This was changed to once every five years in 1893, but this was still not enough to give the Reichstag real control.

- Another of the Reichstag's most significant powers was to pass an annual budget. However, this power was reduced by Bismarck; his switch to protectionism in 1879 brought the federal government increased income and some financial independence from the Reichstag.

- Even though the Reichstag could be dissolved by the Kaiser, it could not be dismissed indefinitely and it had the right to hold elections soon after dissolution.

The Reichstag was elected on a system of universal male suffrage of men over the age of 25. Its members represented constituencies that were arranged in the 1870s. However, the powers of the Reichstag were limited:

- The Reichstag had limited powers to initiate legislation; its primary function was to debate and to accept or reject legislation that was placed in front of it.

- Reichstag members could not become members of the government. If they wished to do so, they had to resign their seats.

- The Chancellor was not accountable to the Reichstag and did not even have to answer its questions. That said, the Reichstag could make trouble for a Chancellor, as Bülow found out in 1909 (see pages 19–20).

- Likewise the military was not in any sense accountable to the Reichstag.

- In order to ensure that only a certain class of person stood for election to the Reichstag, Bismarck included the stipulation that members would not be paid.

The army

The army lay outside the formal constitution because Bismarck did not want to tie its hands by defining its role. But the army was of huge significance in this new state. Its importance in part stemmed from the fact that the German state had been founded on the back of the victories of its army on the battlefield in the 1860s and 1870. As a result, Bismarck did not make the army accountable in law to the Reichstag; instead he made it directly responsible to the Kaiser.

- On the advice of senior military figures, the Kaiser appointed the Military Cabinet (made up of senior military figures).
- The Military Cabinet advised and chose the General Staff.
- The General Staff organised all military affairs from planning to court bodyguard duties.
- The War Minister was a member of the General Staff and was accountable only to the Kaiser and the Military Cabinet.
- The army swore an oath of allegiance to the Kaiser and not to the state.

The army had the right to declare martial law (army rule), which it did from time to time. In terms of social background, the officer class were split; positions in élite regiments such as the cavalry or the guards were held by the Prussian nobility known as Junkers. A sizeable minority, around 44 per cent of officer posts in the army in the period 1898 to 1918, were held by professional soldiers. The point to make is that, whatever the social background, there were few officers in the army who had any respect for democracy. In a sense, therefore, Bismarck had ensured that the army was a 'state within a state'. This means that it ran itself with little or no outside interference beyond that of the Kaiser. This system worked for Bismarck because he was able to manage it. Chancellors who followed Bismarck found it more difficult to cope with.

The bureaucracy

As with the army, the role of the bureaucracy was not identified by the constitution. However, that did not mean that the bureaucrats – the civil servants – did not have an important role to play in the development of policy. Perhaps the best example of their role was that played by Friedrich von Holstein, who was, from 1890 until 1906, the Kaiser's Chief Adviser on Foreign Affairs. His impact on policy decisions and events, therefore, was considerable.

Conclusions

- The constitution created a political structure that was not clear, that was fragmented and that was dominated by the conservative élites.
- Enshrined in the constitution was the dominance and veto of Prussia.

Other conclusions should be drawn out in your discussions as suggested in the discussion point box.

Political organisations

Despite the restrictions on the power of the Reichstag, mass political parties flourished, in part because of the introduction of universal male suffrage. However, because of the limits on the power of the Reichstag, other types of political organisations, which represented different interests, developed.

Discussion points

Discuss the following points in groups:

1 Why might the Prussian voting system provoke protest and who from?
2 After reading through the terms of the constitution, where does real power lie? Reichstag? Army? Bundesrat? Kaiser?

SKILLS BUILDER

In fewer than 300 words, write a summary of the strengths and weaknesses of the German constitution.

These were the main political parties in Germany from 1890 to 1914.

> ## Political parties from 1890 to 1914
>
> **Conservative parties**
>
> **Conservatives**
>
> Groups representing: Junkers, landed interests, especially in Prussia.
>
> Views: Supported the Kaiser, discipline and authority; in favour of a nationalist foreign policy.
>
> **Free Conservatives**
>
> Groups representing: Commercial, industrial and wealthier professional classes from across Germany.
>
> Views: Similar to the Conservatives; strong supporters of Bismarck and protectionism (i.e. the state should protect German business with tariffs).
>
> **Liberal parties**
>
> **National Liberals**
>
> Groups representing: Industrial middle class, Protestant middle class.
>
> Views: Nationalist; believed in a strong nation state and encouragement of a state with a liberal constitution; supported Bismarck's attack on the Catholic Church, the **Kulturkampf**; political allies of the Conservative parties.
>
> **Liberal Progressives**
>
> Groups representing: Middle classes.
>
> Views: Very much in favour of the development of parliamentary government; not so keen on Bismarck's idea of the power of the nation state; views closely shared by the German People's Party.
>
> **Centre Party**
>
> Groups representing: The Catholic Church and its members, essentially based in the south; also support from non-socialist working class and middle and lower middle class interests.
>
> Views: Opposed Bismarck's attack on the Catholic Church, the *Kulturkampf*; feared rise of socialism; anti-Prussia.
>
> **Social Democratic Party (SPD)**
>
> Groups representing: Working classes after Bismarck's Anti-Socialist Laws lapsed in 1890.
>
> Views: Split: Marxists argued for revolution and non-cooperation with the political system; Reformists argued that the party should work within the political system to achieve social reform.

Definition

Kulturkampf

An attack on the Catholic Church from 1871 to 1878. It included the abolition of religious orders and the expulsion of the Jesuits.

Table 1.2 Seats won in the Reichstag 1898–1912

Party	1898	1903	1907	1912
Conservatives	56	54	60	43
Free Conservatives	23	21	24	14
National Liberals	46	51	54	45
Liberal Progressives	41	31	42	42
Centre Party	102	100	105	91
Social Democrats	56	81	43	110
Others	82	63	69	52

SKILLS BUILDER

1 Use Table 1.2 to explain developments in voting and the fortunes of political parties from 1898 to 1912. You might choose to plot this information on to a graph.

2 What impact would these changes have on German politics, given the fact that the Reichstag had an important role in confirming legislation?

What was the extent of German economic growth?

The industries of the first **Industrial Revolution** were heavy – cotton, coal and iron – and up until the middle of the nineteenth century Britain dominated these industries. The extent of German economic growth in the period between unification and the outbreak of the First World War is therefore best illustrated by a comparison with British growth.

Table 1.3 Coal and pig iron production 1870/71 to 1914 in Germany and Great Britain (in thousands of metric tonnes)

Year	Coal (Germany)	Coal (Britain)	Year	Iron (Germany)	Iron (Britain)
1871	37,900	118,000	1870	1,391	6,060
1900	149,000	228,000	1900	7,549	9,003
1914	279,000	292,000	1910	14,793	10,380

By 1914 Germany had become the economic powerhouse of continental Europe, and it was not just in the old industries that Germany excelled. From the 1880s there had been a technological revolution in the new industries of steel, engineering and chemicals that was fuelled and closely linked to the new sources of energy: electricity and petroleum. It was Germany that led the way in many of these new industries.

Definition

Industrial Revolution

Involved the transition to factory based manufacturing and was the most significant economic change of the nineteenth century.

Steel

In 1879 a new method of manufacturing steel, the Thomas-Gilchrist process, made possible the use of phosphoric ores (which were found in abundance in the newly acquired territory of Lorraine) in the manufacture of steel. While manufacturers in Britain were slow to take advantage of this new method, those in Germany most definitely were not: firms such as Krupp of Essen increased production rapidly in the pre-war period. German advantage over Britain in steel was also gained through the size of her companies: only one British firm in 1900 had an annual capacity to produce over 300,000 tons, whereas in Germany there were ten such companies.

Growth in steel production fuelled the expansion of other industries, including armaments and the railways. The Prussian railways expanded from 5,000 kilometres in 1878 to 37,000 kilometres in 1914.

Table 1.4 Steel production 1870 to 1910 in Germany and Great Britain (in thousands of metric tonnes)

Year	Germany	Britain
1870	169	286
1900	6,645	5,130
1910	13,698	6,374

Chemicals

The German chemicals industry was stimulated by the demand for explosives from the military and dyes from textile manufacturers. It was also stimulated by investment in research and training, which meant that on the eve of the First World War there were 58,000 full-time students in advanced commercial and technical training in Germany, whereas in Britain there were only 9,000.

- By 1900 German companies such as Badische Anilin und Soda Fabrik (BASF), which was based at Ludwigshafen, held a virtual worldwide monopoly over the manufacture of artificial dyes.

- In 1914 Great Britain imported around 80 per cent of its chemical dyes, mainly from Germany. When British troops marched off to war in the autumn of that year they were wearing uniforms dyed with German dyestuffs.

- Germany led the way in pharmaceuticals; in 1900 BASF employed a workforce of 6,300 workers and 233 research chemists.

- The film company AGFA produced a million metres of film a year from a factory in Saxony in 1908.

Other industries

It was not just in the chemical industry that Germany led the way. A number of Germans helped pioneer technological change that was to have a huge impact on modern life. In 1897 Rudolf Diesel perfected an oil-based engine; in 1886 Gottlieb Daimler had perfected the high-speed petrol engine. In air transport, Count Ferdinand von Zeppelin launched the first rigid airship in 1900, although the first non-prototype model did not fly until 1908.

Perhaps the most significant of the new industries was the electricity industry, and Germany played a leading part in the development of this

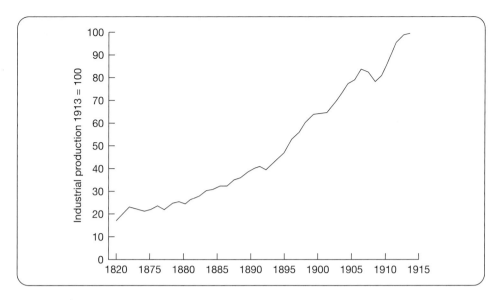

1.4 Index of German industrial production

new source of power, too. By 1907, 107,000 Germans worked as electrical workers, with just under half being employed by two large companies, AEG and Siemens & Halske. By the eve of the First World War, around half of Europe's electrical business was being undertaken by German companies.

Urbanisation

The rapid growth of industries old and new helped stimulate a population boom and changed the structure of German society. The migration from rural to urban life and the rapid expansion of Germany's towns and cities constituted a demographic revolution.

- Such change did not come without its downsides: there was overcrowding in many cities, and poor sanitary conditions and the lack of a clean water supply led to the outbreak of disease. In Hamburg in 1892, 8,600 people died from cholera over a ten-week period. But the outbreak was not met with complacency; it spurred on the city authorities to build a sewerage system, a filtering plant for drinking water and a waste incinerator.

- Better hygiene and medicine improved rates of infant mortality. The introduction of a diphtheria serum in the 1890s cut the number of young children dying of the disease by half.

- The building of tramways meant that people could escape the slum conditions by living in the suburbs and travelling cheaply into town to work.

- Trolley buses, which ran on pneumatic wheels rather than rails, were especially popular in Germany after 1901.

- For those in the urban workforce after 1896, real wages increased because money wages went up more than prices. Another indicator of the rising standard of living was that between 1896 and 1912

Discussion point

Discuss the following in groups of three or four.

German industrial production was fantastic. But why was it significant? Work out five reasons for it being significant. Think outside Germany. Then share your ideas with other groups. Can you arrive at five reasons about which you all agree?

the proportion of taxpayers in Prussia assessed on incomes under 900 marks a year fell from 75 per cent to 52 per cent.

The number of industrial workers in Germany doubled in the period 1882 to 1907, and for many of them life was tough. Overcrowding in insanitary accommodation was one problem. Another was homelessness, with not enough accommodation available to house Germany's booming urban population.

- The Berlin Homeless Shelter Association accommodated 200,000 men a year after 1900.

- The cycle of unemployment was dictated by the cycle of the economy, and perhaps one in every three workers in any year in the 1900 to 1914 period experienced some form of underemployment. The official unemployment figure rose from 1.35 million in 1882 to 3.45 million in 1907.

- However, the unemployed tended to come mainly from the unskilled working class.

- Another consequence of the modernisation of the economy was the increase in the number of lower middle class 'white collar workers' to around 3.3 million by 1907.

Table 1.5 Population statistics, 1870 to 1910

	1871	1900	1910
Total population	41.1 million	56.4 million	64.9 million
Berlin	774,498	1,888,313	2,071,907
Essen	99,887	290,208	410,392
Leipzig	117,818	519,726	644,644

Table 1.6 Population trends from rural to urban, 1870 to 1910 (figures in percentages)

	1871	1900	1910
Rural	63.9	45.6	40.0
Urban	36.1	54.4	60.0

SKILLS BUILDER

1 Using Tables 1.5 and 1.6, summarise population changes in Germany between 1870 and 1910. You might choose to put this on a graph before you answer the next question.

2 What pressures might such changes place on the German state?

Agriculture

While industry boomed, the fortunes of Germany agriculture fluctuated. There were strengths and weaknesses within the agricultural system.

Strengths

Bismarck's Tariff Law of 1879 had been introduced to protect German farmers and was, to a point, successful in doing so. The Junkers certainly benefitted from high prices for their rye, but the peasantry were also protected: the tariff applied to barley, oats and wheat as well as to rye. Perhaps the most significant factor for German farmers in this period was the rapid increase in the domestic population, e.g. 56.4 million in 1900 to

64.9 million in 1910, which created significant extra demand for agricultural products and led to a growth in agricultural prices at start of the twentieth century. Improvements in the chemical industries provided phosphates and nitrates to be used as artificial fertiliser; the result was an increase in yields in crops such as sugar beet. Industrial production helped mechanise German agriculture: in 1882, threshing machines were found on 374,000 holdings, and by 1907 they were to be found on 1,436,000 holdings. This made German farming more efficient and less labour intensive.

Weaknesses

Despite protection, farmers faced challenges that threatened to undermine their livelihoods. Refrigerated ships made possible the importation of meat from the United States, which was cheaper than German meat despite the distance travelled and tariff paid. It became ever harder to make large estates pay. Debt increased, and, as a result, estates were bought and sold more frequently in the 1896–1912 period than before. The growth of the cities (see above) and the promise of better standards of living as an industrial worker rather than as an agricultural hand meant significant migration. As a result, landlords recruited foreign labour from the regions that lay on Germany's borders; on the eve of the First World War there were nearly half a million foreign nationals working in German agriculture, the majority being Poles.

Consequences

The result of these changes was to provide pressures that the political system had to deal with. It is wrong to suggest that the pressures were too much for the system, as some historians have indicated. However:

- There was a contradiction between economic modernisation, which saw Germany's industry flourish and cities grow, and the lack of political reform and the restricted spread of democracy.

- Frustrations were caused as a result of uneven economic growth, which meant rising prices and rising unemployment from 1912 to 1914. The period saw clashes between workers and strikers, notably in the Ruhr.

- Perhaps the greatest manifestation of these pressures was the explosion of participation in politics in Germany in the run-up to the First World War. The challenge for the governing classes was to channel and control the impact of such pressure.

Socialist movement

Perhaps the most significant impact on industrialisation was the growth of the socialist movement. The **Anti-Socialist Laws** of 1878–90 did little to dampen the working class's enthusiasm for political action – indeed, quite the opposite. As has already been indicated, there were elements within the Social Democratic Party (SPD) that were more revolutionary in their politics. This did not mean that the whole socialist movement was revolutionary, far from it. However, the political

SKILLS BUILDER

1 What were the strengths and weaknesses of German agriculture in this period?

2 Given the strengths and weaknesses of German agriculture, what demands were German landlords likely to be making of German governments in the 1900–14 period?

Biography

August Bebel

One of the founder members of the Social Democratic Party (SPD), Bebel was an active socialist and a member of the Reichstag from 1883 until his death in 1913.

Definition

Anti-Socialist Laws

Introduced in 1878. The laws banned socialist groups, meetings and publications. They were upheld by police surveillance and powers given to local authorities.

establishment's perception of the socialist movement was what was important and was what made the rise of socialism such an issue.

By the eve of the war, around 2.5 million German workers were members of trade unions, and 400,000 of them went out on strike at some point in 1913 for better working conditions. In 1910 the SPD had 720,000 members which made it by far and away the largest socialist political party in Europe. The party's membership was predominantly Protestant and working class. By the eve of the war, the SPD was winning 75 per cent of the popular vote in elections in Berlin. The 1912 election, as we will see later in this unit, saw the SPD become the strongest party in the Reichstag with 110 seats. But how much of a threat were the socialists? In 1891 at Erfurt, the SPD party under the leadership of August Bebel committed to a revolutionary Marxist programme. He said that the party:

- would work legally to achieve worker ownership of the means of production
- rejected collaboration with 'bourgeois parties'
- believed that revolution was inevitable.

However, by 1900 many members of the socialist movement agreed more with the 'revisionist' ideas of Eduard Bernstein. In his work *The Presuppositions of Socialism and the Tasks of Social Democracy* (1898) he argued that:

- there was not a crisis of capitalism as the father of communism, Karl Marx, had predicted
- socialists should look for gradual improvement through parliamentary reform
- the SPD should collaborate with other parties when appropriate.

At the Lübeck Conference in 1901, Bernstein was denounced by those on the left of the party, including a revolutionary socialist called Rosa Luxemburg, of whom we will hear much more later. She and her comrades, such as Karl Liebknecht, argued that:

- revolution should be considered
- the movement should use the general strike as a tactic.

The party leadership tended to steer a middle ground but after 1907 steered more towards reformism. However, to the élites, it was their perception of the SPD as revolutionary that stuck.

Pressure groups

Another of the consequences of the economic and social changes was the emergence of pressure groups. These groups were often focused on single issues, but they highlighted the tensions and divisions in Germany.

Nationalist pressure groups

There were three main groups that pressurised for German colonial expansion and the assertion of German interests. They were to have an important impact on the development of policy.

- The *German Colonial League* was founded in 1882 and was concerned with the acquisition of German colonies. It also played a part in ruling various parts of the far-flung Empire; for example in 1884 the Colonial League took control of German South West Africa.

- The *Pan German League* was founded in 1890. It too was committed to the acquisition of colonies but also to German dominance in Europe. The League had strong support from the political establishment, some 60 members of the Reichstag (mostly National Liberals) being members of the organisation in 1914.

- The *Navy League* was founded in 1898 and became highly popular, with a membership of around 1 million. The League played an important role in the successful campaign in and outside the Reichstag to promote naval expansion.

Economic pressure groups

- The *Central Association of German Industrialists* was created in 1886 to protect industrial interests, and from 1878 onwards that meant the implementation of tariffs. In the 1912 election the organisation funded 120 candidates from the conservative and liberal parties, at a cost of 1 million marks. Not surprisingly, it was considered to be the most powerful pressure group in Germany.

- The *Agrarian League* was founded in 1893 to protect agrarian interests. Although Junker-led, it gained widespread support from the peasantry and had a third of a million members by 1914. It pushed for protectionism and subsidies for agriculture.

SKILLS BUILDER

1 There were a number of political parties and pressure groups in Germany. It is important to try and understand where they stood in relation to each other. Plot the groups on a chart going from left wing (on the left) to right wing (on the right). Where you can, draw links between each group and explain the link.

2 What are the divisions in Germany? On a spider chart such as the one shown, and using what you have read so far, plot the divisions in Germany in the period 1900 to 1914. Keep the spider chart because you will be finishing it off at the end of this unit.

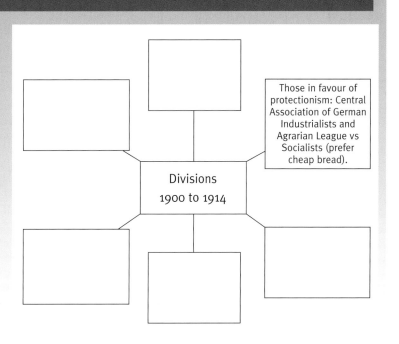

Those in favour of protectionism: Central Association of German Industrialists and Agrarian League vs Socialists (prefer cheap bread).

Divisions 1900 to 1914

Political developments

The main aim of successive German Chancellors was to protect the position of the ruling élites. There were three discernable challenges to the political establishment.

1 *Aggressive foreign policy.* As you have already seen, one significant challenge was from those who wished for a more aggressive foreign policy, the development of which will be dealt with in the next unit.

2 *The demand for constitutional reform.* Another was from the liberals who wished for constitutional reform and a strengthening of the power of the Reichstag. Bismarck had dealt with the liberal challenge by using the tactic of divide and rule. In the 1860s and 1870 he used war and conquest to split the more nationalist minded liberals from those who prioritised constitutional reform. In July 1879 he introduced the Tariff Law which ushered in protection for agriculture, therefore pleasing the Conservatives and the National Liberals but not the Liberal Progressives. While the liberals remained divided, the demands for more power for the Reichstag remained muted. Successive Chancellors were to deal relatively well with the challenge from liberals (and later also socialists) for reform.

3 *The demand for social reform.* Socialists demanded social reform. In October 1878, Bismarck persuaded the Reichstag to pass the Anti-Socialist Law, which banned the SPD and drove all socialist organisations underground. In 1890, the Reichstag, with the Kaiser's backing (and to Bismarck's fury) refused to confirm the legislation, and it was dropped. From then to the outbreak of war, only limited and piecemeal social reform was granted.

Foreign Minister and Chancellor von Bülow

Von Bülow served as Foreign Minister from 1897 to 1900 and then as Chancellor from 1900 to 1909. In that time he devised strategies to protect the interests of the ruling classes.

Sammlungspolitik literally means the politics of concentration. It was von Bülow's aim to build an alliance of conservative interests in the Reich, between conservatives and liberals, Junker and industrialist, which would present a broad front against the threat of socialism. The means by which this would be done would be the creation of a policy of protectionism and the rallying of Germans from all sections of society through the following of a nationalist foreign and colonial policy, *Weltpolitik*, which means world politics. As von Bülow himself explained, 'I am putting the main emphasis on foreign policy, only a successful foreign policy can help to reconcile, pacify, rally, unite.' Integral to the policy of Weltpolitik was the building-up of German armed forces. With the Secretary to the Navy, Alfred von Tirpitz, von Bülow encouraged the development of a *Flottenpolitik*, the building of a navy to rival that of Britain.

Flottenpolitik

In 1898, von Tirpitz steered his first Navy Law through the Reichstag. Supporters of the law were able to argue that a larger fleet was necessary for the protection of Germany's growing number of colonies and for Germany to be taken seriously as a 'Great Power'. It was unrealistic to aim to build a fleet to match the Royal Navy; in 1896 the Royal Navy had 33 battleships, the German navy just six. However, it was Tirpitz's strategy, his 'risk theory', to build a navy of such strength that it would make any other naval power think twice before attacking it. The momentum for *Flottenpolitik* was maintained by the Naval League, which held countless meetings and demonstrations to support Germany's right to build a navy. This was an excellent example of the **synthesis** of popular pressure and government policy.

- In 1900 a second Navy Law sailed through the Reichstag with the proposal to build 38 battleships over the next 20 years. This building programme was one of the main reasons for the leap in production in steel. It brought delight to the members of the Naval League and to industrialists who profited from the commissioning of so many new ships.

- In response to the launch by the Royal Navy of HMS *Dreadnought*, in May 1906 the Reichstag passed the third Navy Law, which added six battle-cruisers to the building programme and widened the Kiel canal to allow the passage of dreadnought-type ships from Germany's main naval bases to the North Sea.

Through this process the navy had become a focus for popular patriotism and nationalism, which in some ways soaked up the pressure and tensions that existed in Germany in this period.

Reforms

Von Bülow's strengths and interests lay primarily in foreign policy. However, in Count Arthur von Posadowsky he had an able and relatively energetic Interior Minister. A series of reforms was introduced to placate both protectionist liberals and socialists.

- The Old Age and Invalidity Law had been amended in June 1899 to increase old age pensions and to extend compulsory insurance to various new groups. In 1900 accident insurance was also extended to new occupations.

- In December 1902 a new Tariff Law was introduced because Caprivi's treaties of the mid-1890s had expired. As a sign of the impact of the influence of the Agrarian League, the Tariff Law restored a higher duty on imported agricultural products, which resulted in higher food prices. The subsequent general election in 1903, however, saw a shift towards the Social Democrats, who strongly opposed the new tariffs and gave the balance of power to the Centre Party.

- In April 1903 the Sickness Insurance Law was amended to give longer and more generous help to workers in ill health, 26 weeks rather than the previous 13 weeks.
- Late in 1908 a law was passed that restricted the hours of factory work carried out by young people and children (no children under 13 to be employed, a six-hour day for children aged 13–14 and a 10-hour day for those aged 14–16).

Weltpolitik

However, few opportunities presented themselves for the type of global expansion demanded by supporters of Weltpolitik. Despite the pressure for colonial expansion from groups such as the Colonial League, the opportunities after 1900 were minimal because most territory had been seized by the other European powers in the preceding 30 years. A tension was therefore created by the pressure for expansion, on the one hand, and the limited opportunity to do so, on the other. The approval in 1899 of the planned extension of the German-built Constantinople-to-Konia railways through to Baghdad kept alive imperialist dreams of extending influence into the Near and Middle East.

The Herero Uprising

Weltpolitik was not always a force for political cohesion, quite the opposite. The SPD stood against imperialist adventure when there was so much social reform needed at home. Up until 1906, the different strands of von Bülow's political policies were sufficient to keep the broad alliance of conservative, liberal and centre parties content. This was known as the Blue-Black Bloc (blue for conservative, black for the clerical Catholic party). However, it was the actions of an arrogant, murderous army and non-accountable colonial administrators who created the conditions for a political crisis in Germany in 1906.

- In January 1904 the Herero people, who were the indigenous people of German South West Africa, rose in revolt against their colonial repressor. They were defeated at the Battle of Waterberg in August 1904.
- The Herero people were then subjected to a deliberate policy of genocide though execution, incarceration in concentration camps and forced migration into the waterless Namib Desert. The Herero population in 1911 stood at 15,000 in comparison to 80,000 before the rebellion.

Some of the more conservative elements of the leadership of the Centre Party were cautious about challenging von Bülow's government. However, the considerable majority of Centre Party members of the Reichstag were scandalised by the reports fed back to Germany by Catholic missionaries in the colonies and highlighted by rising political star Matthias Erzberger.

The affair highlighted two issues:

- the lack of parliamentary accountability for the colonial service and the army
- the need for greater parliamentary financial control of colonial affairs (by December 1906 suppressing the Herero rebellions had cost the state 456 million marks which was the equivalent to building 12 dreadnoughts).

The Hottentot election

On 26 May 1906 the Centre Party joined the SPD in voting down government plans for a new railway in South West Africa, compensation for settler losses in the region and the elevation of the status of the Colonial Department of the Foreign Office into an independent imperial office. In the light of the Centre Party's attitude to the government's colonial policy, the Reichstag was subsequently dissolved. The so-called '**Hottentot**' election of 1907 was fought on the issue of nationalism. Von Bülow entered into the election fray supported by nationalist groups including the Pan-German League, and threatening that the consequences of a Red-Black victory would be an alliance of Centre and SPD Parties. He succeeded in frightening the German voters into backing candidates from the so-called Bülow Bloc, thus delivering a convincing majority.

Discussion points

1 How successful were Bülow's Weltpolitik and Sammlungspolitik?
2 Why was there not an even greater outcry in response to the Herero genocide in Germany?

Daily Telegraph Affair 1908

The Bülow Bloc held together for a short while, but Bülow's government was being undermined by an ever-growing financial deficit, indeed just the kind of deficit the Centre Party was complaining about in 1906 during the Herero crisis. Increased military spending meant that the government needed to raise 380 million marks. Bülow half-heartedly proposed a property tax or an extension of the current inheritance tax. The result was the break-up of the Bülow Bloc, with the conservative parties siding with the Centre Party to oppose such measures. This in itself did not threaten Bülow's position, but what happened immediately afterwards did.

In October 1908 the Kaiser gave an interview to a British newspaper, the *Daily Telegraph*, in which he gave the impression that he wanted a close alliance with Britain. The Reichstag objected to the implication of the article that the Kaiser made foreign policy without consultation (although he virtually did), and he was roundly criticised. The Kaiser blamed Bülow for failing to censor the interview and gave a guarantee to the Reichstag that he would be more circumspect in the future. The Reichstag dropped

Definition

Hottentot

The slang name used to describe the Khoikhoi peoples of southern Africa. It is now considered to be an offensive term to use.

Table 1.7 The 1907 election: the Bülow Bloc (number of seats)

Conservatives	60
Free Conservatives	24
Agrarian League	13
National Liberals	54
Progressives	49
Anti-Semites	16

Definition

Anti-Semites

People who stood on a platform that was anti-Jewish. Anti-Semitism at this moment in German history was popular at court and among some sections of German society. It was further stirred up in 1900 by the publication of Englishman Houston Stewart Chamberlain's book *The Foundations of the Nineteenth Century*, which described history as a struggle for supremacy between the German and Jewish races.

the issue without demanding any restraint on the Kaiser's power. The end of Bülow's Chancellorship came in the summer of 1909 when his budget was formally defeated. But it was not the end of the Bülow Bloc that finished the Chancellor, rather the fact that he no longer had the confidence of the Kaiser.

Chancellor Bethmann-Hollweg

Bülow's successor as Chancellor was Theobold Bethmann-Hollweg. An able administrator, he was an unremarkable Chancellor in domestic policy.

- In 1910, he tried to reform the Prussian voting system, which was so warped that it was blatantly unfair. In the 1908 election to the Prussian Landtag the conservatives won 16 per cent of the vote and 212 seats while the SPD won 23 per cent of the vote and just seven seats. In the face of conservative opposition, he dropped his proposals.

- To please the conservatives he started the process of seizing estates in the east that belonged to Poles, with the purpose of redistributing land to the German peasantry.

- In 1911 the Imperial Insurance Code was introduced, which consolidated all previous workers' insurance laws and amended and extended their provisions. Certain groups of white collar workers were insured against sickness, old age and death by a separate and simultaneous law.

- He introduced a constitution for Alsace-Lorraine in 1911 to try to integrate the province more with the rest of Germany.

1912 election

In the election the SPD polled 4,250,000 votes and became the largest party in the Reichstag with 110 deputies. This improvement in fortunes was partly due to an alliance with the Progressive Liberals. Philipp Schiedemann of the SPD became Vice-President of the Reichstag. The problem was that there were few other parties in the Reichstag that would consider any form of alliance with them. But in 1913 the SPD voted for an Army Bill, which would increase the size of the army by 136,000 soldiers and officers but at a cost of a billion marks. The SPD members were prepared to vote in favour of the Bill because:

- they did not want to be labelled as unpatriotic, especially in the light of what some felt were gathering war clouds

- the money was to be raised from a direct property tax.

The Zabern Affair 1913

An incident of military indiscipline took place in 1913 that escalated into a political crisis that encapsulated all of the contradictions and tensions of the Second Reich.

Background

The position of Alsace and Lorraine in the German Reich was unique. Won as a spoil of war, the region had been initially designated as 'Reichsland Elsass Lothringen' in 1871. Instead of the region being given the same autonomy as all of the other states in the new German Reich, Elsass Lothringen was to be ruled by an imperial governor known as a *Statthalter*. By the Treaty of Frankfurt of October 1872, residents of the region were given the option of emigration or taking German nationality. Around 200,000 French speakers fled to France or the French colonies (notably Algeria) in the handful of years following the annexation. They left behind a minority of French speakers who constituted around 10 per cent of the population. The imperial government tolerated the use of French as the official language in those parts of the province where French speakers were in the majority. In 1911, the imperial government of Bethmann-Hollweg attempted to promote closer assimilation of the region into the Reich by granting it a constitution. This involved the creation of a two-chamber legislature, some regional autonomy, a flag and even a national anthem. Any positive sense created by Bethmann-Hollweg's actions was undermined by events in Zabern in December 1913.

Events

In November 1913 a young German army officer, Second Lieutenant von Forstner, who was stationed in the Alsatian town of Zabern, made some derogatory remarks about the locals to his troops that were printed in the local press. The Governor of Alsace Lorraine, Karl von Wedel, tried to persuade the army to transfer von Forstner away from the town. The local garrison commander, Colonel von Reuter, refused. When von Forstner appeared again on Zabern's streets he was jeered at. Von Reuter's response was to imprison some of the townspeople and, as a result, a state of siege hung over the city. The Kaiser was unmoved by alarmed reports from von Wedel and, on the advice of senior army officers, ordered military reinforcements into the town. A case brought against von Forstner for assault on a disabled shoemaker was dismissed by a military court as self-defence, even though von Forstner was with five colleagues at the time of the assault and the shoemaker was on his own.

Throughout the affair, the Kaiser remained on a hunting expedition at Donaueschingen. He refused to see von Wedel who had requested an audience despite the fact that as Governor of Alsace-Lorraine, von Wedel was the Kaiser's representative in the region. Instead, the Kaiser accepted the explanation of events from the local military commander-in-chief, General von Deimling, which underplayed the incident. As far as the Kaiser was concerned, the matter was a military affair, and he forbade Bethmann-Hollweg to inform the Reichstag that he had sent a senior military officer, Major-General Kühne, to Zabern to investigate matters. On 3 and 4 December Bethmann-Hollweg faced a barrage of questions from critical members of the Reichstag including deputies from the Progressive Liberals, the Centre Party and the SPD. The Chancellor and the War Minister simply defended the military to the dissatisfaction of the Reichstag, which supported a vote of no confidence against the Chancellor by 293 votes to 54.

SPD-inspired protests in the Alsace-Lorraine region in the following days were diffused by the Kaiser's instructions to send the offending regiments out on manoeuvres and by the use of repression.

Impact

The Zabern Affair highlighted the limits to the Reichstag's influence:

- The Reichstag's vote of no confidence was simply ignored by the Chancellor, who was responsible to the Kaiser rather than the Reichstag.

- In the light of events, von Wedel resigned as Governor to be replaced by someone far more reactionary and opposed to the 1911 constitution that had attempted to integrate Alsace Lorraine into the rest of Germany.

- The political parties showed themselves to be far too timid; it took a week after the vote of no confidence for a politician in the Reichstag to demand the Chancellor's resignation. When SPD member Philipp Schiedemann did demand the Chancellor's resignation he was ignored by most of the other politicians in the Reichstag.

- In January 1914 the Reichstag set up a commission to discuss the boundary line between military and civilian authority, but it disbanded after a month.

SKILLS BUILDER

1 In 300 words summarise the events of the Zabern Affair.

2 What does the Zabern Affair tell us about the power of the Reichstag in 1913?

What was the extent of constitutional change 1900–14?

Despite the emergence of the SPD and the growing influence of the Reichstag because of the increase in the weight of business, there was still no great move by 1914 towards parliamentary democracy. On the eve of war the Chancellor still operated independently of party politics and the central points of the constitution remained unreformed. What were the reasons for this lack of political modernisation?

Constituency boundaries

Set in 1871, these remained unformed throughout the period in question. This benefitted the conservative and liberal parties. The urban seats remained the same despite the huge growth in the urban population. Therefore SPD members of the Reichstag, in particular, tended to represent many more constituents than National Liberals. Because of the way that constituency boundaries were drawn, elections were not decided on the popular vote. Indeed, in the 1907 election for the Reichstag the Centre Party and the SPD received 3 million more votes than the Bülow

Bloc but still suffered a comprehensive defeat in terms of numbers of seats gained.

The Kaiser

Afraid of being tarnished as unpatriotic by one or all of the nationalist pressure groups, no political party was prepared to challenge the power of the monarchy. Indeed, even many socialists were bound to the institution of the monarchy by strong bonds of loyalty that meant that they were unwilling to argue in favour of constitutional reform. In 1907 the right wing SPD leader Gustav Noske made a speech stressing the loyalty of the SPD to the 'Fatherland', thereby stressing the deep-seated sense of patriotism that was felt by the majority of German politicians.

Parties as interest groups

This is a theme that will be picked up again later in this book (see pages 70–71). Parties in this period of German history acted as interest groups. They looked after the interests of the groups that voted for them; the Conservatives protected the interest of the landowners, the SPD looked after the workers. This made collaboration between parties difficult. Fear of the revolutionary image of the SPD meant that few politicians from other parties would consider any form of political understanding. The parties did not really trust each other; for example the Social Democrats steered clear of the National Liberals because they had supported Bismarck's Anti-Socialist Laws.

Unit summary

What have you learned in this unit?

You have learned about the German Constitution and how the German political system operated in practice from 1900 to 1914. In particular, you have found out that the German constitution did not change despite the tensions in Germany in the period in question.

You have learned about industrialisation and the development of agriculture and how these had an impact on German society and politics. You are aware that the divisions inherent at the start of the period still existed on the eve of war in 1914.

What skills have you used in this unit?

You will have come to grips with a number of new ideas and concepts. Indeed, it might be quite good for you to have a 'definitions page' in your notes where you can write down some of the new concepts and words that you have picked up. You have discussed a number of issues and you have shown that you understand the significance of various events.

This is the sort of question you will find appearing on the examination paper as a Section A question:

> 'The political establishment in Germany succeeded in maintaining the political status quo through a policy of moderate reform.'

> How far do you agree with this judgement?

Exam tips

The plan

A properly thought through plan is the key to success. In completing the plan you can fully think through your ideas and prepare yourself for completion of the response. In the plan you directly answer the question, using the words in the question. The purpose of the plan is for you to work out in your mind the argument in response to the question.

- The plan should take the form of two or three lines/strands of your argument.
- It is critical that the lines of argument in your plan refer to or cover all of the main issues.
- You then should very briefly highlight what you are going to put in each paragraph as a list of key sections and key points.

Writing analytically

In answering the question set you must ensure that:

- your answer is analytical throughout
- you show an explicit understanding of the chosen factors – you will be credited for pursuing those issues that need to be addressed in relation to the set question
- a wide range of detail is precisely selected and used in your answer to support a developed evaluation of the issues – you will be credited for what you have found out in terms of the content relevant to the topic
- you engage with the stated factor for at least the first third of the essay – you should measure the stated factor against other factors, weighing the factors against each other
- you engage with other factors in your essay, using these factors to set up a *debate* – top marks are awarded to candidates who can show that they can really get inside the debate
- your essay has a substantial conclusion – in your conclusion you should weigh the evidence one last time, judge how each piece of evidence stacks up against other pieces of evidence and make judgements on the basis of the evidence.

Structuring a response

Marks are easily thrown away because your essay technique is not as strong as it should be. The aim of this section is to give you guidance on how to write an assignment that is analytical throughout.

Introduction Once you have written a plan you need to write an introduction that answers the question and defines the key terms.

- The introduction involves writing out the main points from the plan.
- It is essential that you attack the question directly in the introduction.
- Your introduction should be straightforward, direct and should deliver an answer to the question.

Paragraph structure You need to structure your assignment into clear and sufficient paragraphs. To achieve the mark you want, you need to stay direct to the argument throughout. This means that you must explicitly answer the question throughout the essay. The best structure for every paragraph is thus:

- *Argue* At the start of the paragraph you should present a line of argument. The best way to do this is to use the language of argument:

  One should argue that . . .
  It is clear that . . .
  Fundamentally . . .
  Without doubt . . .
  This most obviously . . .

  Try to avoid a descriptive start because this will often lead to a descriptive paragraph.

- *Explain* The next section of each paragraph will explain that line of argument.
- *Evidence* 'The clearest example of this point is the . . .' The next section of the paragraph should give and explain the relevance of detail that you have used to back up your argument. This detail needs to be accurate, well selected and relevant. What is meant by detail? Facts, statistics, names, events, references to historians.
- *Reiterate* The last sentence of the paragraph should be a reiteration, going back to the main theme/argument in the question.

SKILLS BUILDER

1 What are the divisions?

Halfway through the unit you started a spider diagram on which you plotted the divisions in Germany in the 1900 to 1914 period. After reading through the rest of the unit, finish that spider diagram off.

2 What has changed?

What changed in Germany between 1900 and 1914 and what stayed the same? Discuss this question with a work partner and see if you can list three points in each category.

RESEARCH TOPIC

Kaiser Wilhelm II

Kaiser Wilhelm II is a character who interests historians for many reasons. Much has been made of his supposed psychological problems. Given the nature of the Prussian constitution, how much of an impact on German politics did the personality of the Kaiser have?

Using books, articles and the Internet, try to find out as much as you can about the Kaiser's personality. Then complete this assignment:

- To what extent was the course of Germany 1900–14 dictated by the personality of the Kaiser?

2 Controversy: to what extent was Germany responsible for the outbreak of the First World War in 1914?

What is this unit about?

The outbreak of the First World War in August 1914 was not unexpected. Diplomatic tension between the Central Powers (Germany and Austria-Hungary) and the ***entente*** powers of Russia, France and Britain had been rising for a number of years. The first section of the unit is dedicated to explaining developments in German foreign policy up to 1914. The second section deals with the question of the extent to which Germany was guilty of causing the war. This section is different from much else in the book in that the focus is sharply on the controversy of Germany's involvement. In the Skills builder section at the end of the chapter, you and members of your class are invited to undertake research that will broaden your understanding.

You will:

* examine the development of German foreign policy between 1900 and 1914
* work with conflicting interpretations of how and why Germany was involved in the outbreak of the war in 1914.

Key questions

* What were the most significant events in the run-up to war in 1914?
* To what extent can Germany be blamed for the outbreak of war in 1914?
* Why has responsibility for the outbreak of the First World War generated so much controversy?

Definition

Entente

French for 'understanding'. The term is used here because the agreements between Britain, France and Russia were more understandings than formal alliances.

Timeline

1900	June	Second German Naval Law passed, providing for a fleet of 38 battleships to be built in 20 years
1904	April	Anglo-French Entente
1905	March	First Moroccan Crisis – Kaiser visits Tangier
	July	Björkö Treaty signed by Kaiser Wilhelm and Tsar Nicholas of Russia to improve relations between the countries – it comes to nothing
1906	February	Britain launches HMS *Dreadnought*
	April	Act of Algeciras confirms Morocco's independence but France's influence over the country
	May	Germany decides to increase size of its battleships and widen the Kiel Canal
	August	Anglo-Russian Entente

1908	October	Proclamation of the annexation of Bosnia Herzegovina by Austria
1909	February	Germany agrees to recognise French political influence in Morocco in return for recognition of Germany's economic interest
1911	July	Gunboat *Panther* arrives off the Moroccan coast in the Second Moroccan Crisis.
	September	Libyan war breaks out between Italy and the Ottoman Empire
1912	February	British Minister of War, Lord Haldane, visits Berlin
	March	German Naval Bill increases number of ships and personnel
	October	First Balkans War breaks out
1913	May	Treaty of London ends First Balkans War
	June	Second Balkans War breaks out
1914	June	Austrian Archduke Franz Ferdinand is assassinated in Sarajevo

Source A

Economic expansion was the basis of Germany's political world diplomacy, which vacillated in its methods between rapprochement and conciliation at one moment, aggressive insistence on Germany's claims the next, but never wavered in its ultimate objective, the expansion of Germany's power.

From Fritz Fischer, *Germany's Aims in the First World War*, published in 1967

SKILLS BUILDER

What is the impression of German foreign policy given in this source?

German foreign policy c.1900–14

SKILLS BUILDER

We are going to investigate the development of German foreign policy in the years running up to the First World War. Read through this section and then answer the following questions:

- Did the alliance system make war more or less likely?
- What factors turned Britain and Germany into rivals?
- How did the Moroccan crises and Weltpolitik affect international tensions?

Alliances and war plans

German victory in the Franco-Prussian war in 1870 was followed up by the creation of a system of alliances to protect the new empire. The architect of this alliance system was the German Chancellor Otto von Bismarck.

At its heart was the isolation of France, which sought *revanche* for the loss of Alsace-Lorraine and the humiliation of 1870. The pillars of this policy were:

- the ***Dreikaiserbund*** of 1881, which was an understanding of how the peace could be kept between Austria-Hungary, Russia and Germany
- the Triple Alliance of 1882 between Austria-Hungary, Italy and Germany, which was a defensive alliance between the three.

Wilhelm II's accession to the throne in 1888 and Bismarck's subsequent departure from the post of Chancellor was to have a profound impact on German foreign policy. In March 1890, the Kaiser embarked on his 'new course' by refusing to renew the Reassurance Treaty between Germany and Russia that guaranteed that each country would not attack the other. Instead, the Kaiser signalled an even warmer relationship with Vienna, while the Chief of the General Staff of the army, Field Marshall Schlieffen, began to work on a plan that would mean that Germany could fight a war on two fronts by knocking France out of the war before Russia could mobilise. Schlieffen was Chief of the General Staff from 1891 to 1905, and the plan was formulated during his time in office. At the heart of the plan was the idea of a lightning strike of German forces through the Low Countries and northern France before encircling Paris. In Alsace-Lorraine, French armies would maintain a defensive stance. The French were expected to capitulate in six weeks. Once France had fallen, German forces would transfer to the Eastern Front to take on the Russians. The plan relied on slow French and even slower Russian mobilisation.

Germany and Britain

The Kaiser's attitude towards Britain was complex. As a grandson of Queen Victoria, he both loved and loathed the country of his mother's birth in equal measure. In 1896 Wilhelm antagonised British public opinion by

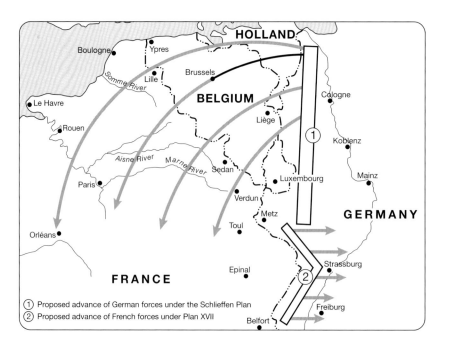

2.1 The Schlieffen Plan

① Proposed advance of German forces under the Schlieffen Plan
② Proposed advance of French forces under Plan XVII

sending a telegram to President Kruger of the South African Republic congratulating him for the defeat of British raiders led by Dr Jameson. There is a possibility that at this point Germany might still have been trying to woo the British into the Triple Alliance, but the following years saw a fundamental sea change in the relationship between Britain and Germany:

- *Flottenpolitik* and a series of Navy Laws (see page 17) were a direct challenge to British naval supremacy and were viewed as such in Britain. Their impact was to spark a naval race between the two nations. The launch in 1906 of the British battleship HMS *Dreadnought* with its ten 12-inch guns prompted Germany into massive naval expenditure to avoid falling further behind.

- German support for the Boers in the Boer War, 1899–1902, further antagonised relations.

- In 1901, the British made overtures towards the Germans for an alliance, but these were spurned by the German Foreign Office, which insisted that Britain would have to commit to the Triple Alliance. Bülow also calculated that the British would not find allies elsewhere, given her colonial rivalries with France and Russia.

- However, over the coming years Britain ended its 'splendid isolation' and her subsequent alliance with Japan (1902) and *entente* agreements with France (1904) and Russia (1907) left Germany over-reliant on Austria-Hungary.

Limits to Weltpolitik

You have read about von Bülow's policy of Weltpolitik in the last unit. The reality was that, despite considerable posturing and pressure from groups such as the Colonial Society, it did not achieve much in terms of new territory.

- In 1897 German involvement in China resulted in her gaining a lease on the port of Kiaochow.

- In 1898 Germany bought the Pacific islands of the Carolines and the Marianas from Spain.

- In 1899 an agreement was made with Britain resulting in Germany taking some of the eastern Samoan islands.

Despite involvement in the Constantinople to Baghdad railway, these gains did not constitute a great success and did not deliver Germany's '**place in the sun**'. However, Russia's misfortune in the Russo-Japanese War of 1904–05 and its subsequent weakening due to revolution in 1905 gave Germany a freer diplomatic hand in the Near East.

The First Moroccan Crisis, 1905–06

In March 1905 Kaiser Wilhelm made a visit to Tangier in Morocco, which was, at least in theory, within the French **sphere of influence** although

Definitions

Place in the sun

A term used to describe the desire to have the same number of colonies as Britain and France.

Sphere of influence

An area in which one nation has control over another or others.

Germany had a number of economic interests in Tangier. Plans by the French to increase influence in Morocco had been discussed with other European powers including Britain and Italy.

- The Germans demanded an international conference to discuss the future of Morocco, hoping to drive a wedge between Britain and France, but the opposite happened.

- They also attempted to prise the Russians away from their friendship with the French by the Treaty of Björkö, which was signed by the Kaiser and the Tsar in July 1905. Aimed at creating closer bonds between Berlin and St Petersburg, this measure failed because of opposition in the Russian foreign office from those who did not want the close friendship with France to be damaged.

- At the Algeciras Conference and in the subsequent Algeciras Act, Morocco was confirmed in the French sphere and the *entente* was strengthened.

The episode had been a humiliation for the Germans, and the highly influential head of the Political Office at the Foreign Ministry, Friedrich von Holstein, was forced to resign. A mentality was emerging that was to have a profound impact on Germany's military and political leaders for the next eight years. At Algeciras the only country that supported Germany was Austria-Hungary, and the launching of HMS *Dreadnought* posed a real threat: for many in Germany, the fear of encirclement was real.

The Second Moroccan Crisis, 1911

In February 1909, the French and German governments signed an agreement to respect each other's interests in Morocco. However, disturbances in the town of Fez in April 1911 led to the military intervention of the French. Germany complained that this action went against the Algeciras Act and they backed their protest by sending the German gunboat *Panther* to moor off the Moroccan port of Agadir. The summer of 1911 was dominated by the talk of war, Germany attempting to bully France into giving her the French Congo in return for Germany giving up all interests in Morocco. Again the Germans attempted to prise the *entente* apart, and again they failed. In his 'Mansion House' speech in July 1911, the Liberal Chancellor of the Exchequer, David Lloyd George, warned Germany against further aggression. The Second Moroccan Crisis resulted in Germany gaining two strips of land in the Congo, but with Germany having to promise to accept French control of Morocco.

Tension mounts

German foreign policy was based on an understanding that the imperial rivalries of Britain and France in Africa, and Britain and Russia in Asia, would mean that Germany would be able to divide and dominate these three countries. Increasingly, this was clearly not the case, and in 1907 Britain and Russia signed an *entente* that put their differences over empire in Asia behind them.

The naval race between Britain and Germany persisted, despite Bülow and Bethmann-Hollweg's attempts to persuade the Kaiser to come to some agreement. He would not compromise, and in March 1909 the British government set aside a budget to build nine dreadnought-class battle ships in the year. The failure of the Haldane Mission in February 1912 marked the last chance for the two countries to come to some agreement:

- Lord Haldane travelled to Berlin in the hope of improving relations between Britain and Germany.

- The Germans would agree to a limit on fleet expansion only if the British agreed to neutrality in any future European land war.

- The Kaiser and Tirpitz were committed to increasing the size of the fleet. In March 1912 the Germans published a new Naval Bill proposing further expansion. The Haldane mission was well and truly sunk.

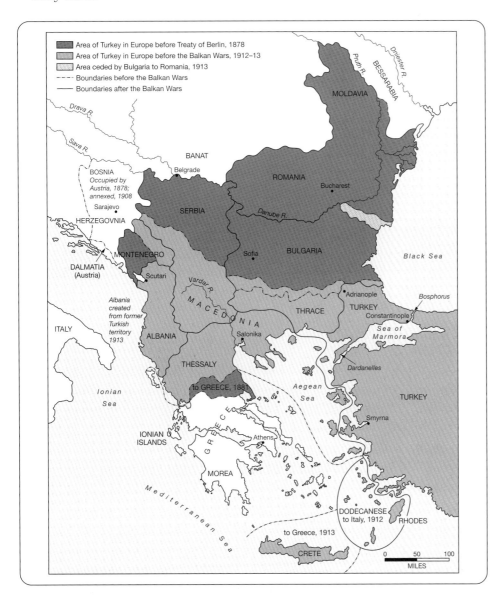

2.2 The Balkans

SKILLS BUILDER

Look carefully at the map of the Balkans. What are the potential tensions in this region?

The Habsburgs

The royal family of Austria-Hungary, one of the most important royal families in Europe.

Ottoman Empire

The Turkish based empire that lasted from the thirteenth century to the twentieth century and, in its prime, controlled the Balkans region of Europe, the Middle East and North Europe.

The Balkans

It was the Balkans that provided the spark for the outbreak of the war in 1914. The Balkans provided the theatre, the stage on which the imperial and racial rivalries were to be acted out. Germany was not a central player in the Balkans, but her one close ally, Austria-Hungary, was. Through her alliance with the **Habsburgs**, therefore, Germany was to be drawn into the politics of Europe's most unstable region. Up until nearly the end of nineteenth century, the Balkans had been dominated by the **Ottoman Empire**. The decline of the Ottoman Empire opened the way for both Russia and the Habsburg Empire to stake a claim for dominance of the region.

- It also paved the way for nationalities such as the Serbs to assert their national identity and independence. For the Habsburgs the problem with the Serbs was that they were Slavs. This meant that they were protected by and allied to fellow Slavs, the Russians.

- In Russia, the concept of protecting fellow Slavs – Pan-Slavism – was popular and strong.

- The Habsburg Empire contained many nationalities that included Serbs, and the Austrians feared that a strong Serbia would lead to unrest and the possible-break up of her multi-ethnic empire. In 1897, the Russians and Austria-Hungary had agreed to work together to resolve tensions in the Balkans and so preserve the status quo in the region, but this was not to last.

Bosnia Herzegovina

In 1903 a strongly pro-Russian dynasty came to power in Serbia. This signalled a more hostile relationship between the Serbs and the Austrians. In 1906 a trade agreement between the two was not renewed, which led to a trade war that became known as the Pig War (because the Austrians blocked the import of Serbian pigs). The real turning point was the appointment of Count Aehrenthal as Austria-Hungary's Foreign Minister in 1906.

- His view, which was supported by the Habsburg Chief of the General Staff General Conrad, was that the best way to deal with the Serbs was to annex the regions of Bosnia and Herzegovina, which the Austro-Hungarian government did in October 1908.

- The Russian Foreign Minister Izvolski had attempted to trade off Russian approval for this action with Austrian recognition of Russian rights in the Dardanelles Straits.

- The deal fell through. The Serbs and the Russian government were furious, and the Austro-Hungarian understanding of 1897, which had kept the peace in the Balkans, was finished.

- When, in February 1909, Austria-Hungary forced Serbia and Russia to recognise the annexation of Bosnia Herzegovina, it did so by threatening war against Serbia. It did so with the full support of Bülow's government,

With a work partner or in groups, discuss the following point.

Russia had been humiliated in 1908–09 over Bosnia and Herzegovina. What was the likely impact of such a humiliation on future relations with Austria-Hungary?

which promised to mobilise the German armed forces in support even though it had not been consulted by the Habsburgs prior to the annexation. The upshot of the Bosnia Herzegovina crisis was that Russia had been damaged and Germany had become involved.

The First Balkans War 1912

The attack by Italy against the Ottoman Empire in Libya in 1911 further highlighted the growing decline of Ottoman influence. It encouraged the forming of the Balkan League of Bulgaria, Serbia, Greece and Montenegro with the purpose of seizing territory from the collapsing Ottoman Empire. In October 1912, the Balkan League launched its attack on the Ottomans. The Austrians were horrified, especially when the Serbs invaded Albania. They were determined to prevent Serbia having access to the sea and creating a Greater Serbia. In November 1912, Austria demanded the creation of an independent Albania. The Serbs, supported by Russia, ignored the Austrians, and the Germans pressed the Habsburgs to make their point. The international crisis was such that the Kaiser called a council of his military advisers to meet on 8 December to consider his options (more of which we shall hear later). Two days later, the Kaiser spoke to the Swiss Ambassador about how 'racial war, the war of Slavdom against Germandom' was now unavoidable. He was prepared to accept that diplomacy might win through this time, and indeed it did – by the Treaty of London of 1913, which ended the First Balkans War. However, the obsession in Berlin that Germany was being encircled and the ever-increasing Slav threat provided the context for much policy over the coming months.

- The Army Bill of June 1913 increased the German army's size by 170,000 troops. The response from the French and the Russians was to increase the length of service in their armies.

- A brief Second Balkans War between the countries of the Balkans League saw Serbia emerge strengthened. In the summer, Serbian troops again entered Albania, and in October 1913 Germany supported the Austrian government in another ultimatum, warning Serbia.

- While it was clear, for the next few months, that neither Germany nor, for that matter, Austria-Hungary were under any immediate threat, the issue was one of fear for the future. A memorandum from 18 May 1914 by Count von Waldersee, Quartermaster-General in the German General Staff, reflects the general impression that, while the Army Bill of 1913 had increased the size of the army by 170,000, the *entente* powers were also increasing the size of their armies and were catching up. The best time for war was the present.

July Crisis

On 28 June 1914, the heir to the Austrian throne, Archduke Franz Ferdinand, was shot by Gavril Princip. Princip was a member of the

> **Discussion point**
>
> This is quite a difficult question but one worth discussing in your group. You may well have some good ideas with which you can answer it.
>
> Why did Germany persistently support Austria-Hungary in its arguments with Serbia despite the fact that Germany had no direct interest in the Balkans?

Serbian terrorist organisation called the Black Hand. On 5 July an Austrian diplomat, Count Hoyos, travelled to Berlin seeking Germany's support for action against Serbia. The Kaiser and the German government, including Chancellor Bethmann-Hollweg, were happy to offer their unconditional support in what became known as the 'Blank Cheque'. Germany had taken what Bethmann-Hollweg called on 14 July a 'leap into the dark'. From now on the series of events acquired a momentum of their own.

23 July	Austria issued Serbia with an ultimatum. Serbia replied in conciliatory fashion but rejected the point that suggested that Austrian officials should be allowed to take part in the enquiry in Serbia about the assassination.
25 July	Russia came out in favour of Serbia, bolstered by French assurances of support.
26 July	The British Foreign Secretary Sir Edward Grey proposed a conference to deal with the Austro-Serb issue. Austria refused to take part.
28 July	Austria declared war on Serbia.
29 July	Bethmann-Hollweg urged the resumption of Austro-Russian negotiations and failed to persuade the British into neutrality. Wilhelm contacted his cousin Nicholas II with the result that the Tsar downgraded an order of general mobilisation to one of partial mobilisation.
30 July	The Tsar changed his mind after being advised that a partial mobilisation was not possible. Russia ordered a general mobilisation despite numerous general warnings from Germany.
31 July	With the Russians mobilising, events were now set by the Schlieffen Plan. Germany sent an ultimatum to Russia giving it 12 hours to cease war preparations on Germany's frontier. The same day Germany refused a request to respect Belgian neutrality.
1 August	France and Germany mobilised their troops for war, and Germany declared war on Russia.
2 August	The German armies invaded Luxembourg and demanded that Belgium should give them access through their country. This demand was refused. The British gave France assurances of support.
3 August	Germany invaded Belgium and declared war on France claiming that her frontier had been violated.
4 August	Britain declared war on Germany in protection of Belgian neutrality as had been agreed in 1839.
6 August	Austria declared war on Russia.

Discussion points

Read the information in the 'July Crisis' section and consider the information in Sources B, C and D. Using all of the information at your disposal, discuss the following questions in groups.

1 What was the point after which there was no turning back?

2 Which country was to blame for war?

3 What are the differences between Sources B, C and D? In answering this question you may well consider differences in what the sources suggest, their tone and emphasis.

Source B

Given these indications that the war would not be localised, there were ample opportunities for Germany to back down. Yet the initial British peace keeping initiatives were given only the most insincere support by Germany. The Germans pressed on, urging the Austrians to make haste, and after 26 July openly rejecting diplomatic alternatives. Only at the eleventh hour did they begin to lose their nerve; the Kaiser first, on 28 July, and then Bethmann who, after hearing of Grey's warning of the 29th to the Germany ambassador [in London] frantically sought the Austrians to apply the brakes. Berchtold tried to respond; but it was the German military which ultimately secured, by a combination of persuasion and defiance, the mobilisation orders, the ultimate and declarations of war which unleashed the conflict.

From Niall Ferguson, *The Pity of War*, published in 1998

Source D

Above all, it is time once and for all to discard Lloyd George's worn out phrase that Europe 'slithered' into war in 1914. Great powers throughout history have rarely, if ever, 'slithered' into major wars; rather, they undertake this most difficult of human endeavours only after carefully weighing the advantages and disadvantages. In this sense and only in this sense can one speak of a 'calculated risk' in 1914.

From Holder H. Herwig, 'Industry, Empire and the First World War', in Gordon Martel (editor), *Modern Germany Reconsidered, 1870–1945*, published in 1992

Source C

Thus to the general necessity inherent in the Schlieffen Plan for the violation of Belgian neutrality and offensive action as soon as possible after mobilisation, the attack on Liège required even more immediate action, since it was scheduled to take place on the third day of mobilisation with such troops as were immediately available. It was, therefore, as Molkte was to argue in a long meeting with Bethmann on the evening of 31 July 1914, essential to launch the attack in the west the moment Russia proclaimed mobilisation, so as to carry out the onslaught on France before Russian mobilisation was complete and before fighting began on the eastern front. And to launch the attack in the west, it was equally essential to capture Liège within three days. The attack on Belgium had therefore to be launched almost immediately after the proclamation of mobilisation and there was no margin for any delay between mobilisation and the start of hostilities. The Liège operation had been kept a deep secret, and it looks as though the Kaiser himself had not been told about it and that Bethmann only grasped its implications on 31 July. While the other powers could order mobilisation and wait what to do next, in the case of Germany mobilisation inevitably meant war.

From James Joll, *The Origins of the First World War*, published in 1984

To what extent was Germany responsible?

The debate as to responsibility for the outbreak of the First World War started almost immediately after the war had ended.

- The Treaty of Versailles of 1919 placed the blame for the outbreak of the First World War squarely on the shoulders of the Germans as you will read in Unit 4. Thereafter, the German authorities published documents selectively to shift the blame for the war onto the shoulders of others because clause 231 of the Versailles treaty explicitly blamed Germany. By the late 1930s a gentle and rather cosy consensus was shared that, in David Lloyd George's words, all of the Great Powers had 'slithered over the brink into the boiling cauldron of fire'.

That consensus survived the Second World War. In 1951 a group of French and German historians met in a Franco-German Historians' Commission. One of the subjects that they discussed was the causes of the outbreak of the First World War. The conclusions drawn by the Commission and accepted by most historians for the period of the next ten years both fitted in with the general opinion of historians before 1939 and the desire to build peaceful and lasting relations between France and Germany.

Discussion point

The history textbooks in France and Germany in the 1950s and 1960s were based on the line expressed by the Franco-German Historians' Commission. In your opinion, was that line accurate?

Source E

The documents do not permit attributing a conscious desire for a European War to any one government or people. Mutual distrust had hit a peak, and in leading circles it was believed that war was inevitable. Each one accused the other of aggressive intentions, and only saw a guarantee for security in an alliance system and continual armament increases.

From the Franco-German Historians' Commission 1951

Definition

Historiographical revolution

Turning points in the writing of history when new ideas are put forward that change how people think. These ideas can constitute a revolution in the writing of history.

The Fischer Controversy

In 1961 a German historian, Fritz Fischer, launched a **historiographical revolution**. In his book *Griff nach der Weltmacht*, which became abridged into the English version *Germany's Aims in the First World War* (published in 1967), Fischer came to some sensational conclusions:

- Germany had gone to war to achieve European and worldwide domination very similar to that aimed for by Hitler and the Nazis in the Second World War: it was a bid for world power.
- Germany had hoped that the 'Blank Cheque' given to Austria in July 1914 would result in war.
- The roots of German expansionism were to be found in the social, economic and political tensions which troubled Germany before 1914.

Discussion point

These views were sensational. Before we go on you should reflect on Fischer's points. From what you know, how far do you agree with Fischer?

Fischer's evidence

Fischer based his evidence partly on a document found in the German archives written by Bethmann-Hollweg's private secretary Kurt Riezler on 9 September 1914, in which he outlines the Chancellor's plans for the peace negotiations, which he expected to take place in the near future. Fischer argued that these plans were the continuation of policy made by politicians, military leaders and industrialists before the outbreak of war in 1914. The plans were not just the ideas of Bethmann-Hollweg or even the leading political, military and industrial figures of the day. To Fischer, these plans had the support of the wider political nation. Indeed the plans in the 9 September programme represented 'a complete revolution in European political and power relations'. The logic was clear: plans for annexation that were being written down in September 1914 did not come from nowhere, they must have been already considered in July 1914. Therefore Germany was not the victim but the perpetrator of war. Fischer's thesis broke new ground in other ways:

- It placed Chancellor Bethmann-Hollweg at the centre of the drive for expansion.

- It removed the distinction between the expansionist military and the supposedly more moderate politicians.

- It linked foreign and domestic policy by suggesting that the proposed annexations were seen as a means of maintaining domestic dominance.

Read the following four sources and study the map.

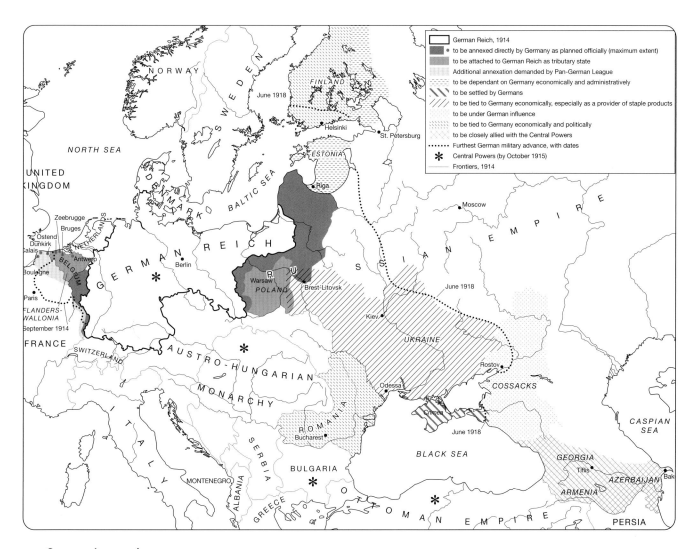

2.3 Germany's war aims, 1914

Source F

Expecting as he did that peace negotiations would be opening shortly, Bethmann-Hollweg describes his programme of 9 September as 'provisional notes on the direction of our policy on the conclusion of peace'. The 'general aim of the war' was, for him, 'security for the German Reich in west and east for all imaginable time. For this purpose France must be so weakened as to make her revival as a great power impossible for all time. Russia must be thrust back as far as possible from Germany's eastern frontiers and her domination over the non-Russian peoples broken.'

The objectives in the east were not yet set out in detail in the programme itself, since peace with Russia was not yet regarded as imminent, but this does not mean that they had not yet assumed concrete form. The detailed explanation of 'individual war aims' was confined to the continental west, where the conclusion of peace seemed within grasp. They ran as follows:

France. The military to decide whether we should demand cession of Belfort and western slopes of the Vosges, razing fortresses and cession of coastal strip from Dunkirk to Boulogne.

The ore field of Briey, which is necessary for the supply of ore for our industry, to be ceded in any case.

Further, a war indemnity, to be paid in instalments; it must be high enough to prevent France from spending any considerable sums on armaments in the next fifteen–twenty years.

Furthermore a commercial treaty, which makes France economically dependent on Germany, secures the French market for our exports and makes it possible to exclude British commerce from France. This treaty must secure for us financial and industrial freedom of movement in France in such fashion that German enterprises can no longer receive different treatment from the French.

And so the document goes on for other countries . . .

From Fritz Fischer, *Germany's Aims in the First World War*, published in 1967

Source G

There is a fundamental flaw in Fischer's reasoning which too many historians have let pass. It is the assumption that Germany's war aims as stated after the war had started were the same as German aims beforehand. Thus Bethmann-Hollweg's 'September Programme' for a separate peace with France – drafted on the assumption of a quick German victory in the West – is sometimes portrayed as if it were the first open statement of aims which had existed before the war. If this were true, then the argument that war was avoidable would collapse; for it is clear that no British government would have accepted the territorial and political terms which the September programme proposed for France and Belgium, as these would have realised the Napoleonic nightmare by giving Germany control of the Belgian coast. But the inescapable fact is that no evidence has been found by Fischer and his pupils that these objectives existed before Britain's entry into the war.

From Niall Ferguson, *The Pity of War*, published in 1998

Source H

Three points deserve emphasis. Firstly German war aims not only exceeded those of any other combatant; they were aspirations to world power. Secondly, there was a greater consensus over those aims that pre-Fischer historians like to admit. Annexationist ambitions were not confined to soldiers like Hindenburg or Ludendorff, or to Pan-Germans and other super-patriots. They were shared by civilian ministers, civil servants, Catholic and liberal politicians, liberal intellectuals such as Max Weber, even by some Social Democrats.

From David Blackbourn, *History of Germany 1780–1918*, published in 1997

SKILLS BUILDER

Read Sources F and G:

1 What is the significance of the September Programme for Fischer and what are Ferguson's criticisms?

2 Who is right?

Using Sources F, G, H and I:

3 Summarise the arguments from all four sources about the extent of German blame for the outbreak of war.

4 To what extent do Sources H and I agree with Sources F and G? Explain your answer fully with reference to the sources and your own knowledge.

Source I

It is now apparent that the 'men of 1914' in Berlin were working to an elaborate and cunning scenario, a secret plot designed either to split the Triple Entente wide open in order to effect a massive diplomatic revolution, which would have given Germany control of the European continent and much of the world beyond, or – a better methods in the eyes of many to achieve the same goal – to provoke a continental war against France and Russia in what appeared to be exceptionally favourable circumstances. If that war could be brought about through a Balkan crisis rather than through some incident in western Europe, they calculated, three highly desirable advantages would accrue to the Reich: Austria-Hungary would be on the front line and would not be able to wriggle out of its alliance commitments to Germany; the German population could be manipulated into believing that Germany was being attacked by 'barbarous' Russia and so would rally to the defence of the Fatherland; and Britain might be persuaded to stay out of the war, at least for the first six crucial weeks during which France would be defeated by means of a lightning attack through Belgium.

From John Röhl, 'Germany', in Keith Wilson (editor), *Decisions for War*, published in 1995 by Palgrave Macmillan

Fischer challenged

Fischer's analysis brought a storm of protest. Historians such as Gerhard Ritter and Egmont Zechlin attacked his thesis. One aspect they objected to was Fischer's portrayal of Bethmann-Hollweg as central to the push for war. The diaries of Kurt Riezler were published in the 1980s by Karl Dietrich Erdmann. He was of the opinion that Germany had slipped into war in 1914. What the diaries suggested to Erdmann was that Germany had been part of the push for war but that it had not been planning for war since 1912, nor did it have grand plans for annexation. While the Riezler diaries have proved useful, there are suggestions by some historians that they were tampered with.

Another challenge made to Fischer's thesis was that there was very little evidence that the outbreak of the war constituted a grasp for world power. Instead, a group of historians including Klaus Hildebrand, Andreas Hillgruber and Gregor Schöllgen maintained that war started because of a sense of encirclement in Germany, especially after failure in the First Moroccan Crisis and after the Anglo-Russian Entente of 1907. They argued that between 1909 and 1914 German foreign policy was almost obsessively focused on the need to break this encirclement. This mentality was partly born from the manner in which Germany was born out of war, partly from geography and partly from events as they unfolded. However, it stresses that the reasons for going to war were defensive, rather than aggressive.

Source J

The picture of Bethmann-Hollweg's policy in the July crisis, such as it emerges from the Riezler diaries, fits neither into the pattern of a Germany pushed into a war against her will, nor of a Germany wilfully pushing into war. Egmont Zechlin found a very adequate term for this attitude. He called it preventive *Abwehr* (preventive defence). This seems to me to be more to the point than 'preventive war', although Bethmann-Hollweg himself, sometime later, called the First World War 'in a certain sense' a preventive war. Fischer shares the opinion that preventive war is not the right term, because on the side of the *entente* there was objectively no intention of attacking Germany. In my view, the term preventive *Abwehr* fits better than preventive war, because Germany, though taking the risk of war, had hope of disrupting the *entente* without war.

From Karl Dietrich Erdmann, *A Judgement on Bethmann-Hollweg*, published in 1964

Source K

The incident that promoted the Kaiser to take further action was the assassination of his close associate, Archduke Franz Ferdinand, the heir to the Austro-Hungarian throne, by a Bosnian terrorist supported by Serbia on 28 June 1914. With emotions running high, William favoured an immediate Austrian action against Serbia. On 5 July, the Kaiser met with the Austro-Hungarian ambassador to Berlin. William II informed the ambassador that 'he expected some serious step . . . towards Serbia' and without consulting with Bethmann-Hollweg, [he said] to the ambassador that Austria could 'rely upon Germany's full support'. The Kaiser was under the assumption that any Austrian action could be localised in the Balkans since 'Russia at the present time was in no way prepared for war, and would think twice before it appealed to arms.'

Later that same day, on 5 July, the Kaiser summoned those of his highest military and political advisers who were available at a moment's notice to a meeting in Potsdam. The German Army was represented by General Eric von Falkenhayn, the Prussian Minister of War and the Chief of the Kaiser's military Cabinet. Bethmann-Hollweg and Zimmermann, both with little knowledge of foreign relations, represented the diplomats at the meeting since Jagow was on leave away from Berlin. At the Potsdam Conference the Kaiser insisted upon Germany supporting Austria-Hungary because its preservation was vital to German security.

From William Young, *German Diplomatic Relations 1871–1945*, published in 2006

Source L

Asquith did not know how little control the Kaiser and Bethmann exercised. A country where the Chancellor hardly dared to ask the General Staff what they were doing was outside his comprehension. He assumed that, when it came to the moment of the decision, the German government would be likely to choose an invasion route which would not force Belgium to call for British military help.

We do not know everything about what happened during the last days of July in Berlin and Potsdam: but we can be sure that events there belied Asquith's assumptions. The General Staff had concealed from the political leaders the worst political horror in their war plans, namely that their first objective was the capture of Liège and its forts. They needed a head start in the war in order to mount a surprise attack there; and they might decide to follow that with a massive bombardment. Bethmann does not seem to have been told this until 31 July. The General Staff were in charge.

From Michael Brock, *The Coming of the First World War*, edited by R.J. Evans and Hartmut Pogge von Strandmann, published in 1990

SKILLS BUILDER

1 To what extent do these sources give the impression that Bethmann-Hollweg drove the agenda for war?

2 What other issues are picked up by these sources?

War of illusions

In *War of Illusions* (1969), Fischer made even greater play of the relationship between German domestic tensions and foreign policy. He argued that:

- The German government used war as a solution to difficult internal problems and the idea that there was a strong 'will to war'.

- War in 1914 was a bold leap forward – *Flucht nach vorn* (flight or push forward) – to establish German dominance and to keep domestic peace.

- The whole decision-making élite had to take responsibility for war. Germany's leaders were culturally pessimistic and needed to break encirclement.

Fischer was able to use the diaries of Admiral Müller, which had been published in 1965 and in which there was reference to a meeting on 8 December 1912 of the Kaiser and his top military advisers. In *War of Illusions* Fisher argued that the 'War Council' of 1912 was evidence that the path to war had already been decided upon. It was, according to Fischer, only postponed because, subsequent to the meeting, Bethmann-Hollweg insisted that Germany had to prepare herself diplomatically and Tirpiz insisted on the military planners waiting for the opening of the Kiel Canal.

How significant was the 1912 'War Council'?

The tensions in European capitals at the end of December 1912 were all too apparent. Serbian expansion to the sea had alarmed Austria to the point that, in November 1912, the Austrian government announced its opposition to such expansion. In response, the Russian government began to mobilise, and Austria sought support from Germany and Italy in the case of a general European war. On 5 December the Triple Alliance was renewed, but two days before the British Minister of War, Lord Haldane, warned the German Ambassador in London that Britain would not tolerate the defeat of France if a war between Russia and Austria led to a German attack on her French neighbours. In this context the Kaiser called a meeting of his top military staff including Molkte, Tirpitz and Admiral Georg von Müller, whose diaries have given historians such an insight into what Fischer called a 'war council'. At the meeting the following points were made:

- The Kaiser insisted that Austria-Hungary should be supported in her actions against Serbia.

- If Russia decided to fight then so be it. Austria would be supported by Turkey, Romania, Bulgaria and Albania, which would leave Germany free to deal with France on land and Britain at sea.

- Molkte thought that war against Russia was inevitable and the sooner the better.

- Tirpitz suggested that the navy needed another 12 to 18 months to prepare the fleet and for the Kiel Canal to have opened to allow large German naval vessels passage from the Baltic into the North Sea.

But while many historians praised much of what Fischer had to say in *War of Illusions*, there has subsequently been considerable debate about the importance of the so-called 'War Council' of 8 December 1912.

Source M

The evidence on the secret 'military-political conference' of 8 December 1912 must be described as unusually abundant. If historians nevertheless encounter difficulties in interpreting this meeting, that is primarily because the 'war council', as Bethmann-Hollweg angrily described it on 20 December 1912, cannot be separated from the emotive controversy on the immediate causes of the First World War. With few exceptions, even those historians who see German policy in the July crisis of 1914 as the main cause of the outbreak of the world war are reluctant to accept that this policy was formulated a year and a half earlier by the Kaiser and his faithful followers in the army and navy meeting in a hastily convened 'war council'.

From John Röhl, *The Kaiser and his Court*, published in 1994

Source N

The meeting [of 8 December] ended with only one resolution, that a press campaign should prepare for war with Russia. There is no evidence that the press chief of the Foreign Ministry attempted to orchestrate such a campaign, or that the newspapers could have been so manipulated if he had . . . Bethmann-Hollweg was not present at the meeting and did not endorse its conclusions. The close relationship between the Kaiser and his service chiefs would probably permit a gathering that excluded the political leadership nonetheless being called a 'war council'. But Bethmann-Hollweg, not the service chiefs, took centre stage in the crisis that did lead to war. The policy which he and Germany followed between December 1912 and July 1914 is not marked by the consistency which would endorse Fischer's argument.

From Huw Stachan, *The First World War*, published in 2001

Source O

What still needs to be investigated is the crucial question of when war was decided upon. The exciting hypothesis is gaining ground, as previously hidden sources come to light, that the decision was not taken in response to the Sarajevo assassination but some time before that event took place, as a result of a long process which began with Germany's perceived humiliation in the Second Morocco crisis [which was in 1911].

In a top secret memorandum of 1 April 1912, Admiral von Tirpitz formulated the question which seems to have informed all military-political thinking in Germany from Agadir to Sarajevo. Under the heading 'Bringing about the War', Tirpitz asked: should we speed up [the outbreak of war] or attempt to delay it?

From John Röhl, 'Germany', in Keith Wilson (editor), *Decisions for War*, published in 1995

Discussion point

Using the information in these sources, as historians what weight should we give to the 'War Council' of 1912? Does it show that Germany was ready to go to war or was it just a meeting at a time of diplomatic excitement?

Primat der Innenpolitik

One of the great traditions of German history was that foreign policy was dictated by events outside Germany. This is known as the *Primat der Aussenpolitik* (the dominance of foreign policy). Fischer turned this idea on its head and stressed the importance of the impact of internal pressures on foreign policy, this idea being known as the *Primat der Innenpolitik* (the dominance of internal policy). The concept has been developed by a number of historians including Hans Ulrich Wehler. He argued that the disruptive impact of industrialisation caused tensions in Germany's social and economic structure. The Junkers, financiers and industrialists resisted attempts by the middle classes to gain greater political power through the Reichstag. The growth of the SPD presented a real challenge, especially when they won 110 seats in the 1912 election. These tensions were diverted outwards, into foreign and diplomatic policy in order to preserve the status quo.

Source P

It would be wrong to analyse foreign policy solely in terms of a theory of the *Primat der Innenpolitk* or to attribute the decision for war to domestic pressures alone. At the same time there is much evidence to suggest that German politicians, generals and admirals were very conscious of the connection between domestic and foreign policy, not only because at certain moments they believed that foreign ventures might contribute to a mood of national solidarity at home, but also because they feared the strength of socialist opposition to warlike policies. The balance between the awareness of internal problems and dreams of world power was always a delicate one; and if recent historical writing had stressed the importance of the internal contradictions of German society in determining German foreign policy and the decision for war and has thus drawn attention to factors which had been largely overlooked by an older generation of historians, we much not forget that for many leading Germans the positive pursuit of world power or the negative securing of Germany's position in what was regarded as a hostile world was something to be undertaken for its own sake regardless of the domestic profit and loss.

From James Joll, *Origins of the First World War*, published in 1984

Source Q

The more direct and immediate consolidation of the Navy Bill was to come from the unifying effects of the naval armaments programme at home. More indirect and more long-range were the stabilising benefits which the government hoped to derive from the navy as an instrument of foreign policy and German imperialism in the twentieth century. But it is not difficult to see that, in the final analysis, the result would be the same. It is in this sense that the decision to build a large battle fleet represented an 'inner-political crisis strategy' designed to contribute to the survival of the Prusso-German political system; with the help of the Navy the monarchy wanted to overthrow the status quo internationally in order to preserve it at home . . . The trouble is, no complex modern society can be ruled like this [as Germany was on the eve of war] for too long. The political system was no longer capable of overcoming internal divisions. The élites were more and more tempted to use war as the catalyst for the renewed attempts to stabilise the monarchy.

From Volker Berghahn, *Germany and the Approach of War in 1914*, published in 1973

Source R

Not many historians nowadays dissent from the proposition that the German government, egged on by its generals, deliberately provoked the war of 1914 . . . In the two years before the July Crisis, Germany's leaders appear to have been gripped by a mood of desperation. In December 1912, for instance, a Crown Council quite seriously suggested that there should be war within a year and a half, that the press should be prepared, that military increases should be undertaken, and that the Reichsbank should build up a larger war chest. The Reichstag could not control the government; at the same time, the Kaiser, surrounded, often enough, by hysterical generals and noblemen, lost any sense of cool raison d'état . . . War squared the circles of German politics. Bismarck had to conquer Germany in order to rule Prussia. Would Bethmann-Hollweg have to conquer Europe in order to rule Germany?

From Norman Stone, *Europe Transformed 1878–1919*, published in 1983

What about Austria-Hungary?

There is not space in this book to outline the role played by other powers in the outbreak of war. However, there is scope within the Skills builder at the end of this chapter for you to research in greater depth. That said, it is important to explore briefly whether there is an argument to suggest that Germany was dragged into war by her closest ally, Austria-Hungary.

SKILLS BUILDER

According to Sources P, Q and R, how significant an impact was domestic politics on foreign affairs in Germany in the run-up to the war?

Source S

In Austria-Hungary there was clearly a sense of desperation at the intractable internal and external problems facing the Habsburg dynasty, and military action, rather than diplomacy, seemed to be the best way to deal with them. By the end of 1913, the majority of ministers wanted to solve the Serbian problem by force . . . [it has been] shown that the policy-makers in Vienna pursued a consistently belligerent policy in 1914 and that there was a fateful meshing of 'aggressive German Weltpolitik' with an even more aggressive, irresponsible 'Habsburg Balkanpolitik'.

From Ruth Henig, *The Origins of the First World War*, published in 1993

Source T

In Vienna in July 1914 a set of leaders experienced in statecraft, power and crisis management consciously risked a general war to fight a local war. Battered during the Balkans Wars by Serbian expansion, Russian activism and now by the loss of Franz Ferdinand, the Habsburg leaders desperately desired to shape their future, rather than let events destroy them. The fear of domestic disintegration made war an acceptable policy option. The Habsburg decision, backed by the Germans, gave the July crisis a momentum that rendered peace an early casualty.

From Samuel Williamson, *Austria-Hungary and the Origins of the First World War*, published in 1988

Source U

The frivolity and arrogance with which Austro-Hungarian statesmen, politicians, military men, publicists and diplomats wished for and decided on war against their small neighbour made them guilty of providing the opportunity that the German military were seeking to wage the preventative war they had been recommending for years. Austria-Hungary bears the responsibility for planning a local third Balkan War against Serbia – the responsibility for the escalation of the conflict into a European war does not lie with Austria-Hungary, it lies in Berlin.

From Fritz Fellner, 'Austria', in Keith Wilson (editor), *Decisions for War*, published in 1995

SKILLS BUILDER

Read Sources S, T and U. What are the different judgements made by the authors of these sources with reference to the role of Austria-Hungary in the causation of war?

Discussion point

What do you think? Is there a relationship between domestic policy and foreign policy? Have you any other examples from history of rulers using domestic policy as a means of deflecting from foreign policy?

Unit summary

What have you learned in this unit?

Germany must carry a fair proportion of the blame for the outbreak of the First World War. The main argument of Fritz Fischer has been accepted by most historians, i.e. that Germany bears some responsibility. However, the reasons why German leaders pushed for war are still a source of some controversy. While Fischer argued that they launched a war of aggression and conquest, many have now suggested that it was more of a defensive war launched to break encirclement. In the 1930s, an argument was presented that Europe 'slipped into war'. Although that is perhaps now discredited as an argument, you have learned that there is an argument to suggest that war started because of the escalation of events.

What skills have you used in this unit?

Your understanding of the sources has been enhanced by an exploration of German foreign policy from 1900 to 1914. You have analysed interpretations in the sources and you have commented on the arguments made.

SKILLS BUILDER

1 Making a judgement

With a work partner, identify five lines of argument brought up by Fritz Fischer. For each point make a scoring judgement. Use the following scores:

Agree	4
Slightly agree	3
Slightly disagree	2
Disagree	1

Now share the lines of argument and scores with another pair.

2 Hypothesis testing

Form yourselves into discussion groups. Discuss the following hypothesis:

'Before 1912 Germany was committed to diplomacy to resolving her foreign policy problems. After 1912, she was committed to using war.'

To what extent do you agree with this judgement? This is quite a complex question to answer and revolves around whether you feel that 1912 constitutes a significant turning point.

3 Debate time

Using the information in this unit, what is your opinion on Chancellor Bethmann-Hollweg:

- guilty of starting the war?
- an innocent bystander?

Exam style question

This is the type of question that will be found in Section B of your examination paper:

'The outbreak of war in Europe in 1914 was due to an aggressive German foreign policy which had been waged since c.1900.'

How far do you agree with this opinion? Explain your answer using the evidence of Sources V, W and X and your own knowledge of the issues relating to the controversy.

Before you start, please read the advice on page 48.

Source V

By 1913 the question of civil war and foreign war had indeed become two sides of the same coin in the minds of the Kaiser and his advisers, and it is virtually impossible to decide which issue obsessed them more. They felt encircled not merely by the Triple Entente, but also by the forces of change. Germany's internal and external enemies, they believed, wanted to destroy them and the monarchical order. While the news was bad on the domestic front, it was arguably worse on the international one. The diplomatic isolation of Germany which started in 1904 had worsened and while Bethmann-Hollweg was making efforts to ease some of the pressure, the generals could only think of further rearmaments expenditure as a remedy. The 1913 Army Bill, which had now unleashed yet another major conflict over the distribution of tax burdens, had in part been a response to growing tensions in the Balkans and the weakening of the position of the Dual Alliance in that part of the world. In view of these developments, it seemed even more urgent to Helmuth von Molkte, the Chief of the General Staff, to fill the gaps which the 1912 Army Bill had left. Yet, rearm as strenuously as they might, the Germany military were unable to check the deterioration of the Reich's international predicament by trying to shift the balance of power in their favour.

From Volker Berghahn, *Modern Germany*, published in 1987

Source W

German responsibility for war should not be restricted to the issue of whether Bethmann, or the German government, or the Kaiser, desired peace in 1912–14 or, for that matter, earlier. Of course they would have preferred to get what they wanted without war. But German actions going back to the 1890s had done much to create international tension. Bethmann personally was a sensitive, passive, fatalistic man, but he was faced with reaping the whirlwind sown by his predecessors. Others bore more responsibility, like Tirpitz, who built a battle fleet aimed at the British but professed his peaceful intentions.

From David Blackbourn, *History of Germany 1780–1918*, published in 1997

Source X

So there emerged right at the beginning of the war the question of who bore the chief responsibility! It was latent controversy between the two allies [Germany and Austria-Hungary] which persisted during the entire war and flared up every time there was a military crisis. However, despite this friction and the English declaration [of war], the German plan to unleash a continental war which had crystallised a month previously during the Sarajevo murder, was fully realised. Only the constellation of forces against the Central powers was unexpected.

From John Moses, *The Politics of Illusion*, published in 1975

Exam tips

- *Plan* your answer before you start. You can use the advice about planning and structure which is given at the end of Unit 1 on pages 24–25.
- Make sure you *analyse* throughout the response, supporting your arguments with well-chosen own knowledge.
- Be very sure you know what '*view*' is being expressed in all three sources.
- Make sure you show that you understand the nature of the *debate* that lies at the heart of the question.
- *Cross-reference* between the sources by focusing on support and challenge.
- Use your *wider knowledge* both to reinforce and to challenge the points derived from the sources.
- *Synthesise* the arguments and points presented in the sources into your analysis.
- Present a *substantiated judgement* as to the validity of the stated view and/or any alternatives in the light of your understanding of the issues of interpretation and controversy.

RESEARCH TOPIC

The roles played by other countries

The focus of this unit has been on the debate surrounding the role played by Germany in the run-up to war and the extent of German war guilt. However, for you to have a full understanding of the reasons for the outbreak of the First World War you will need to undertake some individual research. There are many excellent books on the subject and some informative websites.

You should undertake the research task in groups with an individual or pair choosing one country. This is often best done by drawing lots out of a hat. Here are the countries to be researched:

- Austria-Hungary
- France
- Great Britain
- Russia
- Serbia

For each country you should aim to write up:

- a timeline of events of how your chosen country was involved in the build-up to war up to August 1914

- bullet points of analysis explaining how far your chosen country should be blamed for the outbreak of war.

This information can be circulated to other groups and each group can give a short presentation.

3 What was the impact of the First World War on Germany 1914–18?

What is this unit about?

The First World War was a catastrophe for Germany. The beginning of the war in 1914 was welcomed by a broad spectrum of public and political opinion in the country. However, the war effort was managed by a chaotic bureaucratic system that highlighted rather than covered up Germany's shortcomings insofar as a lack of raw materials and labour were concerned. Huge casualties sapped morale, as did growing hunger on the Home Front. Strikes and an ever more restless Reichstag challenged the military leadership of Generals Hindenburg and Ludendorff. The last two years of war were marked by growing political polarisation. By 1918 the nation was exhausted by war and faced defeat.

You will:
* find out about the impact of war on Germany from 1914 to 1918
* explore changes over the course of the war.

Key questions

* What were the social and economic effects in Germany of the First World War?
* How did the war polarise Germany politically?

Timeline

1914	August	War breaks out; Belgium attacked
	August	On the Eastern Front, German army wins the Battle of Tannenberg
	August	*Burgfreiden* agreed
	September	In the east, Russian army defeated at the Battle of the Masurian Lakes
	September	Advance in the west halted at the Battle of the Marne
	October	Race for the sea
1915	January	Rationing of bread introduced in Germany
	May	*Lusitania* sunk off the coast of Ireland
1916	February	Beginning of the Battle of Verdun
	May	Sea Battle of Jutland inconclusive
	June	Russians launch Brusilov Offensive
	July	Beginning of the Battle of the Somme
	August	Hindenburg and Ludendorff take war command
	December	Auxiliary Labour Law introduced in Germany
1917	January	Decision taken by Germany to wage unrestricted submarine warfare

	March	SPD splits
	April	The United States declares war against Germany
	July	Bethmann-Hollweg resigns as Chancellor
	July	Reichstag passes Peace Resolution
1918	March	Treaty of Brest-Litovsk ends war in the east to Germany's advantage
	March	Ludendorff offensive in the west breaks Allied lines but eventually runs out of steam
	November	Kaiser abdicates
	November	Armistice signed

3.1 *Triptychon Der Krieg* (War Triptych) by Otto Dix, painted between 1929 and 1932

SKILLS BUILDER

What does the painting *Triptychon Der Krieg* show us about the German experience of war?

Reactions to the outbreak of war

The anticipation of war filled many Germans with dread; as a conflict loomed, huge demonstrations against war were held on 28 and 29 July in Berlin (where the crowd was 100,000 strong) and elsewhere across Germany. Once war had broken out and the government presented it as a defensive campaign against Slav aggression, there was a general consensus on the side of national duty and what was understood to be morally right. The image of the cheering crowds on the Unter den Linden is well known. Even better known is the photograph of crowds in the Odeonsplatz in Munich on 2 August 1914 with an excited Adolf Hitler caught on camera cheering the outbreak of war. On 4 August the Kaiser addressed the nation, summarising the feeling of national unity by announcing 'I know no parties any more, only Germans.' To the relief of the **political nation**, the socialists in the Reichstag fell into line and voted for war credits. The political divisions of the pre-war era were over. On the same day, the Reichstag also passed an Enabling Act known as the ***Burgfrieden***; the concept of national unity based on shared suffering, the *Burgfrieden*, was established. The terms of the Enabling Act were to reinforce the pre-war institutional structures rather than challenge them, although there were some important differences.

- The Reichstag delegated all of its legislative powers to the Bundesrat, which was to rule the Home Front by emergency legislation. The Reichstag had the power to review that legislation, but not once in the duration of the war, and 800 laws, did it change anything.

The War Ministry took over the bureaucratic function of running the war, which very much strengthened the hand of the traditional bureaucracy.

Definitions

Political nation

Refers to all of the political parties together.

Burgfrieden

Refers to a castle that is under siege when the defenders put all differences aside in the name of survival.

3.2 Hitler celebrating the outbreak of war in the Odeonsplatz, Munich, on 2 August 1914

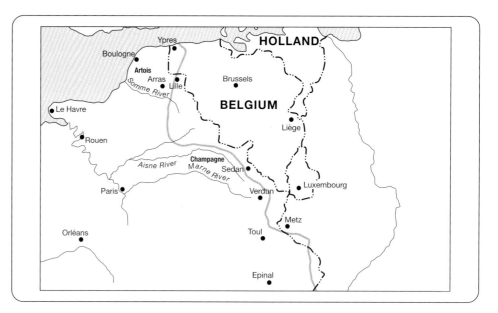

3.3 The Western Front, December 1914

Corporations were set up under the control of the War Materials Section of the War Ministry to ensure the supply of raw materials for the war effort. Also under the wing of the War Ministry, the War Committee for German Industry advised the bureaucrats on industrial policy. Despite this raft of bureaucratic initiatives, most enterprises stayed in private hands for the duration of the war because it was felt that the economy would be more efficiently run that way.

War 1914

On the night of 4 August 1914, the Germans unleashed the Schlieffen Plan, the blueprint for victory on two fronts, knocking out France before turning on Russia.

- Throughout August, the German armies made strong progress, advancing through Belgium despite meeting fierce resistance, especially from the British Expeditionary Force, which was all but wiped out. However, the Schlieffen Plan did not work as expected because the advance slowed as supplies failed to keep pace with it.

- In the east, the German armies, under the command of Generals Hindenburg and Ludendorff, won two great battles at Tannenberg and the Masurian Lakes, victories that turned the two commanders into folk heroes.

- The defining moment of the war came at the end of September. At the first Battle of the Marne the German armies were halted within shelling distance of Paris. They withdrew to the River Aisne and started to dig in. For the rest of the year, both sides attempted to outflank the other in a 'race to the sea'. The result was stalemate: hundreds of miles of trenches and around 650,000 German casualties on both fronts by the end of 1914. Germany's best opportunity for military victory had passed.

War 1915

The new Chief Commander of the General Staff in 1915 was Erich von Falkenhayn. With the Schlieffen Plan a failure, it was his responsibility to devise an alternative strategy, with his colleagues in the Supreme Command of the Army (OHL). The problem was the fighting of war on two fronts, which Germany could not win. The solution was to win a decisive victory on either the Western or the Eastern Front, and the debate within the OHL was over which to focus on. In the end, and against Falkenhayn's instincts, the decision was taken to attack in the east and a hugely successful campaign in Galicia in Poland threw the Russian army back over 250 miles. However, despite massive Russian losses it was not enough to knock Russia out of the war. On the Western Front, the Allies had suffered great losses attacking German defensive positions for little gain, and their campaign against Germany's Turkish allies at Gallipoli had been a dismal failure. The conclusion that Falkenhayn took from 1915 was that the key to German victory lay on the Western Front and in knocking the British out of the war with the use of an aggressive submarine campaign. This was despite the fact that the sinking of the passenger ship *Lusitania* in 1915 drew America closer to joining the war. As 1915 came to a close, German armies were stretched across Europe and were deployed in Asia and Africa.

Food

The German war effort was bedevilled throughout by the shortage of raw materials and consumer basics. On 4 February 1915, the German government announced a submarine blockade of Great Britain. The British government responded immediately by ordering the Royal Navy to seize all goods that were presumed to be destined for Germany. This was to have a considerable impact on the German Home Front. Before the war, Germany was not self-sufficient in food; indeed, in 1914 it imported around 25 per cent of what it consumed. The military taking priority over transport meant that supplies to the cities were hit. The state's response was to assume control for the regulation and distribution of food.

- In January 1915, the Imperial Grain Corporation was set up by the Bundesrat to administer the rationing and distribution of grain. This was to be followed by the creation of over 40 different Imperial Corporations who competed with federal, state and regional governments to administer the food supply.

- To try and bring some coherence to this bureaucratic morass, the state set up the War Food Office in 1916 but without the powers to exert control over all the other organisations and agencies. The chaos of the bureaucratic jungle meant that decisions were often made that were counter-productive; in early 1915 the bureaucracy decided to order the killing of 9 million pigs, primarily because they were consumers of grain and other feed. The consequences for the rest of the war were less pork and less fertiliser, both of which were to have a damaging effect on food production.

Biography

Erich von Falkenhayn

A cautious solider and master of the defence rather than the attack, Falkenhayn believed that the war would be won on the Western rather than Eastern Front. The idea of an all-out war of **attrition** in 1916 was his. After he resigned from being Chief Commander in 1916 he fought in Romania and Palestine. He died in 1922.

Definition

Attrition

One side winning a war by wearing down the other side.

Discussion points

Discuss the following points in groups:

1 After two years of war, what military problems did Germany face for the future?
2 Why did the Schlieffen Plan fail?

Table 3.1 Grain harvests in Germany 1914–18 (figures in millions of tons)

Year	Grain
1914	27.1
1915	22.0
1916	22.0
1917	14.6
1918	17.3

Shortages

Just as significant as the impact of the blockade was the problem of a shortage of labour in the countryside. The mobilisation in 1914 drained the countryside of up to a third of its labour force. By the end of 1914 around half of the agricultural workforce had been called up to serve in the German armed forces. This had an immediate impact on grain production (see Table 3.1 on page 53).

Despite the shortage of labour, the particularly conservative nature of pre-war German society meant that the state did not consider using women in the armed forces and they were not **conscripted** to work. This did not mean that women did not work – quite the opposite. By the end of the war a third of the industrial workforce was women. Women sought work in war industries because it was well paid: 40 per cent of the workers for the munitions maker Krupp, for example, were women. However, most of these women had already been in employment in other jobs such as domestic service. The war gave many working women the opportunity to change jobs for better pay.

In January 1915, the German government introduced rationing of bread, and other items soon followed. This led Germans to look for alternatives. One answer was to introduce substitute/***Ersatz*** goods; Germans soon became used to drinking *Ersatz* coffee made from tree bark or *Ersatz* sausages, which contained no meat. Those who lived in the countryside suffered less because they had immediate access to food. For urban dwellers, the black market provided some relief as did foraging visits (quaintly named in German as *Hamsterfahrt*) to 'relatives' in the country. Added to the problems were the shortages of animal fats, primarily because the government took them off the market because they were needed in the manufacture of glycerine, which is essential for explosives (in 1918 the ration for fats in Germany was only 7 per cent of pre-war consumption).

What was the extent of opposition 1914–16?

The answer to this question is short: minimal. The key to the limits of opposition to the war was the attitude of the SPD and trade union leaders in August 1914. In supporting the war they ended their party's isolation and the mistrust that had been so apparent in the pre-war years. That is not to suggest that all socialists had been in favour of the war.

- In August 1914, 14 of the 110 socialists in the Reichstag argued against the war before accepting party discipline and voting for war credits. At the end of 1914, one SPD deputy, Karl Liebknecht, voted against war credits (money for war) and at the end of 1915, 20 deputies did so. But they were lone voices, as were those members of trade unions or the party who spoke against the war in the first two years.

- A handful of radicals, including Liebknecht and Rosa Luxemburg, argued that the only way to peace was through revolution. Their impact was limited in that they spent most of the war in prison.

Definitions

Conscripted

To be compulsorily enlisted to work or fight for the government.

Ersatz

German for substitute.

Discussion points

With your work partner try to put yourselves in the position of civil servants running the Home Front in Germany at some point in 1915.

- What are the main problems facing Germany from your point of view?
- What can you do about them?

- Small numbers of pacifists attempted to organise in groups such as the German Peace League, but they were also highly marginal and had negligible impact.
- Against them were the party and trade union leadership as well as the Deputy Commanding Generals (the local army commanders), police, press and public opinion.

1916: the year of attrition

The year 1916 was the defining year of the war. Falkenhayn had come to the conclusion that the war could be won only through attrition and endurance: *Ermittlung*. In February, the Germans launched an assault on Verdun with the aim of wearing the French armies down to a point of capitulation (that is, they surrendered). Nothing better summarises the horror of the First World War than the killing field of Verdun where 700,000 casualties from both sides were lost for no gain. In the war at sea in May 1916, the German fleet engaged with the Royal Navy at Jutland. Although the Germans managed to sink more vessels, they disengaged and retreated to port, and the crippling Royal Navy blockade continued. To distract German attention from Verdun, in July 1916 the western Allies opened an offensive on the Somme with equally murderous results. In Galicia in the east the Russians launched an initially successful attack against Germany's Austrian allies. The Germans were forced to send reserves to shore up their Austrian allies, and they eventually managed to halt and then reverse the Russian attack known as the Brusilov Offensive. But the German armies became even more stretched when in August 1916 the Romanians entered the war on the side of the Allies. At the end of the month Falkenhayn had fallen from position, broken by the attrition that he had planned. German war casualties in 1916 totalled 1.5 million.

Hindenburg and Ludendorff

The appointment of Hindenburg as head of the *Oberste Heeresleitung* (OHL, or Supreme Army Command) and Ludendorff as General Quartermaster (which in reality meant Chief of Staff) marked the beginnings of a quasi (semi) military dictatorship that was to last until the end of the war. Ludendorff was now the most powerful man in Germany. There were, however, still some constraints on his powers:

- The Kaiser was still an important figure who needed to be consulted.
- The bureaucracy ran the war effort.
- The Reichstag still held budgetary control and was representative, to a point, of public opinion.

However, from August 1916 it was Ludendorff and Hindenburg who decided on the strategy of the war. Their views on how Germany should proceed with the war were in contrast to those of Chancellor Bethmann-Hollweg:

- They rejected any idea of a negotiated peace.

Discussion point

Given the slaughter that was taking place on the battlefields, why was the number of Germans opposing the war not greater?

Biographies

Karl Liebknecht

A barrister elected to the Reichstag in 1912 representing the SPD. He opposed the war in 1914 and was expelled from the Reichstag in 1916 because of his anti-war views. Liebknecht rejected the post-war democracy as proposed by Ebert.

Rosa Luxemburg

Rosa Luxemburg worked with Liebknecht to set up a revolutionary wing of the SPD as early as 1905. She was imprisoned between 1915 and 1918 for her anti-war views, but she still managed to smuggle out letters from prison calling for a revolutionary end to the war. Luxemburg believed that revolution needed to take place across Germany rather than simply in Berlin for it to be successful. She therefore opposed the Berlin Uprising of January 1919 as being too soon.

- The war had to be prosecuted with all available resources until a conclusion.
- Russia should be knocked out of the war and subjected to a harsh peace settlement.
- The reward for the German people after the war for their toil and sacrifice during it would come from the vast annexations of land which were planned (see map on page 37).

The Hindenburg Programme

The introduction of the Hindenburg Programme marked the beginning of **total war**. The aim of the programme was to compensate for Germany's lack of raw materials by introducing greater efficiencies and drive. All Germany's resources were to be mobilised for the war effort, and all non-essential industries were to be shut down.

This process of rationalisation to transform the German war economy was to be done partly through administrative rationalisation but also through a far tighter control of labour.

- A new War Minister, Hermann von Stein, was appointed to assume overall control of economic mobilisation.
- A new agency, the Supreme War Office, was created under General Groener to oversee the process of economic mobilisation.
- A central pillar of the programme was the Auxiliary Labour Law, which was approved by the Reichstag in December 1916. The purpose of the law was to mobilise all available male labour for the war effort.

The introduction of the Auxiliary Labour Law was a significant turning point for a number of reasons:

- It made it compulsory for all German males between the ages of 17 and 60 to work for the war effort if so required.
- As a gesture to the trade unions, the right to collective bargaining was granted. Union officials would sit on the boards that designated workers to various factories, and arbitration boards were set up to mediate in disputes in companies with over 50 employees. These were considerable gestures given the anti-union stance previously taken by the army.

However, most Germans were not to be deceived; the Auxiliary Labour Law was in all but name forced labour.

Outcome

Whatever the stated aims of the Hindenburg Programme, it failed overall to provide the required efficiency needed.

- The Supreme War Office failed to resolve the bureaucratic chaos. General Groener and his subordinates found it difficult to shut down supposedly 'non-essential' businesses, coming up against a range of vested interests.

Definition

Total war

The mobilisation of all resources within a nation, human and otherwise, for the war effort.

- The Auxiliary Labour Law failed to mobilise large numbers of extra men because they did not exist.

- With an increased demand for the production of munitions, the Hindenburg Programme placed an even greater strain on the already stretched supply of raw materials.

- However the Plan did have an impact on the production of munitions.

Discussion points

1 To what extent was lthe Hindenburg Project a failure? Why?
2 How far did the appointment of Hindenburg and Ludendorff mark a change in how Germany was run?

Table 3.2 German munitions production 1915–17

	1915	1916	1917
Machine guns	6,100	27,600	115,200
Explosives	72,000 tons	120,000 tons	144,000 tons

Shortages 1916–18

The shortages of fuel and raw materials were made worse by the desperately cold winter of 1916–17. Coal production in 1917 was only 90 per cent of the production of 1913 and this despite the increase in demand from war related industries. The freezing of Germany's rivers and railways in the winter of 1916–17 made transportation problems worse. The shortage of animal fats and coal meant a shortage of soap. Clothing was in short supply and, in an effort to save on fuel, local authorities dimmed street lights and cut back on trams. If this was not bad enough, the bad weather had a catastrophic impact on the potato harvest. As the wheat harvest had diminished, in the main due to shortages of labour, many within the German population relied even more heavily on potatoes as the main source of food. It was also an important source of food for livestock. The cold winter of 1916–17 and the damp spring of 1917 led to a potato blight that devastated the winter harvest. The psychological damage was considerable, and for the next two years, despite subsequent improvement in the crop, there was considerable hunger.

Table 3.3 Potato harvests in Germany 1914–18 (figures in millions of tons)

Year	Potatoes
1914	45.6
1915	54.0
1916	25.1
1917	34.4
1918	29.5

Those who suffered most were the urban working class who had no access to cheap food.

- There was also a shortage of other foodstuffs as the shortage of potatoes had a knock-on effect through the food chain; dairy production and animal fats fell by a third in 1917.

- Germans were forced to turn to the turnip as an *Ersatz* potato to the point that the winter of 1916–17 became known as the 'Turnip Winter'.

- Local authorities set up soup kitchens to provide meals. Around 6,000,000 meals were handed out in Hamburg in April alone. Useful though such actions were, there was little the authorities could do to prevent rising levels of malnutrition. The bureaucracy controlled food prices but failed to gain control on the food supply. If, for example, the peasants did not like the price set for grain, they would hoard it.

- Queuing became one of the defining experiences of the war, especially for women, who were forced to do what was nicknamed the **Polonaise**.

Essen was one of the industrial centres in the Ruhr. Table 3.4 tells its own story.

Table 3.4 Food rations in Essen 1916–18

Period	Daily calories	Daily protein intake (g)	Protein require-ments (%)	Daily fats intake (g)	Fats require-ments (%)	Daily carbs intake (g)	Carbs require-ments (%)
Summer 1916	1,326	19	25.0	19	18.4	241	60.3
Winter 1916–17	1,010	35	46.0	13	12.6	290	72.5
Summer 1917	1,176	32	42.1	12	11.6	227	56.8
Winter 1917–18	1,370	57	74.9	16	15.5	401	100.3
Summer 1918	1,353	30	39.4	11	10.7	294	73.5
Winter 1918–19	1,337	30	39.4	10	9.7	284	71.0

Note: An adequate intake of calories per adult is calculated at around 2,500 daily.

Social consequences

The social consequences of the food shortages, hunger, queuing and state intervention were considerable.

- The *peasantry* and other *rural producers* were alienated by government regulations. After 1917 they were especially hampered in their work by lack of labour, despite having 1 million prisoners of war working on the land. State prices were low and did not take into account production costs. There was particular resentment of the Junkers, who maintained their tax privileges until 1916, and the city war profiteers, who seemed to have made their fortunes out of the war.

- The *urban working class* resented state and bureaucratic controls, the lack of food and the Polonaise. They also resented the black market on which between 20 per cent and 35 per cent of food was sold. For this they blamed the middle classes, speculators and, in some cases, the Jews. In Nuremberg and elsewhere, frustrations turned to occasional violence.

- The *middle classes* entered into an insecure world without servants and with savings that were worth less and less. The lower middle classes, the *Mittelstand* (teachers and officials, for example), experienced a greater insecurity as the war closed the gap between those who were salaried and those who were not, and they suffered indignity as they too were hit by the scarcity of food.

Table 3.5 Resources of Allied and Central Powers, 1917

	Allies	Central Powers
Aeroplanes	3,163	1,500
Field guns	19,465	14,730
Heavy artillery	11,476	9,130
Machine guns	67,276	20,042
Military personnel (including reserves)	17,312,000	10,610,000

SKILLS BUILDER

Study Table 3.5. Imagine yourself to be in the position of Hindenburg and Ludendorff. What would your war strategy be in the light of these figures?

Definitions

Convoy system

A system of grouping merchant ships carrying goods and providing warships to accompany them for protection.

Polarisation

When politics on the left and right become more extreme.

War 1917

Your conclusions to the question in the Skills builder box on this page were probably the same as those come to by Hindenburg and Ludendorff. In January 1917 the decision was made by the two military commanders that the only way to bring Britain to its knees was through the use of unrestricted submarine warfare. This was despite the fact that Bethmann-Hollweg, among others, objected to this form of warfare, fearing that it would lead to American involvement in the war. Indeed, in April alone the German navy sank 875,000 tons of Allied shipping. However, the adoption of the **convoy system** by the British soon after meant that such a success was not to be repeated. So Britain had not been knocked out of the war, and in April 1917 the United States of America declared war on Germany in response to the campaign of unrestricted warfare. This was a very important event in the process of **polarisation** of German politics. The United States was a democracy, and for those who believed in greater democracy in Germany, the United States was not a natural enemy.

In March 1917 German troops on the Western Front withdrew to behind two long lines of defensive works known as the Hindenburg and Siegfried Lines. German military commanders began to train élite troops in a new form of warfare, one of movement rather than one that was static. Throughout 1917 the Allies attempted in vain to break the German lines with a series of costly offensives: the British at Arras and Ypres and the French at Chemin des Dames. Such was the high cost to the French that in May–June 1917 troops from 16 Corps of the French army mutinied. In the east, a crushing defeat for the Italians at Caporetto in October, followed by the disintegration of the Russian armies in the wake of another failed Galician campaign and then the Bolshevik revolution in November 1917 augured well for Ludendorff's plan for the breakthrough in 1918.

Opposition

But all was not well on the Home Front. Growing opposition to the war in part stemmed from the huge losses suffered. This is not surprising when the figures are considered: from 1914 to 1918, 13.2 million German men were mobilised to serve, and there were 6.2 million casualties, of which 2.05 million were killed and 4.15 million were injured. Very few German towns, villages and families remained untouched by the carnage of this war. While many accepted their loss stoically, others began to question the sacrifice. In May and June 1916, strikers in Berlin took to the streets carrying placards that demanded 'Freedom, Bread and Peace'. One rally was addressed by Karl Liebknecht, who was arrested for criticising the war. Thousands of workers went on strike in sympathy with Liebknecht and in protest at his subsequent imprisonment for four years. The extra strain placed on the economy by the Hindenburg Programme, the hunger of 1917 and the long hours of work also fuelled resentment.

The events of the Russian Revolution in Petrograd in March 1917 provided an inspiration for the discontented and those opposed to the war. It was as important as the American entry into the war in revitalising opposition to the war and the demand for change. The announcement of a reduction in the bread ration was the catalyst for widespread and large-scale strikes in April 1917. In Berlin alone, over 300,000 workers demonstrated for food and for an end to the war. Some workers formed workers councils, copying their Russian comrades. The trade union leaders objected to the formation of these councils, as did the majority of SPD members in the Reichstag. But they were supported by a minority of SPD members of the Reichstag who, on being thrown out of the SPD in March 1917 for refusing to vote in favour of war credits, formed their own breakaway party, the Independent Socialists (USPD), the following month. By 1918 the party had 100,000 members across Germany who spread its message of:

- an immediate end to the war to be followed by social reform
- an immediate repeal of the Auxiliary Service Law
- no more war loans.

The split in the Socialist Party and the creation of the USPD was a very clear sign of growing polarisation.

July Crisis

The leaders of the majority SPD continued to support the war, but only tentatively. The entry of America and the ending of the Russian autocracy made it harder for them to convince their members that the war was a just one. The Kaiser was persuaded by Bethmann-Hollweg to give a hope of reform, and on 7 April 1917 in his so-called 'Easter Offer' the Kaiser promised in somewhat vague terms to end Prussia's three-class system of voting and reform the Bundesrat after the war had ended. Such promises did little to convince the growing numbers inside and outside the Reichstag who felt that it was time to negotiate a 'peace without victory' rather than wait for a 'victorious peace'. In the debate on war credits in the Reichstag at the start of July 1917, the Centre Party and majority SPD tried to link more money to the search for a 'peace without victory'. Bethmann-Hollweg did not share this view and was in an impossible position: he had lost the confidence of both the Reichstag and the military command. He resigned, to be replaced by a Ludendorff nominee, George Michaelis. On 19 July, and quite sensationally, the Catholic deputy Matthias Erzberger persuaded a majority in the Reichstag to vote (by 212 votes to 116) in favour of a 'Peace Resolution' that promoted the idea of peace without annexation of land.

The fault lines for the polarisation of German politics were clear to see and were to become even clearer.

- In August 1917, Pope Benedict XV issued a peace note urging the warring states to consider a seven-point peace plan. The idea was ignored by Ludendorff but it cheered those who had supported Erzberger's 'Peace Resolution'.

- In September 1917 a pressure group, the German Fatherland Party, was founded. Supported by Ludendorff, Tirpitz and other leading military figures, it promoted the cause of a victorious peace through the type of excessive annexation of territory as proposed by Ludendorff. By the turn of the year it had 1 million members.

- The founding of the German Fatherland Party prompted the creation of a rival pressure group, the Peace League for Freedom and Fatherland, which promoted the idea of a more moderate peace.

- In October 1917, Michaelis was sacked as the Reichstag passed a resolution supporting reform of the Prussian voting system. He was replaced by Count Hertling of the Centre Party, who made conciliatory noises about constitutional reform. In the following months the Prussian parliament continued to debate reform of their voting system although the conservatives made it clear that they were not quite prepared to accede to parliamentary reform.

- In August 1917, Richard von Kühlmann became German Foreign Secretary. He was a sophisticated man who hoped to bring a negotiated peace without annexation but to extend German influence to the east. His moderation and subtlety were far too much for Hindenburg and Ludendorff, who helped engineer his dismissal in July 1918.

SKILLS BUILDER

1 Use a spider chart to answer the following question: why did the July Crisis 1917 come about?

2 Summarise in your own words the main issues that polarised German politics in the second half of 1917.

3 How far were the divisions in Germany in the second half of 1917 the same as the divisions of the Kaiserreich pre-1914 (see pages 1–23)?

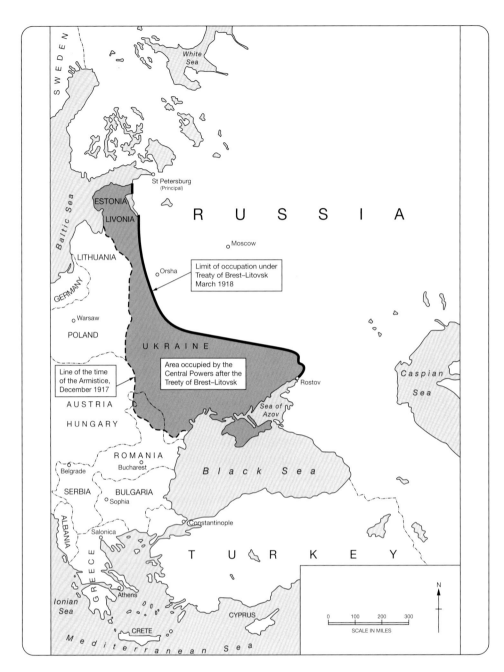

3.4 The Treaty of Brest-Litovsk, March 1918

War and peace 1918

In January 1918 a series of huge strikes gripped Berlin and other industrial centres. Munitions factories stopped work. The strikes had been inspired by the USPD but because of the size of the demonstrations (over 1 million workers took part), the leadership of the SPD and the trade unions attempted to seize the initiative. The strikers wanted:

- an end to the war
- more food
- democratic rights.

However, the political initiative quickly swung back to the military with the settlement that followed victory in the east. The type of annexation Hindenburg and Ludendorff were keen to see was written into the Treaty of Brest-Litovsk, which was signed by the Russian government in March 1918. It handed over to the Germans the regions of Poland, Lithuania, Finland, the Baltic provinces, part of the Caucusus and the Ukraine. To put this into perspective, Germany seized three-quarters of Russia's coal and iron, virtually all of its oil and cotton, and a third of its population. Bolstered by the victory of the war in the east, all parties in the Reichstag except the USPD voted in favour of the Brest-Litovsk Treaty.

The Ludendorff Offensive

The military significance of the treaty was that it allowed the transfer of half a million troops from the Eastern to the Western Front in anticipation of the great offensive. The aim of such an offensive was to deliver the Allies such a blow that they would withdraw from the war. Such thoughts were wishful thinking, given the fact that the Allies already had superiority in men and materials and they had yet to tap America's full potential. On 21 March the Germans launched their attack, pushing Allied troops back considerable distances. By July they had advanced 80 miles and were spent. They were exhausted, having suffered half a million casualties. Ludendorff's last throw of the dice had failed. The Allies counter-attacked, and by September the German army had been thrown back to the Hindenburg Line. By this point, German morale had been severely dented. Ludendorff described the day of 8 August, when the German army was pushed back at Amiens by the British, as 'the blackest day of the German army'.

What was the impact of defeat?

The news of the surrender of Bulgaria in late September seems to have shaken Ludendorff. On 29 September 1918 General Ludendorff of the German High Command demanded of his government that it should enter into armistice talks with the Allies and the United States. By late 1918, Germany and her allies were exhausted by four years of bitter war. On 4 October, Prince Max of Baden was chosen as Chancellor and immediately formed a coalition government, which included members of the Centre and Progressives parties and the socialist SPD. It was at this point, and only at this point, that the Kaiser was prepared to concede constitutional change:

- Parliament was to be able to consider foreign and military affairs.
- The vote to the Prussian parliament was to be democratic.
- Cabinet government was to be recognised by the constitution.

Prince Max began the process of negotiations with the Allies and the United States. Ludendorff resigned his command on 27 October to be succeeded by General Groener.

- The prospect of defeat and peace sparked off mutiny in the naval ports of Wilhelmshaven on 29 October 1918 and Kiel on 2 November.

Biography

Friedrich Ebert

Ebert was a moderate 'reformist' socialist. He became chairman of the SPD in 1913 and supported the war in 1914. At the end of the war, Ebert's preferred option was for a reformed monarchy to lead Germany. In 1919 Ebert was elected President of Germany, a post he held until his death in 1925.

Biography

Friedrich Ebert

Ebert was a moderate 'reformist' socialist. He became chairman of the SPD in 1913 and supported the war in 1914. At the end of the war, Ebert's preferred option was for a reformed monarchy to lead Germany. In 1919 Ebert was elected President of Germany, a post he held until his death in 1925.

Discussion point

Working in pairs, imagine you are in the position of the SPD leaders Friedrich Ebert and Philipp Schiedemann. What are your three main priorities for your government in November 1918? When you have decided, discuss these priorities with another pair. Are your priorities the same? If not, why not? Try to come up with a list of priorities with which your whole group agrees.

- The mutiny soon spread to other ports as sailors refused to go to sea to fight the Royal Navy.
- Councils of workers and soldiers (called soviets) were set up in towns and ports, including Rostock, Bremen, Hamburg and Lübeck.
- In Munich, a revolt on 8 November headed by socialist Kurt Eisner led to the proclamation of a democratic and socialist republic in Bavaria.

The Allies had demanded as a condition of an armistice that the Kaiser be forced to abdicate. This call was now taken up by the socialist members of Prince Max's government. On 10 November the Kaiser slipped into Holland after his abdication was announced by Prince Max.

Despite the Kaiser's abdication, the leading members of the SPD withdrew their support from Prince Max's government, and Friedrich Ebert of the SPD became the Chancellor of a new government consisting solely of members of the SPD and USPD. Meanwhile, at Compiègne, near Paris, the German armistice commission was forced to agree to stiff ceasefire terms:

- The German army was to withdraw east of the Rhine.
- The Treaty of Brest-Litovsk and the Treaty of Bucharest (the terms of Romania's surrender to the Central Powers in May 1918) were to be renounced, and German troops were to be withdrawn from Russia, Romania, Austria-Hungary and Turkey.
- Germany was to surrender 150 submarines and a number of large naval vessels.

On 11 November German delegates met with representatives of the Allies at Compiègne and signed the armistice that ended four years of war.

Unit summary

What have you learned in this unit?

You have learned how the First World War was fought and lost. You have read how the war had an impact on the Home Front and how the shortages of labour and raw materials undermined the war effort. You have learned about the roles played by Hindenburg and Ludendorff and how their military gambles did not pay off. In this unit you have also learned that the socialist movement supported the war for the majority of its duration. You have learned how opposition grew during the second half of the war and how there was significant political polarisation. Labour unrest and serious food shortages had an impact in radicalising opponents of the war. You have learned that it was only in the last weeks of the war that serious constitutional reform was offered.

What skills have you used in this unit?

You have been asked to make a number of decisions. You have had to use your skills of empathy to answer many of the questions. You have done a lot of analytical work regarding the positions of governments, generals and administrators.

Exam style question

This is the sort of question you will find appearing on the examination paper as a Section A question:

'The First World War increased rather than narrowed Germany's political divisions.'

How far do you agree with this judgement?

Exam tips

You have read at the end of Unit 1 how to approach these types of questions. To reiterate, planning is crucial, as is the structuring of your paragraphs.

To give a full answer you need to look at both sides of the quotation:

- First, how and when during the war was there a narrowing of political divisions.
- Then, at what point were divisions made worse and how?
- On balance, what was the greatest impact of the war on political divisions?

You are now ready to write up your answer.

SKILLS BUILDER

Asking questions

As a historian, it is one of your tasks to ask questions of a particular period. In formulating questions you get to understand the most important issues. What are the eight questions that you might ask of Germany during the First World War? Here are two examples to set you on your way.

- At what point did Germany have a serious opportunity of winning the war?
- Why did Germany wage unrestricted submarine warfare when it carried with it the risk of the USA joining the war?

RESEARCH TOPIC

There are a number of individuals and events related to the First World War that you might find useful to research, for example:

- Verdun
- Käthe Kollwitz
- Rosa Luxemburg
- Karl Liebknecht
- The sinking of the *Lusitania*

What if?

Many historians believe that it is useful to ask the question 'what if?' as part of the process of understanding what actually did happen. Other historians dismiss this counter-factual approach as being too speculative, arguing that it is the role of the historian to study what did happen rather than what might have happened. However, we are going to put the latter group's concerns aside for the time being. In groups, discuss all or some the following:

What if:

- the German Army had got to Paris in 1914?
- the Russian Army had collapsed after defeat in 1915?
- Falkenhayn had stayed in post as Commander in Chief for the next two years?
- the Peace Agenda had been followed in the summer of 1917?
- Germany had conscripted women to work?

What were the problems faced by the Weimar Republic, 1919–23?

What is this unit about?

This unit explores the first four years of the Weimar Republic from its creation in 1919 to the economic and financial crisis at the end of 1923. It looks at the threats to the Republic from left and right and the attitude of the establishment to the new state. It explains the impact of defeat in the First World War, the Treaty of Versailles and the Weimar Constitution.

You will:

- find out about the instability of the Weimar Republic in its first four years
- consider and discuss important turning points and issues as part of the process of enhancing your understanding of these years of the Weimar Republic.

Key questions

- What were the more significant threats to the stability and survival of the Weimar Republic in the years 1919 to 1923?
- Why, given the threats, did the Weimar Republic survive?

Timeline

1918	November	Attempted revolution in Munich; German Republic declared; government led by Friedrich Ebert
	November	Ebert–Groener agreement
	November	Political parties agree to hold elections to a national Constituent Assembly
1919	January	Spartacist revolt in Berlin crushed by army and *Freicorps*
	January	National Assembly elected
	February	Friedrich Ebert chosen as President
	April	Soviet Republic declared in Bavaria
	May	German government presented with Treaty of Versailles
	June	German fleet scuttled at Scapa Flow
	June	Terms of Versailles settlement accepted
	July	Weimar Constitution adopted
1920	March	Kapp-Lüttwitz Putsch
	June	Elections for a Reichstag sees fall in votes for the Weimar Coalition
1921	May	Germany accepts reparations terms
	August	Matthias Erzberger assassinated
1922	April	Treaty of Rapallo with Russia
	June	Walther Rathenau assassinated

1923	July	Law for the Protection of the Republic
	January	French and Belgian forces occupy the Ruhr
	September	Gustav Stresemann becomes Chancellor
	November	Attempted Nazi *putsch* in Munich
	November	Rentenmark is introduced

What does this mean?

This is Article 231 from the Treaty of Versailles. From what you know about the causes of the First World War, is this fair?

Article 231

The Allied and Associated Governments affirm and Germany accepts the responsibility of Germany and her allies for causing all the loss and damage to which the Allied and Associated Governments and their nationals have been subjected as a consequence of the war imposed upon them by the aggression of Germany and her allies.

A Republic is born

The new state was born against a background of defeat and national humiliation at Versailles. As Article 231 shows, Germany was even forced to accept responsibility for the war. Other threats to the Republic came from revolutionary activity and economic crisis. Indeed the legitimacy of the state's existence and constitution was questioned by many of the country's élite, including members of the judiciary and army. It was also challenged by political extremists, most noticeably by communists, monarchists and ex-soldiers (the *Freikorps*). Together, these threats endangered the very existence of the Republic.

Threats from left and right

With peace declared and the Kaiser gone, the most important task facing Chancellor Ebert was to ensure political stability. On 25 November 1918 a conference of representatives of the new state governments from across Germany agreed to elections for a National Constituent Assembly. However, the parties in Ebert's government were divided on the best way ahead.

- The USPD were more revolutionary, and many challenged the decision to hold democratic elections, hoping for some kind of workers' seizure of power.

- Members of the more moderate 'majority SPD' wanted a democratic Germany. They did not want revolution. There were examples of working class hostility to the purveyors of revolution. For example, in December

1918 the First Congress of Workers' and Soldiers' Councils in Berlin refused to allow Rosa Luxemburg and Karl Liebknecht, who were known revolutionaries, to address them.

The Spartacists

The new government faced threats from left and right. In December 1918 a group of revolutionaries, known as the Spartacists and led by Karl Liebknecht and Rosa Luxemburg, broke away from the USPD. Their aspirations were revolutionary:

- They hoped to provoke a revolution on similar lines to that in Russia in 1917 followed by an alliance with the new Russian state led by Lenin.
- They wished to see the cancellation of the election for the National Assembly and all power transferred to workers' and soldiers' councils.
- They promised to nationalise and seize all large-scale industries and large and medium-sized farms, which would then become the property of the state.
- The police and the army would be disarmed and workers' militias would be created.

Ebert–Groener agreement

Another potent threat to the new Republic was the opposition to its existence from the pre-1918 military, judiciary and civil service. Their influence in the new Republic was by no means guaranteed when the Kaiser abdicated. However, they resumed that influence as a result of the actions by the leaders of the SPD in late 1918. In November 1918 Ebert made an agreement with General Groener. The threat of revolution from the Spartacists was clear and Ebert and his colleagues could not necessarily rely on the support of the army. So a deal was made:

- Ebert promised the army supplies and protection of its status against the armed militias of the workers' and soldiers' councils.
- In return the army promised to put down revolutionary activity with force.

Ebert turned to the army as the means by which forces of moderate socialism could defeat a more radical left of the USPD and then the German Communist Party (KPD) and the Spartacists.

The Spartacist revolt

On 1 January 1919, members of the Spartacist Union held their first congress in Berlin. With the support of other left wing groups they formally created the German Communist Party, the KPD. This was followed by a revolutionary uprising in Berlin that began on 5 January.

- Newspaper offices were seized and revolutionary committees were formed.

- But the uprising was poorly planned and easily crushed by troops from the regular army and *Freikorps* troops led by General Walther von Lüttwitz.
- On 15 January 1919, members of the Horse Guards Division of the army murdered Karl Liebknecht and Rosa Luxemburg.

The alliance of Ebert and the 'majority Socialists' with the army in crushing the revolutions of 1918–19 possibly saved Germany from a widespread communist uprising. However, this alliance came at a price; from now on the governments of the new Republic were tied to using anti-democratic forces, i.e. the army and the *Freikorps*, to restore so-called 'order'. Throughout this period, one of the gravest problems for the state was the fact that the instruments that it used to end violence were often the organisations that initiated it – as we will see throughout this unit.

Red Bavaria, 1919

In February 1919 Kurt Eisner, the USPD leader in Bavaria, was assassinated by a right wing student. The assassination, in conjunction with news from Hungary of a soviet revolution, triggered revolution in Bavaria. On 6 April 1919, the Bavarian Soviet Republic was declared. It was led by communist leader Eugene Levine, who embarked on a series of radical reforms that included seizing the property of the wealthy. He raised a 'Red Army' of workers, members of which soon started rounding up well-known right wingers, including the wonderfully named Prince von Thurn und Taxis, and summarily executing them. In early May 1919, the Army and *Freikorps* sent a force of some 30,000 troops into Bavaria, and the Soviet Republic was crushed after some bitter fighting that claimed the lives of 1,000 members of the 'Red Army'. After the fighting ended, the *Freikorps* rounded up 800 known communists, including Levine, and executed them.

German party politics

Chancellors of the Weimar Republic, 1919–23

Friedrich Ebert (SPD)	November 1918 to February 1919
Philipp Scheidemann (SPD)	February 1919 to June 1919
Gustav Bauer (SPD)	June 1919 to March 1920
Hermann Müller (SPD)	March 1920 to June 1920
Konstantin Fehrenbach (Centre)	June 1920 to May 1921
Joseph Wirth (Centre)	May 1921 to November 1922
Wilhelm Cuno (non-aligned)	November 1922 to August 1923

Who can work with whom?

Read through the descriptions of the parties. Which are the more likely coalition partners?

Discussion points

In groups, consider the following questions. See if your group can come up with three strong reasons for each.

1 Why do you think that the army was prepared to strike such a deal with Ebert's government?
2 Why do you think that the *Freikorps* responded with such violence to the creation of the Bavarian Socialist Republic?
3 For Ebert and democratic government in Germany what was the impact of their alliance with the army, in the short and the medium term?

The parties

Party: Social Democratic Party (SPD)

Founded: 1863.

Constituency: The working class; mainly urban industrial workers and craftsmen. Main strength in Prussia including Berlin and the Ruhr.

Leaders: Friedrich Ebert, Philipp Schiedemann, Gustav Bauer, Hermann Müller.

Attitude to the Republic: Divided. Many within the party, including Ebert, strongly supported parliamentary democracy. Others were more ideologically driven, seeing the Republic as a 'bourgeois democracy' and therefore rejecting the idea of full collaboration with other parties or taking full responsibility for forming government.

Domestic policy: Committed to the 'class struggle'. Supported social reform and the idea of an extension of social welfare including unemployment benefit.

Foreign policy: Supported the policy of fulfilment.

Party: Independent Socialists (USPD)

Founded: Broke away from the SPD in 1917.

Constituency: Industrial workers disillusioned by the policies of the SPD, especially Ebert's use of the Army and *Freikorps* and cooperation with the Centre Party and German Democratic Party (DDP).

Leaders: Rosa Luxemburg and Karl Liebknecht.

Attitude to the Republic: Wanted the replacement of parliamentary democracy with workers' soviets.

Domestic policy: The party supported the idea of revolution but was bitterly divided as to how to proceed and which policies to follow. In October 1920 it split into two wings, the left wing joining the KPD and the right wing eventually merging in 1922 with the SPD.

Foreign policy: Opposed the war and Versailles treaty. Followed the foreign policy dictated by Moscow through the Comintern (the international communist organisation).

Party: German Democratic Party (DDP)

Founded: Created in November 1918 from the left wing of the National Liberals.

Constituency: Business interests, the middle classes and intellectuals.

Leaders: Hugo Preuss (author of the constitution), Erich Koch-Weser.

Attitude to the Republic: Fully supportive of the Republic and constitution in the early years of the Weimar Republic. From 1928 joined with the Young German Order and from 1930 fought elections as the State Party, which became increasingly less supportive of Weimar democracy. Members of the DDP/State Party served in virtually every cabinet of the Weimar Republic.

Domestic policy: Supported constitutional reform, democracy, some social reform, civil liberties.

Foreign policy: In favour of a policy of fulfilment.

Party: German People's Party (DVP)

Founded: December 1918 from the right wing of the National Liberals.

Constituency: Business interests, industrialists and white-collar workers.

Leaders: Founder and dominant leader of the party until his death in 1929 was Gustav Stresemann.

Attitude to the Republic: Ambivalent. Recognised the Republic but instinctively preferred a return to a more autocratic system of government.

Domestic policy: Pro-business, anti-union and anti-labour.

Foreign policy: Instinctively hostile to the Versailles treaty but foreign policy of fulfilment driven by Stresemann.

Party: German National People's Party (DNVP)

Founded: 1918.

Constituency: Conservative, nationalists, landowners, upper middle classes.

Leaders: Count Westarp, Karl Helfferich, Alfred Hugenberg.

Attitude to the Republic: Consistently hostile to the Republic, which it believed to be illegitimate. Wished for a return to the Imperial Reich and the restoration of the Kaiser. Only participated in two governments, both times with unsatisfactory outcomes.

Domestic policy: Conservative, anti-socialist and anti-Semitic.

Foreign policy: Strongly nationalist and rejected Versailles treaty. Proposed union with Austria.

Party: Centre Party

Founded: At the unification of Germany in 1870.

Constituency: The party representing Germany's Catholics.

Leaders: Konstantin Fehrenbach, Wilhelm Marx, Franz von Papen, Ludwig Kaas.

Attitude to the Republic: Initially strongly supportive of the Republic as a barrier against revolution. An important element in virtually every cabinet of the Weimar Republic. From 1930 onwards was less supportive of democracy.

Domestic policy: Essentially on the moderate right, a party of political compromise. Supported social reform but also socially conservative (against abortion, contraception and pornography). Looked to protect the interests of the Catholic Church.

Foreign policy: Supported the policy of fulfilment.

Party: German Communist Party (KPD)

Founded: By members of the Spartacist Union in December 1918. Held its first conference in Berlin on 1 January 1919.

Constituency: Communist revolutionaries. Attracted many ex-members of the USPD. Mainly working class.

Leaders: Paul Levi, Ernst Thälmann.

Attitude to the Republic: Hostile to the Republic, which it believed to be a bourgeois capitalist political system dedicated to exploiting the working classes. Committed to overthrowing the Republic by revolution.

Domestic policy: Supported the idea of violent revolution and the destruction of capitalism. Violently opposed to the SPD, which it viewed as 'social fascism'.

Foreign policy: Dictated by the foreign policy of the Soviet Union.

Party: National Socialist German Workers' Party (NSDAP)

Founded: As the German Workers' Party in 1919 and the National Socialist Workers' Party in 1920.

Constituency: Ex-servicemen, radical anti-Semites.

Leaders: Adolf Hitler, Gregor Strasser.

Attitude to the Republic: Extremely hostile, condemning the 'November Criminals'.

Domestic policy: The restructuring of society on racial grounds. The creation of a People's Community.

Foreign policy: Destruction of Versailles treaty, non-payment of reparations, destruction of communism, *Lebensraum* (living space).

SKILLS BUILDER

The coalition game

It is your job to try to build coalitions. You can include more than one party in a coalition. Suggest the following:

- obvious coalitions of parties
- possible coalitions of parties
- unlikely coalitions of parties.

When you have finished, compare, explain and discuss your coalitions with a work partner.

The National Assembly, January 1919

Elections to the new National Assembly were held on 19 January 1919 against the backdrop of the Spartacist uprising. Participation in the election was high, with around 85 per cent of those eligible voting. The election was a triumph for those parties (SPD, Centre Party and DDP) that supported the concept of a parliamentary democracy; 76 per cent of the electorate voted for them. The first Reich President of the Weimar Republic was the leader of the SPD, Friedrich Ebert, and the first coalition cabinet was led by Philipp Schiedemann, with ministers from his own party (the SPD), the Centre Party and the DDP.

- The clear winner of the election was the SPD with 37.9 per cent of the vote, the minority USPD receiving only 7.6 per cent.

- The important feature of the result was the strength of the performance of other parties occupying what might be termed the centre ground, with the Centre Party achieving 19.7 per cent of the vote and the DDP 18.5 per cent.

- The strength of the DDP's vote compared the performance of the DVP which polled only 4.4 per cent demonstrated the overwhelming support of the liberal middle classes for democracy and the Republic.

- The main party contesting the election on a platform opposing the new democracy, the nationalist DNVP, only received 10.3 per cent of the vote.

Table 4.1 Elections to the National Assembly, January 1919

Party	DNVP	NSDAP	DVP	Centre	DDP	SPD	USPD	KPD	BVP*
Votes (in millions)	3.121	–	1.345	5.980	5.641	11.509	2.317	–	–
Seats	44	–	19	91	75	165	22	–	–
Percentage of vote	10.3	–	4.4	19.7	18.5	37.9	7.6	–	–

* Bavarian People's Party

Discussion point

What does the outcome of January 1919 elections tell you about German public opinion in January 1919?

The Treaty of Versailles

The most important issue facing the government was the terms of the peace treaty. Throughout the war, the German government propaganda machine had stressed to the German people that Germany was fighting a 'just war' against the aggression of the Entente Powers. The abdication of the Kaiser and the transition to a democracy supported by the majority of Germans in the January 1919 election gave rise to the hope among Germans that their country would be treated leniently and that the final peace settlement would be based on President Woodrow **Wilson's Fourteen Points**. Those who thought this way had paid little attention to the following facts:

- the aggressive terms of the November 1918 armistice
- the fact that neither the German government nor their representatives had been invited to Versailles to participate in the deliberations
- the united domestic opinion in the Allied countries, and France in particular, that Germany should be harshly punished and made to pay for the war
- the fact that Germany was in no position to fight on, and was therefore in no position to negotiate or influence the Allies.

The victorious powers had different ideas about the future shape of Europe and the peace settlement. The Peace Conference at Versailles opened on 18 January 1919. The victorious Allies and the United States alone debated the future of Germany and Europe. The most influential leaders at Versailles were Georges Clemenceau (the Prime Minister of France), David Lloyd George (the Prime Minister of the United Kingdom), Vittorio Orlando (the Prime Minister of Italy) and President Woodrow Wilson (the President of the United States of America). As the so-called Council of Four, they debated the main issues to be resolved.

- The priority of President Woodrow Wilson of the United States was the creation of the League of Nations. To Wilson the League was the means by which peace could be maintained by compromise. Wilson believed that the way to build a peaceful Europe was through national self-determination. His Fourteen Points were very clear in defining his agenda for peace, and through their application Wilson hoped to bind Germany into an international structure based on peace.
- For President Clemenceau of France the overriding principle was that of security. Clemenceau's main aim (and in this he was supported by public opinion in France and Britain) was to end the German threat for good by imposing a damaging **Carthaginian peace**. His priority was to ensure that never again would France be vulnerable to attack from Germany. Clemenceau's agenda was to propose the confiscation of territory and restrictions on German military strength. The French also encouraged the strengthening of Poland at the expense of Germany. At the back of the minds of the leading politicians at Versailles was the unpredictable nature of the new Bolshevik state in Russia. A strong Poland could therefore act as an important barrier against Soviet expansion.

Definition

Wilson's Fourteen Points

Revolved around the idea of self-determination for all nationalities and a 'just peace'. (You will be asked to research these in greater depth at the end of this unit.)

Definition

Carthaginian peace

A peace settlement that is particularly harsh and designed to maintain the inferiority of the loser. It is named after Rome's defeat of Carthage in 202 BC and the subsequent humiliating settlement.

- While the British Prime Minister David Lloyd George was also concerned to contain Bolshevik Russia and German militarism he did not wish to see an over-strengthened France. As a result, Lloyd George and Wilson argued against the French annexing the land on the left bank of the Rhine and the coal-rich Saar basin. Instead, the Rhineland was to be demilitarised. However, Lloyd George came under significant political pressure from home to support the French idea of imposing damaging reparations on Germany. To establish Germany's liability for reparations, Article 231 was included, making Germany solely responsible for the outbreak of war (despite Woodrow Wilson's objections).

- Prime Minster Orlando's domestic issues revolved around the acquisition of the so-called **irredentist** lands from Austria and were not directly relevant to the German question.

Definition

Irredentist

The lands containing Italian speakers that many in Italy argued should belong to Italy.

SKILLS BUILDER

1 To what extent was there agreement between the Council of Four, and how did their hopes for the future differ?

2 What were the priorities for the leaders at Versailles?

The Versailles settlement

In May 1919 the terms of the treaty were presented to a horrified German delegation, which was led by Foreign Minister Count Brockdorff-Rantzau. There was great resentment in Germany at the Article 231 'war guilt' clause and the fact that the treaty was harsher than Wilson's Fourteen Points had originally suggested it would be. There was also anger that the terms of the treaty were not in line with the conditions on which Germany had laid down her arms. Count Brockdorff-Rantzau suggested open refusal of the treaty, in part because he claimed that its terms would be impossible to fulfil and that it would lead to bitter resentment among the German people. Chancellor Scheidemann spoke for virtually the whole nation when he said to the National Assembly on 12 May:

'What hand would not wither that binds itself and us in these fetters?'

Rather than accept the Treaty, Scheidemann's government resigned on 20 June. The following day, German sailors scuttled their fleet moored at Scapa Flow in the Orkneys in an act of protest and defiance. The new government was led by Chancellor Gustav Bauer of the SPD and Vice-Chancellor Matthias Erzberger of the Centre Party. Both accepted, as did the German Parliament sitting in the town of Weimar, that Germany did not have the means to resist an Allied invasion and that they therefore had no choice but to sign the treaty. On 28 June the Treaty of Versailles was signed on behalf of the German government by Foreign Minister Herman Müller (SPD) and Minister of Communications Johannes Bell (Centre).

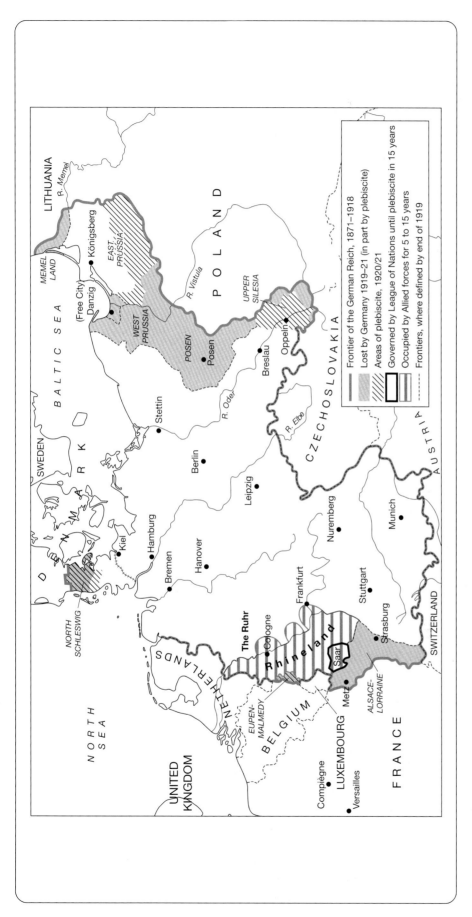

4.1 Provisions of the Treaty of Versailles

Legend:
- Frontier of the German Reich, 1871–1918
- Lost by Germany 1919–21 (in part by plebiscite)
- Areas of plebiscite, 1920/21
- Governed by League of Nations until plebiscite in 15 years
- Occupied by Allied forces for 5 to 15 years
- Frontiers, where defined by end of 1919

LITHUANIA
R. Memel
MEMEL LAND
Königsberg
EAST PRUSSIA
POLAND
(Free City) Danzig
WEST PRUSSIA
R. Vistula
POSEN
Posen
UPPER SILESIA
Breslau
Oppeln
BALTIC SEA
Stettin
R. Oder
CZECHOSLOVAKIA
R. Elbe
SWEDEN
Berlin
Leipzig
AUSTRIA
DENMARK
Kiel
Hamburg
Bremen
Hanover
Nuremberg
Munich
NORTH SCHLESWIG
NORTH SEA
UNITED KINGDOM
NETHERLANDS
Frankfurt
The Ruhr
Cologne
Rhineland
Stuttgart
Saar
Strasburg
SWITZERLAND
EUPEN-MALMEDY
BELGIUM
Metz
ALSACE-LORRAINE
LUXEMBOURG
Compiègne
Versailles
FRANCE

By the terms of the Versailles settlement Germany suffered significant humiliation as shown in the map setting out the provisions of the Treaty of Versailles.

Territorial provision

Germany lost territory of economic importance (up to 20 per cent of coal production and 15 per cent of agricultural resources) as well as territory of symbolic importance, such as West Prussia and Posen, which were given to Poland. Other areas to be lost without a vote included Alsace-Lorraine to France, Memel to Lithuania, Eupen and Malmedy to Belgium, and Danzig to be a free port under the control of the League of Nations. It was the loss of land to Poland that perhaps caused the greatest upset in Germany as the majority of people in West Prussia and Posen were German speakers. Many Germans argued that the terms of the treaty were hypocritical in asserting the principle of self-determination for the peoples of Europe, but not for Germans.

- After plebiscites (popular votes on important issues), all of North Schleswig (in 1920) was lost to Denmark and parts of Upper Silesia (in 1922) were lost to Poland.
- The Rhineland was to become a demilitarised zone to act as a buffer between France and Germany. It was to be occupied by the Allies for 15 years.
- The Saar was placed under the control of the League of Nations, and its rich coalfields were to be controlled by France.
- The Kiel Canal was opened to warships and merchant ships from all nations.
- *Anschluss* (union with Austria) was forbidden by Article 80 of the treaty.
- All Germany's colonies were to be handed over to the Allies. Who would govern the colonies would be decided by the League of Nations through the creation of mandates. For example, German East Africa became a British mandate, and German South West Africa became a South African mandate.

Military terms

- Germany's military capability was destroyed – the army being limited to 100,000 men and the navy to six battleships, six cruisers and twelve destroyers but no submarines.
- Germany was to have no military aircraft.

War guilt and reparations

- Britain, France, Belgium and all the main countries that had fought against Germany demanded that Germany be made to pay for the war. They had spent a huge amount of money, and all countries had borrowed heavily from the United States of America; for example, in 1923 it was calculated that the French owed the Americans $4000 million.

- President Wilson disagreed; he thought that Germany should be made to pay reparations in compensation only where international law had been broken, e.g. the invasion of Belgium or where civilians had suffered damage to their property.

- British and French public opinion were strongly in favour of Germany being made to pay heavy reparations. Lloyd George insisted that war pensions and money paid to bereaved families be paid for by the Germans. In April 1919 President Wilson agreed to the French and British demands because he did not wish to see Lloyd George or Clemenceau voted out of office in their respective countries for failing to deliver on reparations.

- The Allies agreed to set up a Reparations Commission to decide on the exact amount to be paid.

- In order to make Germany pay, the Allies and America had first to assert the principle of German liability. The result was the inclusion of Article 231. The German response to the idea of war guilt was one of anger and bewilderment. However, such a judgement became quickly widened into a moral question of the extent of Germany's supposed 'war guilt'. The politicians of the Republic who were faced with this clause attempted to have it dropped from the final treaty but to no avail.

- Reparations were not set until 1921. However, in the meantime Germany was to hand over all merchant ships of more than 1,600 tons, half of those between 800 and 1,600 tons and a quarter of its fishing fleet. It was to build 200,000 tons of shipping a year for the Allies for the next five years. Germany was forced to bear the cost of the army of occupation. It was forced to agree to the sale of German property in Allied countries.

A compromise treaty

The Treaty of Versailles was a compromise solution. This was due to the differences between the leaders and the fact that it was not solely concerned with limiting the power of Germany. There were other considerations for the leaders of the Allies:

- Of particular importance was the need to contain Bolshevik Russia, which made the breaking-up of Germany unrealistic.

- A large Poland (with the subsequent German loss of Posen and West Prussia) was created in the context of Wilson's ideal of self-determination but also with the creation of a state of substance next to Russia in mind.

In reality, although the Versailles treaty left Germany humiliated and scarred, the treaty also left Germany potentially strong. The terms of the Treaty of Versailles did not in themselves threaten the existence of Germany, nor did they prevent a new Germany from being reborn as a diplomatic power in Europe. There was disillusion in Germany about being excluded from the League of Nations, but the treaty left Germany as a

Discussion points

1 As you have read, the treaty caused bitter resentment in Germany. In groups, discuss the following.

What were the most humiliating aspects of the Treaty of Versailles for:

- the German government
- the German military
- the German people?

2 How fair was the treaty?

united nation state with the potential to regain its status as an important diplomatic power, even in the short term. This was proved by the Treaty of Rapallo in 1922 between Germany and the Soviet Union, by which both rejected reparations. Of equal importance was the fact that the Treaty of Versailles left Germany as the power most likely to dominate Central and Eastern Europe. These are important points because they place German opposition to the treaty into context.

How did the Treaty of Versailles threaten the Republic?

Hindenburg and the myth of the 'stab in the back'

It is important to separate the reality of the extent of the damage the treaty inflicted on Germany as a great power from the psychological damage it inflicted on the national consciousness. The German government signed the treaty because it was advised by the German army (including Field Marshal Hindenburg) that it was in no state to resist an Allied invasion. There was also little public support for further conflict. Months later, in November 1919, Hindenburg gave evidence to the Investigation Committee of the National Assembly (a committee of the German parliament studying the Treaty of Versailles).

- His testimony backed up the suggestions of the right wing parties and the press that the Versailles treaty was a humiliating **Diktat** and a shameful peace (*Schmachfrieden*) that should not have been signed. Given the fact that it was Hindenburg who had, with Ludendorff, suggested an armistice in September 1918, this was an example of hypocrisy.

- That the treaty was signed, according to Hindenburg and his political allies, was because of the anti-patriotic sentiments of the clique of left wing politicians, the so-called 'November criminals' who had founded the Republic, e.g. Ebert, Müller and Erzberger. They were also blamed for the '**stab in the back**' of the armed forces that led to military collapse in 1918.

Such theories were very useful to the anti-Republican right. They absolved the military from responsibility for their own failings in 1918 and they played on popular resentment of the treaty, thereby gaining support. As you can see from Table 4.1 on page 72 and Table 4.2 on page 85 the nationalist DNVP's percentage of the vote increased from 10.3 per cent in January 1919 to 14.9 per cent in June 1920. The other point is that such accusations became widely accepted. This was because they were simple and they gave many Germans an acceptable framework by which they could explain defeat. They acted to reduce support for the Republic and the parties that were involved in its creation. Such accusations of treachery gave the anti-Republican right a misplaced belief in the morality of their illegal actions. It was these myths that were developed as a result of the Versailles treaty that were to cause one of the greatest threats to the Republic's legitimacy.

Definitions

Diktat

The Treaty of Versailles being dictated to Germany without negotiation.

Stab in the back

The idea that Germany's armed forces had been undermined by politicians and others in Germany who wanted peace in late 1918.

The Weimar Constitution

On 15 November 1918 liberal lawyer and democrat Hugo Preuss was appointed Secretary of State in the Ministry of the Interior with the responsibility for drawing up a new constitution for Germany. In January 1919 a cross-party group from the new National Assembly was created to consider the possibilities. The task facing Preuss and his colleagues was considerable:

- Germany had been defeated in war and the Kaiser had abdicated so the new state and constitution were born out of defeat and crisis. The Kaiserreich had been an authoritarian rather than a democratic political system. The introduction of democracy would represent a significant change.

- Not only that but the constitution was to be written and discussed against the background of revolution. Above all else, Germany needed a constitution that would ensure stability.

- Equally significant was the fact that there had been some constitutional changes over the summer of 1918, most noticeably a shift in power from the executive to the Reichstag. The issue was whether or not the new constitution would reflect this shift and give more power to the Reichstag.

- The elections of January 1919 had made the socialist SPD the largest party in the Reichstag with 165 out of 423 seats, but it did not have an absolute majority. Instead it relied on the support of the Catholic Centre Party, which had won 91 seats, and the Democrat DDP, which had got 75 seats. The first government was, therefore, a compromise between those in the SPD arguing for moderate socialist change and those who wished for the establishment of a liberal democracy. This compromise was to be reflected in the constitution.

There were also a number of specific questions for Hugo Preuss, and his team to answer including:

- How much power should the executive (i.e. the President) be given?

- How powerful should the Reichstag be?

- Should the state be a unitary or a federal state? If the latter, what should be the balance of power between the central government of the Reich and the governments of the individual states that made up the Reich, the *Länder*?

- What civil rights, if any, should be enshrined in the constitution?

Preuss attempted to build on the traditions of German politics as well as balance power between the different institutions of the state. After much discussion, the Weimar Constitution (as it became known) was adopted on 31 July 1919.

4.2 National Socialist election poster encouraging the electorate to vote for List 1

What were the main features of the constitution?

The new Reich was to be a federation of 18 regional states known as *Länder*. Each *Land* was to have its own parliament.

The constitution provided for a strong executive in the form of a President elected on a seven-year tenure and with strong powers to counterbalance those held by the central parliament.

The constitution created the Reich (state) as a parliamentary democracy with the Reich Chancellor and the cabinet needing majority support in the Reichstag.

The new central parliament was made up of two houses. The upper house, the Reichsrat, had the power to delay laws. Its members were chosen by

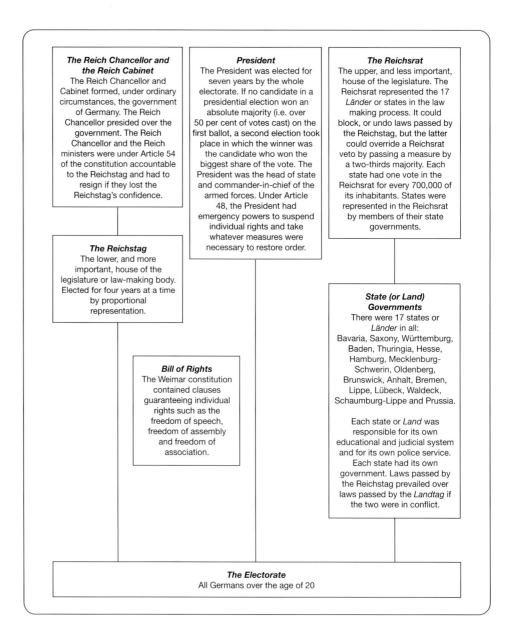

4.3 The Weimar constitution

the parliaments of the *Länder*. The lower house, the Reichstag, was to be elected every four years. By the Reich Election Law that accompanied the constitution, it was decided that the Reichstag would be elected by proportional representation:

- Each party contesting an election would draw up a list of candidates (see Figure 4.3 the election poster).
- The electorate would vote for a list rather than for a specific candidate.
- Every party received one seat in the Reichstag for every 60,000 votes cast for that party.
- All men and women over the age of 20 could vote.

This system was very different to the '**first past the post**' electoral system that is used in Britain. Its introduction was supported by all the main parties: the socialist SPD argued that this was the fairest system; its opponents believed it was the best way of preventing the SPD gaining a majority of seats in the Reichstag. This is not surprising given the fact that the socialists received nearly 50 per cent of the vote between them in the 1919 election.

A Bill of Rights guaranteed individual rights such as freedom of speech and the right to belong to a union.

Did the constitution weaken the Republic?

Proportional representation

Many historians have suggested that the Weimar constitution of 1919 was a source of weakness for the Republic.

- *Argument for* This argument is based on the idea that the constitution was flawed and that its main features – e.g. proportional representation, parliamentary government and civil liberties – were not widely accepted. The constitution was the product of a compromise between the most successful parties in the January 1919 election to the National Assembly, i.e. the majority Social Democrats (SPD), the Centre Party and the DDP. Yet at no subsequent election did these three parties poll even close to the number of votes they had achieved in 1919 (in 1919 they polled 23.1 million votes between them; the next highest was 14.3 million in 1928). One might therefore argue that the constitution's base was narrow and unrepresentative.
- *Argument against* The Weimar constitution, compromise as it was, reflected a broader spectrum of political opinion than the initial coalition that put it together would suggest. It even included those on the nationalist right such as the DNVP. It reflected successful constitutional practice at the time and had built into it checks and balances that, if used carefully, might have helped create some semblance of political stability. The problem with the Weimar constitution was not its design but its misuse by the new state's opponents.

Discussion point

What are the potential strengths and weaknesses of the Weimar constitution in the post-war period?

Definition

First past the post

When the candidate in an election with the most votes wins the seat even if he or she has not got a majority of the votes cast.

The importance of proportional representation

Proportional representation led to **coalition governments**, which rose and fell with spectacular consistency. In the period up until 1923, a series of minority governments failed to establish themselves; the longest in office in the period in question was that led by Joseph Wirth, which lasted the 18 months between May 1921 and November 1922. In a period of such political instability, it has been assumed that a majority system of voting might have been more effective in combating attacks from left and right, and might have been more effective in guaranteeing Weimar's stability and survival. However, such a view ignores the complexity and subtlety of the German political and party system of the time. In fact, proportional representation was essential to ensuring continuity in party politics from pre-1914.

- The introduction of proportional representation was accepted by most across the political spectrum. It was an ideal to which the SPD were committed. For many of the SPD's political opponents it was the means by which the socialists could be prevented from having total control over the government.

- The main political groupings, e.g. socialists or conservatives, were represented in the same proportions in the Reichstag of 1919 as they had been in 1912. Parties in pre-1914 Germany were more representative of sectional interests, which were often but not necessarily linked to class. For example, the Centre Party gained much of the Catholic vote. Proportional representation allowed these sectional interests to continue to be represented – an important factor for stability in such uncertain times. It was not until the late 1920s, when these sectional interests broke up, that voting patterns altered.

- The coalition governments did not fail because the voting system forced them into being but because the leading political parties chose not to operate the system effectively. This was particularly the case with the SPD, whose leaders found it difficult to break the habit of opposition and accept the compromise offered by Weimar.

Executive powers and Article 48

Between 1919 and 1923 the checks and balances written into the constitution acted to strengthen the political system. The aim behind the authors of the constitution was clear. By insisting the President was elected directly by the people and for a period in office of seven years and by giving him the power to disband the Reichstag and dismiss the government, they created a counterbalance to any potential 'elected parliamentary dictatorship'. There had been no tradition in Germany before 1914 of **parliamentary sovereignty**. The creation of strong executive powers through Article 48 should been seen at a further attempt at creating political continuity. The excessive use of Article 48 by President Hindenburg from 1930 onward focused attention on the excessive powers granted to the Reich's President by the constitution. But President Ebert used Article 48 as an instrument for the preservation of the Republic. One of the best examples of its use was in November 1923 when he used it to give power to the army to put down the Munich **Putsch** (see page 116). Although the constitution allowed Hindenburg and others legally to undermine Weimar democracy later in the decade, it allowed government sufficient flexibility to overcome the main problems facing the Republic between 1919 and 1923.

A federal state

By building in checks and balances, and a long list of civil rights, the constitution's authors attempted to prevent any one group/region dominating the Republic. The relationship between the central government and that of the regions (the *Länder*) was complex. In recognising an element of regional authority, e.g. over police, and regional influence, e.g. representation of the *Länder* in the national second chamber (the Reichsrat), the constitution again reflected pre-1914 practice. For the political system to succeed, it was essential that it was recognised as legitimate by the majority of the population.

What were the threats in 1920?

Kapp-Lüttwitz Putsch, 1920

Causes

The threats to the Republic from the forces of the right were apparent and real early in 1920. The Versailles treaty demanded a reduction in the size of the German army from 650,000 to 200,000 in November 1919 and 100,000 thereafter. This reduction was too much for a number of right wing nationalists who demanded that the terms of the Versailles treaty be rejected and that the Weimar state be overthrown. The figurehead of the movement was General Ludendorff, but the leaders were Wolfgang Kapp from the right wing and marginal Patriotic Party and General von Lüttwitz of the *Freikorps*. In March 1920, the government's Defence Minister, Gustav Noske, ordered that the Ehrhardt and Baltikum Brigades of the *Freikorps* disband as part of the scaling down of the armed forces. A group of army officers led by Lüttwitz refused to disband and instead demanded the resignation of Ebert and the government and new elections to the Reichstag.

Events

On the night of 12 March and the morning of 13 March, Lüttwitz led his *Freikorps* brigade into Berlin where they seized the government district of the city. The Defence Minister, Noske, ordered the army to act. The commander-in-chief, General Reinhardt, was prepared to act in defence of the Republic, but the Head of the General Staff, General von Seeckt, ordered his troops to stay in their barracks, declaring that '**Reichswehr**

SKILLS BUILDER

1 From what you have read above what do you think were the priorities for Hugo Preuss and his colleagues when drafting the constitution?

2 Were they successful in achieving their aims?

Definition

Putsch

A takeover of power.

Definition

Reichswehr

The name given to the German armed forces from 1921 to 1935.

does not fire on the Reichswehr'. Kapp was declared Chancellor by Lüttwitz. The government fled to Dresden, but before it left it appealed to the workers to strike in defence of the Republic. The response was immediate; a large general strike paralysed the capital, and the rebels failed to win the support or recognition of the civil service or financial institutions including the Reichsbank. After four days the Kapp regime collapsed, and he and Lüttwitz fled to Sweden.

Impact

The Kapp-Lüttwitz Putsch posed a significant threat to the Republic. It revealed the army's reluctance to support the Republic and the dubious loyalty of the *Freikorps*. Noske was forced to resign as Defence Minister, but only one army officer was imprisoned for his role in the plot. In Bavaria, army officers sympathetic to the *putsch* forced the elected SPD led state government to resign and replaced it with a government of the right. Ultimately, however, the events of the Kapp-Lüttwitz Putsch underline the fact that the Republic relied nearly exclusively on unreliable forces to maintain a semblance of 'order'.

The Ruhr revolution, 1920

In response to the threat from the *Freikorps*, workers in the Ruhr formed a 'Red Army', which was essentially a workers' militia. On 15 March they seized power and set up a government in Essen with the aim of setting up a soviet state. The government sent in the *Freikorps* and a willing army to crush the revolution. This was very ironic; the government was using the very same forces that had just shown themselves to be of dubious loyalty. The army's attack on the 'Red Army' in the Ruhr was ferocious with no prisoners taken and anyone suspected of being a revolutionary being shot on the spot. The fighting was heaviest around Essen, with the 'Red Army' finally defeated on 7 April. The Ruhr revolution of 1920 was over.

How much of the threat to the Republic were the left?

The fear in Germany of the communist revolution spreading across Europe was considerable. Not only had the spectre of revolution reared its head at Kiel in November 1918 and in Bavaria in April 1919 but street violence and industrial unrest seemed to suggest more serious unrest. Not only that, but revolution in Germany was a central element of Soviet leader Lenin's foreign policy; exporting their revolution was the means by which their own revolution could be secured. The Russian–Polish war of April–October 1920 heightened fears in Germany, especially with the Soviet Red Army at the gates of Warsaw in August 1920. Although the Poles pushed the Soviets back, the perceived 'Red Threat' barely diminished.

But the revolutionary left was divided and weakened by the lack of widespread support. The KPD benefited from a split in the Independent Socialists (the USPD) in October 1920 as it brought them a large portion of

> **Russo–Polish War 1920**
>
> The armies of the government of the new Polish State fought against the forces of Bolshevik Russia. By August 1920 the Soviet Army had reached the gates of Warsaw but was pushed back.

the USPD's membership. The issue that brought many socialists into the party was the KPD's membership of the **Comintern** and its close alliance with the Soviet Union. However, this also alienated large sections of the working classes. Similarly, the tactic of head-on revolt against the state was counterproductive and never threatened to succeed in its objective of prompting a Bolshevik style takeover.

There are similarities between the significance of the revolutionary left and the Treaty of Versailles, in that it was not so much the reality of each that most threatened the Republic but the perception of each. The most important consequence of this perception was that it deflected attention from the most serious threat to the democracy – the anti-Republicanism of right wing nationalism. Indeed, the threat of revolution encouraged many to share the analysis of the right that the Republic was based on weak government and should therefore be replaced.

Table 4.2 Elections to the Reichstag, June 1920

Party	DNVP	NSDAP	DVP	Centre	DDP	SPD	USPD	KPD	BVP
Votes (in millions)	4.249	–	3.919	3.845	2.333	6.104	5.046	–	1.238
Seats	71	–	65	64	39	102	84	–	21
Percentage of vote	14.9	–	13.9	13.6	8.3	21.7	17.9	–	4.4

The government led by Gustav Bauer collapsed in the wake of the Kapp-Lüttwitz Putsch and the Spartacist rising in the Ruhr and was replaced by a government led by Hermann Müller (also of the SPD). The Müller government was eager to bring forward the elections to the first Reichstag of the Weimar Republic (which was to replace the National Assembly). Called for June 1920, they were to be overshadowed by the bitter disappointment of the Versailles treaty and the continuing political unrest. The votes cast highlighted a distinct polarisation and a swing away from the parties of the 'Weimar Coalition'. The parties supporting the Republic saw their votes collapse by 6 million in comparison to the 1919 election. An upsurge in support for parties opposed to the Republic, the DVP, DNVP and USPD, reflected widespread disenchantment among the electorate.

The election result was to have a very important impact on the Republic. The 'Weimar Coalition' received only 44.6 per cent of the vote, and the majority of the Reichstag were unsympathetic or hostile to the new Republic. This was to have very serious implications for the Republic:

- From now on the main opposition groups such as the DNVP and the USPD did not act as a government in waiting; they opposed the new Republic.
- The largest party in the Reichstag, the SPD, were reluctant to work with other parties in coalition governments for fear of further alienating their supporters.

Definition

Comintern

An international communist organisation founded in Moscow in 1919 and dominated by the Soviet Union. It was also known as the Third International.

Discussion point

Looking at the table on the 1920 elections and referring back to the elections of 1919, what changes in voting have taken place?

Political violence

After the failure of the Kapp-Lüttwitz Putsch many of the *Freikorps* brigades were disbanded because of their sympathy with the uprising. But this did not stop ex-members of the *Freikorps* from agitating against the Republic. The means by which the *putsch* was defeated convinced many nationalists and those on the far right that the Republic was propped up by the communist-inspired unions. A few joined secret organisations, such as the Consul organisation, that were dedicated to a campaign of intimidation and violence against their enemies. Despite the intense violence of extremist groups, they were tolerated by the Bavarian government led by Gustav Ritter von Kahr. Groups on both left and right of the political spectrum resorted to such violence, but the vast majority of murders between 1920 and 1922, 354 out of the 376 that took place, were carried out by members of right wing organisations.

- The years 1921 and 1922 witnessed an escalation in political violence and the assassination of some important political figures. The murders of USPD leader Karl Gareis and Centre Party politician Matthias Erzberger in the summer of 1921 caused considerable dismay across the political spectrum. The case of Erzberger was particularly revealing. As a leading member of the Centre Party, he had promoted the cause of peace during the war and had campaigned for the signing of the Versailles treaty. He was the epitome of the Republic and was, therefore, singled out by right wing radicals for death. On 26 August 1921 Erzberger was murdered in the Black Forest by the extremist right wing Consul organisation.

- Erzberger's death did not mark the end of the violence. On 24 June 1922, the Foreign Minister, Walter Rathenau, was shot by the Consul organization. Jewish, wealthy, the architect of the Treaty of Rapallo that set up closer relations with Soviet Russia; Rathenau was an obvious assassination target for the extreme right. The assassination of the Foreign Minister was a direct challenge to the Republic to the extent that Chancellor Wirth blamed the right for destabilising the Republic, claiming in the Reichstag that 'the enemy is on the right'. The political response to Rathenau's death was the Law to Defend the Republic that set up special courts to deal with assassins and terrorists. But, as will be explained, the judiciary were lenient is their dealings with those on the right; Rathenau's assassin, Count Arco, was given a short prison sentence.

Discussion point

What were the dangers for the Weimar democracy of such high levels of political violence?

What was the attitude of the establishment towards the Republic?

Case study 1: the judiciary

The judiciary were drawn from a pre-war caste and their interpretation of the law and constitution shows very clearly where their sympathies lay.

- By Article 54 of the Weimar constitution, the judiciary maintained their independence. This privilege was often used to undermine the spirit of the constitution. It was the judiciary's interpretation, or rather misinterpretation, of the constitution that posed a threat to the Republic. Essentially, many judges showed bias against the Republic and were lenient towards those who tried to destroy the new democracy.

- The examples of judicial bias are many, their significance being that they helped create an atmosphere that suggested that challenges to the state had some semi-legal status. The role played by the judiciary in the Erzberger case in 1920 is an example. Matthias Erzberger was hated by the enemies of the Republic as a politician who had argued in favour of signing the Versailles treaty. In early 1920, the leader of the DNVP, Karl Helfferich, accused Erzberger of fraud and corruption. Erzberger accused Helfferich of libel and took the case to court. But the judiciary found against Erzberger, and the result was the resignation of Erzberger, which was a real blow to the Weimar political scene in which he had been such an important player. The judges' decision was dubious at best.

- Even more significant was the failure of the Law for the Protection of the Republic, which was passed in July 1922 in the wake of Walter Rathenau's murder (see page 86). The law stiffened the powers of the state against conspiracy for murder and the operation of extremist parties. In the Reichstag it was opposed in its passage by the nationalist DNVP, the BVP (Bavarian People's Party) and the KPD. Once it had passed into law, the judiciary failed to use it to the full – and if they did it was against the forces of the left. In Bavaria, the law was ignored and its functions taken on by a Bavarian special court.

- In October 1922, Felix Fechenbach, who had been secretary to Eisner (the leader of the Bavarian revolutionary government in 1918), was given eleven years imprisonment for violating the Press Law. In contrast, in 1924 the leader of the Munich Putsch (see page 116), Adolf Hitler, was given only five years for high treason, and his co-conspirators were acquitted. During the trial, the judges and even Bavarian State Prosecutor Stenglein showed considerable sympathy towards Hitler and his cause. So the judiciary were foremost among the forces that attempted to undermine the Republic.

Case study 2: the army

We have already seen how the contrasting speed and urgency with which the Reichswehr tackled *putsch* attempts from left and right highlighted its unreliability. In effect, the army stood to protect its own interest and not that of a state to which it felt it owed no allegiance. In 1923, this imbalance continued.

- The attempts of the KPD and its allies to unleash a German 'October Revolution' in Saxony and Thuringia in 1923 failed because of the prompt deployment of willing units of the Reichswehr. It was highly effective in stamping out the *putsch* and in arresting Saxony's KPD and SPD cabinet members.

SKILLS BUILDER

1 Why were the attitudes and actions of the judiciary and the army between 1919 and 1923 potentially so damaging to the Weimar Republic?

2 Why did they dislike the Republic so much? See if you can come up with at least three points in response to this question.

Definitions

Milliard

A thousand million, so 132 milliard gold marks is equivalent to 132,000,000,000, for example.

Fulfilment

Germany's policy of fulfilling the terms of the Versailles treaty so that the terms could be shown to be unjust and unworkable.

- A month later, General von Seeckt initially refused to send in the troops to deal with an attempted coup by the right in Munich (see page 116). The local Reichswehr leader, General von Lossow, had made it clear that he would refuse to obey the orders of the Weimar Republic. In the case of the subsequent Munich Putsch, Seeckt was saved the dilemma of having to order the army into battle against comrades on the nationalist and military right. The intervention of the Bavarian police saved the Reichswehr's blushes. Similarly, Seeckt and the army had their hand forced by Ebert who transferred all power of the Reich to Seeckt on the night of 8 November 1923. As Seeckt was not prepared to risk a split in the army he acted in the interests of the Republic in ordering the disbanding and banning of the NSDAP.

Reparations

The means by which the French attempted to effect a revision of the Versailles treaty was via reparations. The treaty had established Germany's war guilt and, therefore, Germany's obligation to pay for war damage. Between 1919 and 1921, 23 conferences were held to discuss the levels of reparations to be paid.

- In July 1920 the Spa Conference agreed that reparations payments would be received in the following proportions: France, 52 per cent; British Empire, 22 per cent; Italy, 10 per cent; and Belgium, 8 per cent, with the smaller powers to receive the rest.

- At the Paris Conference in January 1921 the Reparations Commission decided on a figure of 226 **milliard** gold marks. The German government rejected this demand as excessive and France sanctioned the occupation by French troops of the German cities of Düsseldorf, Duisburg and Ruhrort.

- The London Conference on reparations met on and off from February to May 1921. In April 1921 the Reparations Committee set a new figure for reparations of 132 milliard gold marks to be paid by Germany in annual instalments of 2,000 million gold marks in addition to 26 per cent of the value of its exports. Germany was to pay 1,000 million gold marks by the end of August 1921. Failure to agree or to pay the first instalment would result in the invasion of the Ruhr by French forces.

- The German government led by Konstantin Fehrenbach resigned in protest, and a new government was formed under the leadership of Julian Wirth. On 11 May 1921, Wirth's government accepted reparation terms and raised a loan in London to pay the first instalment. Wirth complied under its policy of **fulfilment**.

Growing financial crisis

One of the greatest threats to the Republic came from the consequences of the currency collapse in 1923. As with all nations that had participated in the First World War, successive German governments had huge problems in coming to grips with economic readjustment and debt. Reparations simply made matters worse. In 1919 the national debt stood at 144 milliard marks; by late 1922 it had increased to a staggering 469 milliard marks. Without meaningful currency reform and a balancing of the budget, the Republic was set on a course for **hyperinflation**. In July 1922 the government asked for permission to suspend reparation payments. This request was refused by French Prime Minister Poincaré, who demanded, as conditions for a moratorium, various 'productive guarantees', including 60 per cent of the capital of the dyestuff industry on the left bank of the Rhine as well as the state mines of the Ruhr. So, rather than have to sack state employees or try to reform the currency, which might have destabilised the country further, the German government printed more money to cover its debts. This move was taken by the Allies, and the French, in particular, to be a deliberate sabotage of reparations. In November 1922 the new government led by Wilhelm Cuno was faced with financial disaster. At the end of the year, the Reparations Commission declared that Germany had failed to deliver promised coal and timber to the Allies.

Ruhr crisis, 1923

This political and financial crisis was the most serious in the period 1919–23. The German defaulting on reparations led to the Franco/Belgian occupation of the Ruhr in January 1923 with 60,000 troops. Germany was outraged, and Cuno's government encouraged the workers and population of the Ruhr to offer **passive resistance**. The French and Belgian authorities responded by arresting mine owners and by taking over the mines and railways.

On the one hand, passive resistance led to a sharp reduction in the amount of coal delivered to France and Belgium. But the government had to pay out millions of marks to those who had lost revenue as a result of passive resistance. The lack of income from tax meant that the government simply printed even more money; by August 1923 there were 663 billion marks in circulation and the German currency collapsed into hyperinflation.

Table 4.3 Hyperinflation in Germany (bread prices in marks)

1918	January 1923	September 1923	November 1923
0.63	250	1,500,000,000	201,000,000,000

As the currency collapsed, so did the policy of passive resistance. The German economy also collapsed; by the end of 1923 only 29.3 per cent of trade union members were working full time. Although the crisis did not result in the collapse of the Republic, it shook the faith of many Germans. The examples of those who were affected are many – from the thrifty middle class who saw their savings destroyed to the waged working class who saw their income drop in real terms. The blame for the crisis of 1923 and the threat to the Republic is a matter of contention. There is little

Definitions

Passive resistance

The refusal to work or collaborate with the French and Belgian forces of occupation.

Hyperinflation

Occurs when the amount of paper money in an economy increases and pulls prices up to the point where the spiral of printing money and price rises goes out of control.

Discussion point

With a work partner, discuss whether you think that the level of reparations set was fair or not.

doubt that the management of the German currency and financial policy from 1919 was a contributory factor in the financial collapse of 1923. However, to implement strict currency and fiscal reform before 1923 was politically impossible.

Stabilisation of the currency

In August 1923, a new government led by Gustav Stresemann was formed. It began to take measures to stabilise the situation.

- In September 1923 payments of reparations were resumed, and the French agreed to set up a commission to study the problem of the German economy.

- In November 1923 the Rentenmark was established by the Finance Minister Hans Luther to replace the old mark. Mortgage bonds on industrial and agricultural assets covered this new currency, and the printing of it was strictly limited. Luther also sacked over 700,000 state employees as part of an attempt to balance the budget.

- Also in November a Rentenbank (shortly to become the Reichsbank) was opened, and Hjalmar Schacht was appointed as Currency Commissioner. It was Schacht's task to oversee the replacement of the worthless currency with the Rentenmark (which became the Reichsmark in 1924).

Unit summary

What have you learned in this unit?

There were elements of the Weimar Republic's constitution that were to cause problems later on. However, the document itself was a pragmatic attempt to reflect the need for compromise and continuity with pre-war Germany. It is inaccurate to suggest that the constitution itself threatened the survival of the Republic. Similarly, while the perceptions of the Versailles treaty were to bring the Republic criticism, it was not the terms of the treaty that caused the greatest threat to the new state. The threat to the Republic came from those who attempted to revise the treaty or interpret it to the detriment of Germany.

The Republic was also threatened by repeated attacks from its internal enemies on the left and right. Many Germans feared a Bolshevik-style revolution. A far more potent threat came from the forces of right wing nationalism, those who despised the new democracy. However, it was the rejection of the Weimar Republic by those who dominated important institutions within the state; the army, judiciary and civil service, that posed the most serious threat to the democracy.

What skills have you used in this unit?

You have discussed a number of issues and weighed factors against each other to come to a conclusion. You have answered a number of questions that are central to this topic, and you have interpreted a number of tables.

SKILLS BUILDER

1 Read the following statements and then answer this question: How damaging to Germany was the Treaty of Versailles?

- The Treaty of Versailles was a compromise as it was not solely concerned with limiting the power of Germany. There were other considerations for the leaders of the Allies. Of particular importance was the curtailment of the threat from Bolshevik Russia, which made the breaking-up of Germany unrealistic.

- The Versailles treaty did not damage or limit Germany to the extent that many of her enemies, especially the French, had wished. Indeed, the 1945 settlement on Germany, in which the country was divided, was far harsher.

- The Treaty was not the 'Wilsonian Peace' hoped for in Germany but neither was it the 'punishing peace' as hoped for by many in the victorious countries.

- The creation of a substantial Poland was implemented in the context of Wilson's ideal of self-determination but also with the creation of a state of substance next to Russia in mind, hence the addition of West Prussia and Posen.

- Loss of territory in the east was acutely felt and revision of the treaty's terms became an aim for most German politicians. The differences emerged in ideas about how and how quickly this revision could be brought about.

- Fear of the spread of communism into Central Europe was an important consideration for Britain and the USA. So the treaty left Germany humiliated and scarred but potentially strong.

- The treaty was certainly not as punishing as the Brest-Litovsk Treaty imposed by Germany on Russia in early 1918, nor did it take as much land off Germany as the German Chancellor Bethmann-Hollweg planned to snatch from Germany's conquered foe in 1914.

- There was disillusion in Germany because it had been excluded from the League of Nations, but the exclusion was temporary.

- The treaty left Germany as a united nation state with the potential to regain its status as an important diplomatic power. Given the collapse of Imperial Russian power, the treaty left Germany as the power most likely to dominate Eastern Europe.

2 Question time

Try to answer this question in writing:

'To what extent were the 1920 elections to the Reichstag the most important turning point in the political development of the Weimar Republic?'

3 Discussion point

This unit has described in detail the threats to the Weimar Republic from 1919 to 1923. The question for you to discuss in groups is:

Given how considerable those threats were, why did it survive?

To start your discussion, here are a few clues:

- legality
- fear of revolution
- division of opponents.

Exam style question

This is the sort of question you will find appearing on the examination paper as a Section A question:

'The main threat to the stability of the Weimar Republic in the period 1919 to 1923 came from the political violence of the extreme right.'

How far do you agree with this judgement?

Exam tips

- Plan before you start writing. In your plan identify the lines of argument that you intend to follow. Then write out a running order of paragraphs.
- Make sure that you deal effectively with the core factor. In this question it is the impact of political violence.
- Weigh the relative significance of other indentified factors.
- Stay analytical throughout.
- Illustrate your response with accurate detail.
- Make a clear judgement in your conclusion.

You are now ready to write up your answer.

RESEARCH TOPIC

Going into detail

There are some areas of interest that you might choose to research in greater detail. For each of the following, identify the causes, events and impact.

- Wilson's Fourteen Points
- the Ruhr crisis, 1923
- hyperinflation.

5 How stable were the 'Stresemann Years' of the Weimar Republic, 1924–29?

What is this unit about?

The so-called 'Stresemann Years' were named after the politician Gustav Stresemann, who was Reich Chancellor in 1923 and Foreign Minister from 1924 to 1929. Throughout these years there was a failure to rectify the structural political defects of the Weimar state (as detailed in the previous unit). The weaknesses that were to contribute to a breakdown of democracy in the early 1930s can be traced to the middle of the 1920s. This period also saw the beginnings of economic depression and social discord, which were to worsen after 1929. It was in foreign policy that Stresemann excelled, and the period 1924 to 1929 witnessed an improvement in the nation's diplomatic standing. The view that stability was reflected in the cultural flowering of the Weimar period is not fully accurate; the modernism of 'Weimar culture' stood in stark contrast to the conservatism of large sections of a disapproving society. These years were ones of cultural polarisation, which was to be reflected in the events of the early 1930s and beyond. Any stability in these years is relative to the periods that immediately preceded and followed them.

In this unit you will:
- discover the extent of the stability of the Weimar Republic in the mid to late 1920s
- consider and discuss important turning points and issues as part of the process of enhancing your understanding of these years of the Weimar Republic.

Key questions

- To what extent should the period 1924 to 1929 in Germany be described as the 'Golden Years'?
- What were the main economic, social and cultural developments of the period?

Timeline

1924	May	Nationalist vote increases in Reichstag elections
	August	Reichstag accepts the Dawes Plan
1925	February	Death of President Ebert
	April	Hindenburg elected as President
	October	Locarno treaties signed
1926	September	Germany admitted to the League of Nations
1927	August	Commercial treaty signed between France and Germany
1928	May	Number of socialist votes in Reichstag elections increase

1929	September	Allies begin military evacuation of the Rhineland
	October	Gustav Stresemann dies
	December	Referendum upholds the decision to adopt the Young Plan

5.1 Berlin street scene, 1927

Biography

Gustav Stresemann

A leading member of the DVP party, Stresemann was a nationalist and a monarchist. However, he accepted the Weimar Republic and worked within its framework of fulfilment to restore Germany's diplomatic status. He served briefly as Chancellor in late 1923 and then as Foreign Minister until his death from a heart attack on 3 October 1929.

What impression does the photograph of a Berlin street scene in 1927 give you of life in Berlin at that time?

Relative political stability

The middle years of the Weimar Republic were marked by an absence of the attempts at extra-Parliamentary action typified in the 1918–23 period by the Spartacist uprising, Kapp-Lüttwitz Putsch and 'German October' or Munich Putsch (see page 116). That said, it is still inaccurate to describe these years as ones of political stability as the parliamentary system failed to mature and develop, despite the reduction in the threat from the extreme left and right. There are many reasons for this, primary among which was the failure of the coalition system to produce governments that had sufficient support to tackle the problems that faced the new democracy. The blame for this failure should be placed with the political parties.

Before 1914, political parties in Germany had not all had the experience of forming governments or compromising to create viable governments. This naivety and cultural deficiency became highly apparent during the Weimar years when the parties still acted more as interest groups representing their own sectional interests than as national parties of government. This is significant because the Weimar Republic's electoral system was based on proportional representation, as explained in the last unit. Parties needed to act in a spirit of compromise and consensus, but, as we will see, most did not; for example, the DVP's ever-increasing association with the interests of business caused it to refuse coalition with the SPD in 1926. The result was frequent political paralysis. The inability of successive coalitions to act or legislate with any cohesion meant that many of the structural problems Weimar faced, both economic and political, were not tackled. With these facts in mind, this could hardly be labelled a period of political stability.

Chancellors of the Weimar Republic, 1923–30

Gustav Stresemann (People's Party)	August 1923 to November 1923
Wilhelm Marx (Centre Party)	November 1923 to January 1925
Hans Luther (no party)	January 1925 to May 1926
Wilhelm Marx (Centre Party)	May 1926 to June 1928
Hermann Müller (SPD)	June 1928 to March 1930

Election May 1924

Gustav Stresemann's government lacked the support of a majority in the Reichstag and it collapsed in late November 1923 to be replaced by one led by Wilhelm Marx of the Centre Party. However, Stresemann continued to serve as Foreign Minister until 1929. The Republic, because of the financial collapse was in a state of emergency, which was only lifted in early 1924. In the Reichstag elections of May of that year the Nationalist and Communist Parties made significant gains at the expense of the more moderate parties of the centre.

Discussion point

The May election of 1924 saw some important shifts in voting patterns. Look back at the election figures from 1920 (see page 85) and draw five conclusions about the extent of the changes.

Table 5.1 Election, May 1924

Party	Number of votes (in millions)	Percentage of votes cast	Number of seats
DNVP	5.6	19.5	95
DVP	2.7	9.2	45
Centre	3.9	13.4	65
BVP	0.9	3.2	16
DDP	1.7	5.7	28
SPD	6.0	20.5	100
KPD	3.6	12.6	62
NSDAP	1.9	6.5	32
Others	n.a.	9.8	n.a.

The Dawes Plan

Stresemann believed that a policy of fulfilment was the best course of action in dealing with the Allies. Above all else, Germany needed raw materials, new markets for its goods and new sources of capital; it also needed to restore confidence in its economy. According to Stresemann, this was even more so the case because the Treaty of Versailles had removed Germany's military strength. He therefore willingly collaborated in an American initiative to consider the issue of reparations. The Dawes Plan was put together by a committee of economists and other experts chaired by the American banker Charles Dawes. In April 1924, the committee produced its proposals.

- The French would leave the Ruhr, and further sanctions would be made harder to apply.
- Reparations would be paid over a longer period of time, and credit would be advanced to help rebuild the German economy. In the first years of the plan, an international loan of 800 million Reichsmarks would be granted to cover four-fifths of the reparation payments of 1,000 Reichsmarks a year. The higher level of 2,500 million Reichsmarks a year set by the London Payments Plan would be paid after 1929.
- The Reichsbank would be reorganised under Allied supervision. Reparation payments would be paid in such a way as not to threaten the stability of the German currency.

The foremost challenge for the government of Wilhelm Marx was the passage through the Reichstag of the Dawes Plan. The main problem was that the plan involved Germany accepting that it would have to continue to pay reparations. The collapse of the SPD vote in the May 1924 election, down from 171 to 100 seats, and their ideological divisions over whether they should take part in 'bourgeois coalitions', made the task of pushing through the agreement on a two-thirds majority even harder. The plan was approved in the Reichstag on 29 August 1924 with the necessary support coming from members of the DNVP, which was the largest party of the right throughout the period in question. As a large party it was a broad church, including former members of groups as diverse as the pre-1914 Conservative Party, the National Liberals and Christian Social groups. Although many within the party opposed both the Versailles treaty and the democratic republic, there were others who were prepared to work within the system to improve the lot of their constituency. However, in a foretaste of what was to come, the willingness of some of the nationalist DNVP to align themselves with the government led other factions of the coalition, the DDP and the Centre Party, to withdraw their support.

SKILLS BUILDER

Explain why, at this point in 1924, the majority of German politicians in the Reichstag were prepared to vote in favour of the Dawes Plan despite the fact that it insisted that Germany must continue to pay reparations?

Election, December 1924

Table 5.2 Election, December 1924

Party	Votes cast (in millions)	Percentage of votes cast	Number of seats
DNVP	6.2	20.5	103
DVP	3.0	10.1	51
Centre	4.1	13.6	69
BVP	1.1	3.7	19
DDP	1.9	6.3	32
SPD	7.9	26.0	131
KPD	2.7	9.0	45
NSDAP	0.9	3.0	14
Others	n.a.	7.8	n.a.

In December 1924, a new election brought a revival in the fortunes of the SPD, which gained 31 seats (mainly at the expense of the KPD who lost 17 seats).

Obstruction by the SPD

The new coalition of January 1925 was led by Hans Luther. The coalition excluded the socialists but included members of the nationalist DNVP for the first time. This was to prove the undoing of this government as the DNVP objected to the terms of the Locarno treaties (see pages 108–109) negotiated by Stresemann, which were passed in November 1925 only because of support from the SPD. A new coalition was sought, but the SPD still objected to joining a coalition with 'bourgeois parties' (i.e. the DDP, Centre Party or DVP). Indeed, the problems for the Republic's political system of coalition governments were made considerably worse by the behaviour of the SPD.

- Between early 1924 and June 1928 the SPD resisted becoming involved in forming viable coalition governments despite its position as the Reichstag's largest party. The main reason for this course of action was a belief that coalition with the 'bourgeois' parties would lead to a compromise of the party's ideals. This belief was strengthened by the adoption at the 1925 party conference of the Heidelberg Programme, a Marxist-based series of policies to transform the capitalist system of private ownership of the means of production to social owners.
- The consequence of such action was to reduce the influence of the SPD in the Reichstag, although their tacit support for governments such as that of Wilhelm Marx in 1926 was often the key to that government's survival. However, such rejection of political responsibility also weakened the whole process of democracy as it contradicted the concept of representation and accountability.
- The reluctance of the SPD to join coalitions was made worse from mid-1925 by the election of President Hindenburg, who was instinctively anti-socialist. His attempts to exclude the SPD from influence in government were to help create an atmosphere in which constructive

political consensus was at best unlikely. Yet such consensus was essential if the Republic was to tackle the political and economic problems it faced.

So the actions of the SPD played into the hands of the opponents of the Republic and weakened its political legitimacy.

Election of President Hindenburg

This stalemate was reinforced by the new President – Hindenburg – who was elected to office on 26 April 1925. Hindenburg's election was to have serious consequences for the survival of the Republic, in particular when one takes into account the powers invested in the presidency by the constitution. As a veteran of the Franco-Prussian War and as the victor of the Battle of Tannenberg in 1914, he was much respected. He won the election because of the split in the anti-right vote, gaining 14.6 million votes in comparison with 13.7 million votes for Marx of the Centre Party and 1.9 million for Thälmann of the KPD. Hindenburg was to make it very clear that he would not accept SPD participation in a coalition government.

Hindenburg was instinctively conservative and anti-socialist. Many of his supporters hoped that, on election, Hindenburg would swing to the right and deal the new democracy a blow. He was not prepared to do this because he was tied by his oath as President of the Republic to protect the constitution. However, his election had a huge impact on how the constitution and democratic politics operated.

- From the very beginning of his period in office, Hindenburg used his presidential powers and therefore had a far greater influence than Ebert ever had on the membership of coalition governments. From the moment of his election as President in 1925 Hindenburg worked tirelessly to create coalitions that would exclude the SPD. The exclusion of the SPD meant that Chancellor after Chancellor found it difficult to build working and sustainable coalitions. When the socialists were included in government, e.g. the Müller government that was formed in June 1928, those governments were beset with problems. Many within the DVP and the Centre Party shared Hindenburg's reluctance to accept SPD dominance of a government despite the fact that they were by far the largest party in the Reichstag.

- Whenever possible, Hindenburg insisted on the inclusion of the DNVP as part of a government coalition. This had the impact of limiting the scope of many coalitions. The fourth Marx government, formed in 1927, included the DNVP on the insistence of Hindenburg and thereby ruled out the possibility of a 'grand coalition' covering the political spectrum.

- Hindenburg made it very clear indeed that he did not wish for any constraints on his presidential power. In 1926 the Ministry of the Interior produced a draft law defining the use of Article 48. Hindenburg blocked the draft law from proceeding. Even though he did not look to use Article 48 in the 1925 to 1929 period as extensively as he did later, it was clear that he believed that the President's powers should be unrestrained.

It what became an ironic spiral, as parliamentary government failed to fulfil its potential so there was increasing scope for the interference of the President. The blame for this should not be placed with the constitution itself but with those such as Hindenburg who worked to undermine it.

Political instability

In January 1926, Hans Luther formed a minority coalition involving the Centre Party, the DVP and the DNVP, but this cabinet was not to last for long, foundering on the instructions it gave to the country's diplomatic corps to use the old **imperial flag**. The Reichstag passed a vote of no confidence in May 1926, and Luther was replaced by William Marx as Chancellor. On 20 June 1926 a referendum took place on the confiscation of royal property, the vote failing to reach the required majority. The Marx cabinet relied on the support of the same parties as its predecessor and, until late 1926, had the tacit support of the SPD. That support was removed in late 1926 and the cabinet fell. It was replaced in January 1927 by another Marx government, which this time included the nationalist DNVP. There was always a strain on the cabinet, the interests of the involved 'bourgeois' parties of the DNVP, BVP and DVP being divergent. Nevertheless some important social legislation was passed, including a comprehensive reform of unemployment insurance, passed in July 1927. The coalition collapsed in February 1928 over the issue of religion in education.

Election May 1928

The election of May 1928 was an important turning point for the Weimar Republic. The left made important gains, the SPD increasing its share of the seats by 22 to 153 and the KPD showing a rise of 9 seats to 54. More significantly, as the parties of the centre and right saw their share of the vote drop, so there was a rise in the vote of splinter parties such as the Bauernbund, which represented farmers' interests (23 seats and 4.5 per cent of the vote). By the time the SPD was prepared to form a coalition after the May election victory of 1928, the political polarisation that was a developing feature of the period meant that forming a stable majority government had become nigh on impossible.

Table 5.3 Election, May 1928

Party	Votes cast (in millions)	Percentage of votes cast	Number of seats
DNVP	4.4	14.2	73
DVP	2.7	8.7	45
Centre	3.7	12.1	62
BVP	0.9	3.1	16
DDP	1.5	4.9	25
SPD	9.2	29.8	153
KPD	3.2	10.6	54
NSDAP	0.8	2.6	12
Others	n.a.	14.1	n.a.

SKILLS BUILDER

Write down on a spider chart the arguments suggesting that from the start of his presidency, Hindenburg acted to undermine the democracy and acted against the spirit of the constitution.

Definition

Imperial flag

The black, red and white tricolour.

Discussion point

What are the significant trends emerging in the election results of the Weimar Republic, notably those relating to the smaller, more extreme parties?

Biography

Alfred Hugenberg

A leading nationalist and industrialist of the Weimar period. By the late 1920s he was considered the most influential newspaper and film company owner in the country. He used his extensive media interests to attack the Weimar constitution. He served as a member of Hitler's first cabinet in 1933 but was forced to sell his media interest to the Nazis.

The DNVP moves right

It is important to point out that the drift of German politics towards political extremes pre-dated the Wall Street Crash. A very good example of the drift to extremes was the changing nature of the DNVP from a party covering a broad coalition of groups to one with a narrow anti-Republican outlook. The sharp fall in the DNVP vote (down from 20.5 per cent of the vote in 1924 to 14.2 per cent in 1928) was to cause convulsions within the party. The publication of what became known as the Lambach Article in 1928 was the trigger for a shift in the party's policy. Written by Walter Lambach, the piece urged DNVP members to renounce their nostalgic monarchism and become reconciled to the permanence of the Republic. Such was the backlash among party members that Alfred Hugenberg was elected leader of the DNVP in October 1928 on an avowedly anti-democratic platform. Similarly the Centre Party saw a drift to the right, which resulted in the election of Monsignor Kaas as party leader in December 1928.

The Young Plan

In June 1928, a ministry dominated by socialists was formed, led by Hermann Müller and including members of the DDP, DVP, Centre Party and BVP. The main task of this so-called 'grand coalition' was to steer through the Reichstag the Young Plan of 1929. This plan dealt with the issue of reparations and had been drawn up because, under the terms of the Dawes Plan, Germany was due to pay reparations at a higher rate from 1929. In September 1928, the Müller government requested that France evacuate the Rhineland. The French were only prepared to consider such a proposal alongside plans for the future payment of reparations. The Young Plan included the following proposals:

- The timescale for the repayment of reparations was set. Germany was to make payments for the next 59 years until 1988. It was to pay 2,000 million marks a year, rather than the 2,500 million marks a year as laid out by the Dawes Plan.

- Responsibility for paying reparations was passed to Germany. Exchange of payments from German marks into other currencies was to be handled by a new institution, the Bank for International Settlements in Basle, Switzerland.

- Payments were to increase gradually and, from 1929 to 1932, Germany was to pay 1,700 million marks less that it would have paid under the Dawes Plan.

- As their side of the bargain the French promised to evacuate the Rhineland by June 1930, five years ahead of schedule. This was an important diplomatic victory for Stresemann.

The Freedom Law

However, despite the concessions won by Stresemann in the negotiation of the Young Plan, many German politicians were not impressed. They were particularly incensed that Germany still had to pay reparations. Under Article 73 of the Weimar Constitution, it was possible to petition for a referendum. The leader of the DNVP, Alfred Hugenberg, formed the Reich Committee for a Referendum to oppose the Young Plan. The committee won the support of a range of anti-Republic groups including the Stahlhelm, whose leader Franz Seldte helped raise some four million signatures for the petition. The campaign was particularly important because it included, on the invitation of Hugenberg, the leader of the NSDAP, Adolf Hitler. In being associated with respectable figures such as the industrialist Fritz Thyssen or the leader of the Pan-German League, Heinrich Class, Hitler's stature among those of the right grew considerably. By the so-called Freedom Law, the Reich Committee demanded a repudiation of Article 231 of the Versailles treaty and an immediate evacuation of areas occupied by Allied powers. The number of signatures was enough to ensure a referendum on the issue, and this was duly held on 22 December 1929. It resulted in a defeat for the right; only 13.9 per cent of those who voted supported the Freedom Law despite the support for their campaign from the President of the Reichsbank Schacht. The Reichstag eventually passed the relevant Young Plan legislation in March 1930, although events were increasingly becoming overshadowed by the collapse of the New York stock exchange in October 1929.

Collapse of the grand coalition

Much of the economic recovery of the mid-1920s had relied on short-term loans from abroad. As the Depression deepened, those who had lent money demanded repayment. One consequence of the deepening Depression was growing unemployment and an increasing strain on the unemployment benefits system. As unemployment rose in the late 1920s, so employers increasingly protested at the increasing cost of social security payments. In 1927 the law on unemployment insurance changed. The Reich Institution in charge of unemployment benefits was to pay a fixed benefit to all of those out of work. In 1927 the number of Germans unemployed was around 1.3 million, and the system worked relatively well. By February 1929 the number of unemployed had increased to around 3.6 million, and the Reich Institution was forced to borrow from the government to pay the benefits. By late 1929, it had borrowed 342 million Reichsmarks, which put a tremendous strain on the government's finances. The coalition partners had different views as to how the problem should be addressed:

- The SPD believed that central and local governments as well as employers should increase their contribution to the unemployment benefits fund by 4 per cent.

- The DVP disagreed and argued that contributions should not be increased but benefits cut.

- The Centre Party negotiated a deal whereby a decision on the issue would be put off until the autumn of 1930.

Biography

Fritz Thyssen

A nationalist and anti-democrat. In the early 1920s he donated considerable amounts to the NSDAP, having inherited a fortune from the family steel making business. He supported the campaign in late 1932 to persuade President Hindenburg to make Hitler Chancellor. However, he eventually fell out with the Nazi regime and was imprisoned in concentration camps during the war.

In March 1930 the SPD deputies rejected the Centre Party's compromise solution and brought down Müller's government. The inability of the parties to agree was indicative of a narrowing of the interests of the mainstream parties that would eventually be a cause of their decline, with voters looking increasingly to parties of the extreme, which could represent their wider concerns. The actions of the SPD deputies in bringing down the Müller government were tantamount to political suicide.

Were the years 1924–29 a period of economic stability?

Most historians argue that 1924–29 were years of slow growth and 'relative stagnation' in the German economy. Some suggests that the main reasons for this were that trade union power kept wages high and therefore squeezed profits and middle class income and that the Weimar economy was structurally weak and generally unstable before 1929.

Monetary stability

Foreign investment

Between 1924 and 1929 there was significant monetary stability, which was particularly important to those classes who had suffered because of the hyperinflation of 1923. This stability was due mainly to the establishment of the Rentenmark and the consequences of the Dawes Plan. In the wake of the plan, there was a significant influx of foreign capital, 25.5 billion marks, between 1924 and 1930. The vast majority of this capital came from the USA, and it enabled the reconstruction of German industry to take place. However, such a policy had its potential dangers, a downturn in the world economy could lead to the rapid withdrawal of such investment.

Delay of reparation payments

The growth in available capital was also due to the delaying of payments at the highest rate stipulated by the Dawes Plan, thereby stimulating some inward capital investment (the Dawes Plan allowed the Germans to pay at the rate of only 1 million marks a year until 1929, when the rate would be increased to 2.5 million marks). As a consequence, national income was 12 per cent higher in 1928 than in 1913, and industry experienced spectacular growth rates. The collapse of the economy in 1929 is often seen as the catalyst for increasing economic discord and polarisation of employers and labour. This is too simplistic an analysis. While the period 1924–29 saw currency stability and economic growth, it did not experience peace in industrial relations.

Agricultural problems

While there was monetary stability in this period, it was based on foreign capital. Other areas of the economy suffered continuing change and unrest. Of particular note was the collapse in food prices from 1922, which led to widespread rural poverty.

Industrial unrest

The period 1924 to 1929 was one of economic growth, yet the term 'stability' is an inappropriate one to apply, in particular with industrial relations in mind. There is much to be gained from drawing conclusions from the political sphere. There is little evidence in the voting figures of a return of confidence in the mainstream parties of the Republic; in fact, as has been shown, quite the opposite is true. While the vote of the Centre Party held up from 1920 to 1929, it and the DDP saw a considerable drop from the election of 1919. Similarly, the number of votes won by the DVP fell from 3.9 million in 1920 to 2.7 million in 1928. Unemployment figures also tend to bear out the view that many of the later economic problems may have had their roots in the supposed years of stability; for example, in late 1928 the number of those without work stood at 3 million, or 15 per cent of the workforce.

The main problem for many Germans was to adjust to a period of relative normality in comparison with the recent years of turbulence. Yet that turbulence left a legacy that made industrial peace virtually impossible. This legacy also had serious social and political repercussions.

- For employers, the main issue from 1923 to 1929 was to claw back the initiative that they felt they had lost to labour from 1918 to 1923. Although all sides had temporarily accepted the spirit of cooperation expressed in the constitution of 1919, the mid-1920s saw an increasingly concerted attack by employers on the rights of labour. In 1923, the legislation of 1918 that enforced an eight-hour day was altered to allow employers to institute a ten-hour day in some circumstances.

- The union demands for higher wages in this period were resisted by employers to the extent that between 1924 and 1932 around 76,000 cases were brought to arbitration. There is little doubt that employers increasingly resented having to use such a procedure, and in late 1928 in the Ruhr the ironworks owners locked out over 210,000 workers rather than accept the findings of arbitration.

- The fight by the DVP on behalf of industrialists who opposed increasing unemployment insurance contributions in 1929–30 was symptomatic of a growing economic polarisation that had manifested itself in the refusal of the DVP to collaborate constructively with the SPD from the mid-1920s. In fact, the growing antagonism between the parties that made coalition government nearly impossible had its roots in increasing conflict between the groups the parties represented.

Were the years 1924 to 1929 a period of social change?

The welfare state

The constitution

The foundations of the German welfare state were laid at the end of the nineteenth century. What made the Weimar period different was that the

> **Discussion point**
>
> Work in pairs. What are the arguments for and against the period 1924 to 1929 being described as a period of financial and economic stability? One of you should summarise one side of the argument while the other should summarise the alternative view. Whose argument is the more convincing?

concept of a German welfare state was enshrined in Hugo Preuss's constitution. The proposed welfare provision was to be paid for from an increase in taxation. The plans in the constitution were bold, although some of them were not realised because of employer opposition or lack of available funds. These are some of the points written into the constitution:

- The family lay at the centre of German life (Article 119) and it was the responsibility of adults to protect and nurture young people (Articles 135–141).

- Religious freedom was guaranteed (Articles 135–141).

- Economic life was mentioned in a number of articles of the constitution. These included respect for private property, a commitment to build new housing (Article 155) and a commitment to employee protection (Article 157).

The need for an inclusive welfare state had been made ever greater by the impact of the war, which had created new classes of claimant from orphans and war widows to disabled soldiers. The Reich Relief Law and the Serious Disability Laws, all passed in 1920, provided the framework for support. In 1924 the system for claiming relief and assessing the needs of the claimants was codified. However, despite such changes, many claimants continued to receive benefits at a subsistence level. In 1927 the Labour Exchanges and Unemployment Insurance Law introduced unemployment insurance, which, as you have already read, became an important political issue.

Housing and public health

Before the First World War the state had built public housing. Public spending on housing grew rapidly throughout the 1920s. By 1929 the state was spending 33 times more on housing than it had been in 1913. Indeed, between 1927 and 1930, 300,000 homes were either built or renovated. The effect of the house building programme was to improve the quality of homes for many Germans. Better health insurance meant better medical provision and a reduction in deaths from certain diseases (see Table 5.4).

Table 5.4 Public health statistics 1909–30

Before 1914	After 1914
Deaths from tuberculosis in 1913, 143 in every 10,000	Deaths from tuberculosis in 1928, 87 in every 10,000
Deaths from pneumonia in 1913, 119 in every 10,000	Deaths from pneumonia in 1928, 93 in every 10,000
4.8 doctors per 10,000 Germans in 1909	7.4 doctors per 10,000 Germans in 1930
63.1 hospital beds per 10,000 Germans in 1910	90.9 hospital beds per 10,000 Germans in 1930

Women

The role of women and the debate about their status was an important aspect of society in Weimar Germany. The proportion of women who worked outside the home during the Weimar period remained roughly the same as before 1914. The jobs that they did were also very similar (see Table 5.5).

Table 5.5 Women in employment in Germany between 1907 and 1925 (figures are percentages of female workforce)

Type of employment	1907	1925
Domestic servants	16	11.4
Farm workers	14.5	9.2
Industrial workers	18.3	23
White collar and public employment	6.5	12.6
Percentage of women in employment	31.2	35.6

The most obvious change was in the growing number of women in new areas of employment such as the civil service, teaching or social work. There was also an increase in the number of women working in shops or on the assembly line. However, attitudes towards women working were generally conservative, and the vast majority of women who had worked full time in so-called 'men's jobs' during the war gave this work up once the war was over. There was considerable debate in Weimar Germany about whether or not married women should work. Condemnation of the so-called **Doppelverdiener** increased after 1924 when rationalisation of some businesses saw men laid off. Criticism of married women working became even sharper during the Depression, and in 1932 the Law Governing the Legal Status of Female Civil Servants was passed. This made possible the dismissal from the civil service of women who were *Doppelverdiener*. There was some opposition to this measure from certain sections of society, not least the 20,000 women who were university students in 1932. However, most Germans accepted the legislation.

Definition

Doppelverdiener

'Second earners' in English.

Youth

The Weimar State intervened in an attempt to improve the upbringing of the nation's children. The Reich Youth Law of 1922 claimed the right of all children to a decent upbringing. But such a claim was general and difficult to fulfil in reality. The issue of juvenile crime and rehabilitation of young offenders was covered by the Reich Youth Welfare Law of 1922 and the Reich Juvenile Court Law of 1923.

Weimar culture

The development of a modern 'Weimar culture'

The years 1924–29 saw the development of a style which was unique to the Weimar Republic, that of *Neue Sachlichkiet*. This was essentially a

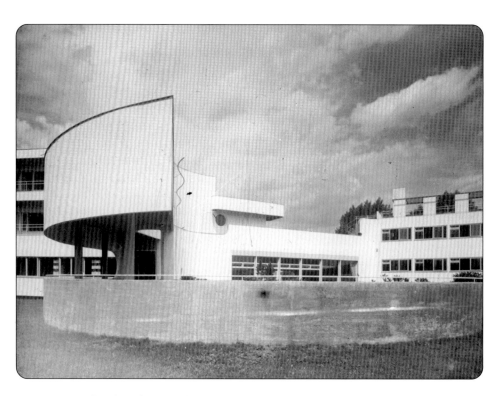

5.2 An example of Bauhaus architecture c.1926

stress on objectivity and matter-of-factness and manifested itself in a variety of media.

- Architecture and consequently many other art forms were dominated by the Bauhaus movement associated with Walter Gropius. He stressed the relationship between art and technology, the functionality of design and freedom from the past. The influence of the Bauhaus should not be underestimated; it provided the inspiration for creativity as diverse as the painting of Kandinsky and the design of the new towns in the mid-1920s, in particular Weissenhof near Stuttgart in 1927. The picture on this page shows how modern the architecture was.

- Mirroring the departure from tradition in art was the music of Schönberg and the ironic literature of the *Neue Sachlichkeit* writers such as Alfred Döblin or the satirist Kurt Tucholsky.

- The theatre and the cinema in the mid-1920s were dominated by plays that reflected social issues with a seriousness that also permeated much of literature. In particular, this period saw the publication of numerous works based on the First World War, of note being the pacifist *All Quiet on the Western Front* by Erich Maria Remarque, published in 1928.

- Alienation from the Weimar Republic was a common feature of writing on the left and right, but it was also prevalent among an artistic community that attacked its failure to construct a viable new political culture. This is best represented in Ernst Toller's *Hoppla, wir leben!* (1928) in which a revolutionary is released from an asylum after many years of incarceration, only to find that society and politics have stagnated.

- *Neue Sachlichkeit*, with its matter-of-fact style, was used to expose the weaknesses and injustices of Weimar society as it had developed by the mid-1920s. In the theatre, the works of writers such as Friedrich Wolf and Peter Lampel became the dominant forces of the mid-1920s, concentrating on a range of issues. An excellent example was Lampel's *Revolte im Erziehungshaus*, first performed in 1928, which led to a prolonged debate on education reform. That the movement summed up the public mood is a debatable issue, for as will be seen, the public mood was very much divided. What it did reveal was disenchantment with Weimar and scepticism about its ability to reform. This is very clear in the writing of authors such as Alfred Döblin, who in the 1929 novel *Berlin Alexanderplatz*, castigates the decline of the Weimar years.

Continuity – the conservative side to 'Weimar culture'

What is popularly described as 'Weimar culture' was only one manifestation of cultural expression in the mid-1920s. The objectivity of the *Neue Sachlichkeit* contrasted with the nostalgia, romanticism and escapism of popular literature, the modernity of Bauhaus with the traditional taste of the majority of the population.

- *Literature* Many writers on the political right such as Arthur Möller and Oswald Spengler contributed to an anti-democratic German 'destiny' literature which glorified the experiences of the First World War trenches. This became highly popular through the work of authors such as Ernst Jünger and Werner Beumelberg. This was countered by the anti-war offerings of Erich Remarque and Ludwig Renn. And it was not only in its treatment of war that literature was divided. While the *Neue Sachlichkeit* authors described social issues, so in the cinema films such as *Die Freudlose Gasse* (1925) by G. W. Pabst discussed the topical in a rational manner. Yet there was a parallel culture at this time that very much rejected the objectivity of *Neue Sachlichkeit* and found refuge in escapism. This was reflected in the increased sales of authors such as Hans Grimm or Hermann Löns.
- *Cinema* In the cinema, escapism found its expression in the films of Charlie Chaplin. The significance of their popularity was that their works of comedy, fantasy, nostalgia and mythology were in direct contrast to the modernity of *Neue Sachlichkeit*.

Conclusion – a clash of cultures

Cultural divisions ran deep, which very much reflected the political and social polarisation of the period. The cultural developments of the period did little to help stabilise the Republic but became part of the process by which it was undermined. The war's legacy was to create division within Germany and this was reflected in culture. The important point is that neither of these two poles of cultural expression gave support to the regime or the values that underpinned it. Instead they stood as opposites yet both in antipathy to the Republic. So while the Weimar Republic

SKILLS BUILDER

Answer the following question using the information from pages 102–107:

'To what extent could the period 1924 to 1929 be described as one of economic, social and cultural stability?'

became identified with cultural change and liberation, these forces did not act as a foundation for stability.

Foreign policy

Better relations with the Allies

From 1919 to 1924 relations between the Allies and Germany were poor. The Treaty of Versailles, Germany's agreement with the Bolsheviks at Rapello in 1922, the Ruhr crisis and other problems all contributed to a continuing mistrust. After the antagonism in relations between Germany and the Allies, 1924 saw brought a change in attitudes on all sides.

- The election of a Labour Government led by Ramsay MacDonald in Britain in January 1924 produced a friendly attitude towards Germany, and subsequent British governments maintained this.
- The victory of the left in the French general election of May 1924 marked a sea change in French attitudes to Germany. The architect of the hard line policy against Germany, Raymond Poincaré, resigned in the wake of the election defeat, and the new French government led by Édouard Herriot was far more open to constructive dialogue with Germany.

For the German Foreign Minister, Gustav Stresemann, this created opportunities to negotiate for a revision of the Treaty of Versailles and reparations through constructive diplomacy.

Locarno

One of Germany's foremost diplomatic priorities was evacuation of the French from the Rhineland. In early January 1925 the Allies issued a statement to the effect that they would not vacate Cologne by the due date of the 10th of that month. Stresemann's response in February 1925 was to propose a Rhineland mutual guarantee pact. In April, the new French Foreign Minister Aristide Briand accepted the invitation to join the British and German governments in discussions about the future of the Rhineland and the settlement of France's eastern border with Germany. Months of negotiations followed, ending in meetings at Locarno in October 1925. The resulting Locarno Treaties included the following points:

- A treaty of mutual guarantee of the Franco-German and Belgium-German borders was signed, with Britain and Italy guaranteeing the agreement.
- All parties agreed not to use force to alter these frontiers.
- A series of arbitration treaties were signed at Locarno between Germany and France, Poland, Czechoslovakia and Belgium.

Stresemann held out against a Locarno-style settlement for Germany's eastern borders, hoping for revision of them at some later date. He succeeded in avoiding being drawn into such an arrangement and even secured guarantees from France that it would not attack Germany in the event of a Polish-German war in which Germany was not the aggressor. The French agreed to move some troops out of the Rhineland, but despite further talks on the subject between Stresemann and Briand in September 1926, there was no further movement on this issue until 1929. In August of that year, and just before Stresemann's death, the Hague Conference approved the Young Plan, and the Germans were rewarded for their acceptance of the plan with an agreement from the Allies to evacuate the Rhineland before June 1930.

The League of Nations and other developments

From the post-Locarno period until 1929 Germany's diplomatic standing and relationships improved. One bone of contention was the fact that Germany had been excluded from the League of Nations when it was first created in 1919. This meant that German diplomats had been unable to work from within the structures of the League of Nations for a revision of the terms of the Versailles treaty. As part of the Locarno agreements, Germany was admitted to the League of Nations on 8 September 1926. It was agreed at the Locarno talks that although Germany was granted a permanent seat on the Council, it was free from the military obligations as laid out in Article 16. This was in part to reassure the Soviet Union, which expressed doubts about Germany's admittance.

- In April 1926, the Treaty of Berlin was signed between the Soviet Union and Germany, each country reconfirming the terms of the Treaty of Rapallo and both stressing neutrality in the event of attack by a third power.

- Relations between Germany and the Allies continued to improve. In late 1926, the allied occupation forces in Germany were reduced by a further 60,000, and in January 1927 the Allies withdrew the Inter-Allied Military Control Commission (IMCC), which had been set up to oversee German disarmament as demanded by the Treaty of Versailles.

- There were economic side effects to the improvement in diplomatic relations; for example, a commercial treaty was signed between France and Germany in August 1927.

Case study: Gustav Stresemann – a successful Foreign Minister?

Introduction

There is little debate among historians as to the aim of Gustav Stresemann's foreign policy, which was to restore Germany to 'great power' status. A more controversial debate has revolved around the question of the extent of the success of Stresemann's foreign policy. Some have claimed that Stresemann failed in his main foreign policy objective of revising the Versailles treaty. This has been countered by those who point to Stresemann's considerable success given the difficult international situation in the context of which he was operating.

> **Discussion point**
>
> In pairs, come up with two reasons why the Locarno Treaties might have been considered a diplomatic triumph for Stresemann and two reasons why they might not. When you have your reasons, discuss them with another pair. Can you reach agreement?

The argument for

- *Fulfilment* Significant progress was made towards the revision of some of the articles of the Versailles treaty that so dominated the foreign policy of the period. This was done by Stresemann through the policy of 'fulfilment'; that is, by fulfilling the terms of the treaty Germany could show how unjust and unworkable they were.

- *Soviet Union* Simultaneously, Germany worked towards agreement with the Soviet Union as shown by the Treaty of Berlin of 1926, which prompted the Western Powers into a more sympathetic approach to Germany.

- *Locarno* The achievements of German diplomacy in the Stresemann era are considerable and in particular the greater understanding with France as reflected in the Locarno Treaties of 1925. There was a very real possibility at the end of 1924 that an Anglo-French agreement would be brokered to address the issue of French security. Stresemann saw this possibly leading to the prolonging of the occupation of the Rhineland and therefore proposed a settling of the security issue.

- *Revision of Versailles* Soon after the treaties in 1925, the first evacuation from the Rhineland took place. This contrasts with the attitude of the French government to the German moratorium on repayment of loans in 1923 and the consequential invasion of the Ruhr. Yet one must not over-exaggerate the extent of the French change in attitude towards Germany. The meeting between Stresemann and Briand at Thoiry in September 1926 failed to find a solution to the contentious issue in Germany of France's continued occupation of the Rhineland, as there was not sufficient political willpower in France to withdraw. However, the fact that a solution to the problem of the Rhineland was linked to reparations repayments by the Young Plan in 1929–30 was testimony to both the desire of all parties to find a collective solution to the problems facing them and the success of Stresemann's tactics to effect a revision of the Versailles treaty.

- *Growing diplomatic influence* Most importantly, Stresemann's policies resulted in Germany regaining diplomatic influence and the ability to influence the Allies. The absence of a Locarno-style settlement of Germany's eastern borders in 1925 is a case in point as is the acceptance of Germany into the League of Nations in 1926 with a permanent seat on the Council. Perhaps the most important aspects of the revision of the Versailles treaty were the two plans to reorganise reparations, Dawes and Young, which gave Germany some breathing space to develop her economy. The removal of the Inter-Allied Military Control Commission (IMCC) in 1927 and the French withdrawal from the Ruhr all point to the success of the policy of fulfilment in achieving positive outcomes for German interests.

- *The Dawes Plan* There is little doubt that the Dawes Plan was fundamental in strengthening the German industrial base and in developing better relations with the USA, in particular improving trade.

- *The Young Plan* The Young Plan of 1929 was Stresemann's last major diplomatic achievement. Most importantly, it linked the evacuation of the Rhineland to the successful revision of the reparations programme. There were considerable other benefits to Germany, including a rescheduling of the debt to 2,000 million Reichsmarks, to be paid yearly until 1988. Stresemann did not see the treaty ratified, his death coming in October 1929.

The argument against

The success Stresemann enjoyed was not recognised universally in Germany, where there was no apparent consensus on the best tactics to force a revision of the Versailles treaty. In this sense, therefore, it is impossible to conclude that Stresemann's diplomacy resulted in domestic political stability.

- *Treaty of Versailles* The main issue of Versailles, Article 231, reparations and the 'stab in the back', continued to undermine the Weimar Republic. While 'fulfilment' brought some relief, the policy did not alter the humiliation felt in large sections of German society. There are numerous examples of this, not least the referendum of December 1929 on the Freedom Law, which opposed the signing of the Young Plan. The fact that 5.8 million Germans were prepared to vote for a law that rejected Stresemann's policy and labelled him a traitor is suggestive of the perceived limitations of the success of the 'fulfilment' policy. The issue of the Versailles treaty plagued politics and was the main cause of disagreements between the DNVP and the DVP/DDP; for example, their coalition in 1925 collapsed over Locarno.

- *Lack of room for manoeuvre* There is little doubting Stresemann's achievements, in particular with regards to Locarno. Through the lack of military means at his disposal, there were precious few options available other than to follow the peaceful policy he persued. Although his policy did lead to greater economic stability, the gradual approach to the restoration of German power meant that those who proposed more radical action to end the Treaty of Versailles were still able to act as a destabilising influence on German politics. It was not the policy of Stresemann that was responsible but the existence of the Versailles treaty.

Unit summary

What have you learned in this unit?

You have learned that it is with great care that one should use the term 'stability' to describe the years 1924–29 in Germany. While recognising that there was a return to comparative normality after the turbulence of the immediate post-war years, stabilisation was only relative.

The work of Stresemann in foreign policy, the consequential restabilising of the currency, economic growth and the decline of the extremist threat to political stability are the much-used indicators of a return to stability.

> **Discussion point**
>
> Take part in a class debate about the success or otherwise of Stresemann's foreign policy. There are two stages to this process:
>
> - Working in pairs, decide which points of argument you wish to make. You will need to flesh out these points of argument with examples.
> - One of the two of you delivers a speech to the rest of the group explaining your argument.

The advice for answering this question remains the same as at the end of the last unit. However, it is worth reiterating.

- Plan before you start writing. In your plan identify the lines of argument that you intend to follow. Then write out a running order of paragraphs.
- Make sure that you deal effectively with the core factors. In this question they are political calm, economic development and social progress.
- Weigh the relative significance of other identified factors.
- Stay analytical throughout.
- Illustrate your response with accurate detail.
- Make a clear judgement in your conclusion.

You are now ready to write up your answer.

However, it should be argued that these indicators are essentially superficial ones. The structural weaknesses of the political system remained. In the failure of the political system to develop and in the development of presidential influence one sees the causes of the collapse of the Weimar democracy in the 1930s. Monetary stability disguised worsening industrial relations and growing unemployment. These factors were to worsen after 1929 but, again, one sees signs of instability in the mid-1920s. This underlying instability was mirrored in the cultural diversity and conflict of the mid-1920s, which acted not to legitimise the Republic but to further undermine it.

What skills have you used in this unit?

You have made a series of judgements against the hypothesis that the years 1924 to 1929 were 'Golden Years'. You have also evaluated judgements and dealt with the concepts relevant to this period.

Exam style question

This is the sort of question you will find appearing on the examination paper as a Section A question:

'Germany experienced a period of political calm, economic development and social progress in the mid-1920s.'

How far do you agree with this judgement?

SKILLS BUILDER

1 Obituary

After undertaking the relevant research, write an obituary of Gustav Stresemann. You should decide the main focus of the obituary and whether it will be positive or more critical.

2 Discussion point

From what you know about Germany in the 1918 to 1929 period, why have some historians painted the middle period of the 1920s as the 'Golden Years'?

3 Thinking ahead

Draw a spider chart. Your task is to speculate ahead from the standpoint of late 1929 (the Wall Street Crash has just happened). With a partner, discuss your fears for the future of Germany and then list them on your spider chart.

6 What are the reasons for the rise of the Nazi Party, 1920–33?

What is this unit about?

This unit explores the rise of the Nazi Party from obscurity to power. It focuses on the party's formation and early development. It explains the changes in tactics and organisation in the mid-1920s that allowed the party to take advantage of changes in circumstance later on. The unit looks at the impact of the 1929 Crash and the growth in support for the Nazis. It explains the collapse of democracy and the circumstances in which Hitler was made Chancellor of Germany in January 1933. The unit the looks at how the Nazi regime consolidated power in 1933.

Key questions

- Why was there a growth in support for the Nazi Party in the late 1920s and early 1930s?
- Why was Hitler made Chancellor in January 1933 and how far had the Nazis consolidated power by the end of 1933?

Timeline

1919	January	German Workers' Party (NSDAP) founded by Anton Drexler
1920	February	Twenty-Five Points programme published, which outlines Nazi ideology
	December	NSDAP buys and publishes the *Völkischer Beobachter* (Peoples' Observer)
1921	July	Adolf Hitler becomes chairman of NSDAP
1923	November	Munich Putsch, which leads to Hitler's imprisonment
1926	February	NSDAP Conference at Bamberg established *Führerprinzip*
1928	May	Elections to the Reichstag and breakthrough for NSDAP
1929	October	Wall Street Crash
1930	March	Heinrich Brüning becomes Chancellor
	July	Reichstag rejects budget that Hindenburg passes using Article 48
	September	NSDAP vote increases in elections for the Reichstag
1932	March	Hindenburg beats Hitler in presidential election
	May	Brüning resigns as Chancellor to be replaced by Franz von Papen
	July	Von Papen Putsch against Prussian government
	July	In Reichstag elections the NSDAP becomes the largest political party
	November	Von Papen resigns as Chancellor to be replaced by von Schleicher
	November	NSDAP vote in Reichstag election down from July

1933	January	Adolf Hitler appointed Chancellor
	February	Reichstag Fire and the Decree for the Protection of People and State
	March	NSDAP largest party in Reichstag elections but fails to win a majority
	March	Enabling Act passed by Reichstag, which destroys constitution
	April	Law for the Restoration of the Professional Civil Service
	May	Trade unions banned and the German Labour Front (DAF) created
	July	All political parties except the NSDAP banned
	July	Concordat between Catholic Church and state

Propaganda

Source A

6.1 Break the Dawes Chain: a Nazi election poster from the September 1928 election

Source B

6.2 The National Socialist Workers' Party: a poster from the September 1930 election. The words coming from the snake are: usury, Versailles, unemployment, the lie of war guilt, Marxism, Bolshevism, lies and betrayal, inflation, Locarno, Dawes Pact, Young Plan, corruption, Barmat, Kutistker, Sklarek [three Jews involved in major financial scandals], prostitution, terror, civil war

Source C

6.3 'Our last hope': poster from the November 1932 election campaign

SKILLS BUILDER

1 What is the message given by this political party in these posters?

2 What makes this party stand out from the other parties of the Weimar Republic?

Biographies

Anton Drexler

A Munich locksmith, Drexler founded the German Workers' Party as a nationalist and anti-Semitic organisation.

Ernst Röhm

Influential among the *Freikorps* – groups of nationalist soldiers – Röhm helped to ease Hitler's introduction into politics and created the Nazi storm troopers, the SA. Although estranged from Hitler from 1925 to 1930, he returned to run the SA until he was killed on the order of Hitler in the 'Night of the Long Knives' purge in 1934.

Definition

SA

Stands for *Sturmabteilung* or storm troopers. They were the Nazi street fighters.

Origins

The Nazi Party was born of humble origins. Anton Drexler founded it in January 1919 as the German Workers' Party. It developed against a background of political turmoil as the new Weimar Republic struggled to establish itself. It assumed its new name, the National Socialist German Workers' Party (NSDAP), and set out its Twenty-Five Point programme at the Hofbräuhaus meeting in Munich in February 1920. Included in this manifesto – written by Drexler and an up and coming member of the party, Adolf Hitler – were themes that remained constant throughout the 1920s and beyond: the revision of the Treaty of Versailles; the ending of reparations; the destruction of the establishment; the creation of *Lebensraum* (living space) for the German people; the creation of a *Volksgemeinschaft* (a national community); and anti-Semitism.

Because of the work of Hitler and other new members, including Ernst Röhm, Alfred Rosenberg and Dietrich Eckart, the new party became one of the more noticeable among the many splinter groups of the right. In December 1920, the party increased its membership and was able to buy a local newspaper, which it renamed the *Völkischer Beobachter* (Peoples' Observer). In the following three years, Hitler consolidated his leadership of and influence on the party, becoming chairman of the party in July 1921. This was followed by the creation of the **SA** which was to become the paramilitary wing of the party. As Germany was in political turmoil, the SA was involved in widespread political violence

Discussion point

With a work partner, discuss how you would describe the Nazi Party in its early years from 1919 to 1923. Try to come up with a least three points each.

Definition

Führerprinzip

Established the complete authority of the leader, Hitler.

and thuggery, primarily aimed at the communists. On 4 November 1921 it engaged in a running battle with socialists at a political meeting in Munich and in street violence against the same foe in Coburg in October 1922.

Munich Putsch, 1923

By mid-1923 the party had some 55,000 members, many of whom were attracted by the 'catch all' manifesto and the radical nationalism of the movement. Throughout the Ruhr crisis of 1923, Hitler and the Nazi press kept up its barrage against the Weimar Republic. After a failed attempt at direct action on 1 May, tension arose between the Reich government and that in Bavaria over the refusal of the latter to arrest nationalists. The confusion spurred the Nazis into believing that the time was right for a seizure of power. The aim of the uprising was to create a dictatorship with General Ludendorff as President. Subsequent events turned out to be a shambles; the attempted coup of 8/9 November resulted in 17 dead and the arrest of Hitler. His trial for high treason in February/March 1924 was transformed into a propaganda coup by giving him and his comrades a nationwide platform for his beliefs. The sympathy of the judges ensured he received the minimum term of five years' imprisonment.

Imprisoned in Landsberg Castle in 1924, Hitler wrote *Mein Kampf* (My Struggle), which was to become his enduring political testament. In what is a generally incoherent and rambling text, Hitler attempted to explain his *Weltanschauung* (world view or outlook). The main points were the elimination of the Jewry from German life, the provision of *Lebensraum* (living space) for the Germanic peoples in the east and the destruction of communism.

Party reorganisation

A crucial factor in the rise of Nazism was the ability of the party to expand and provide a political home for those discontented with their lot, in particular after the crash of 1929. This should be put down to the flexibility of the party structure as created or developed in the 1920s. In May 1924, the Nazis, in alliance with other parties of the right, won an impressive 1.9 million votes (6.5 per cent) in elections to the Reichstag. Two months after Hitler's release from prison on 27 February 1925, the NSDAP was re-founded following a poor showing in the December 1924 elections, in which they received only around 907,000 votes (3.0 per cent).

- Throughout the year the party was reorganised into a centralised, bureaucratic entity, and an index of all members was created.
- At the party conference at Bamberg in February 1926, a new autocratic and centralised structure was discussed, which stressed complete obedience to Hitler and the *Führerprinzip*, and adherence to the 'Programme of 1920'. This conference was held as some of the party's

regional leaders or *Gauleiter* were beginning to suggest policies independently of Hitler; those based in the north-west of the country wanted to follow the more radical anti-capitalism of Gregor Strasser. Hitler's programme was formally accepted at a membership meeting of the party in May 1926.

Definition

Gauleiter

Leaders of *Gaue* or districts.

- Also important was the failure of the challenge of Gregor Strasser to the insistence of Hitler that all action had to be dictated by the policy of 'legality'.

- As part of this drive for at least a semblance of legality, Hitler attempted to quell the SA. The staged march past SA members at Weimar in July 1926 was intended to show the public at large the extent of party control over its paramilitary arm. In the summer of 1926, Captain Franz von Pfeffer was appointed leader of the SA to implement guidelines on the movement's role. From now on the SA was to undertake more mundane roles such as training and the stewarding of rallies. This did not prevent SA street fighting in cities such as Berlin and Munich, a fact that was to cause considerable tension within the movement.

There were other administrative and organisational reforms undertaken in these years. In 1926 the Hitler Youth and the Nazi Students' Association were founded. At the Nuremberg Party Congress in 1927 further reorganisation took place, with unsuitable *Gauleiter* being replaced and the central bureaucracy further reorganised. Despite such changes, the performance of the party in the election of May 1928 was dismal; it registered only around 800,000 votes (2.6 per cent) and held only 12 seats in the new Reichstag. Such a poor overall result masks the fact that when campaigning on specific regional issues, the Nazis were able to attract a significantly higher proportion of the vote – for example, in 1928 in the agricultural north-west.

Further reorganisation

The disappointment at the ballot box in May 1928 acted as a stimulus for further reorganisation.

- October 1928 saw the creation of the first Nazi professional body, the Association of National Socialist Jurists. This was to be followed in 1929 by similar bodies for doctors, teachers and students. It was this structure that enabled the party to rapidly transform into a mass movement and to spread propaganda at elections.

- Most importantly, the existence of groups to represent specific sections of the community gave the party the wide base that was at the root of its appeal to the establishment, which wanted to use that base for its own brand of authoritarian rule. There are many examples of these organisations, among the most important being the Agrarpolitischer Apparat (AA), founded in 1930 to draw a largely discontented peasantry into the movement. Not only did it achieve its aims within a relatively short space of time but it managed to infiltrate and dominate other important agrarian based organisations such as the Reichslandbund, which was important in pressing for Hitler's appointment in 1932–33.

SKILLS BUILDER

1 What was the purpose of Hitler's policy of 'legality' and what do you think that it meant in practice?

2 What was the purpose of the *Führerprinzip*?

3 What was the benefit to the NSDAP of the reorganisation undertaken in the 1920s?

- Part of the work of the AA, as envisaged by its founder Walther Darré, was to create a network of party members to undertake propaganda activities. This local activity effectively complemented the 'saturation' propaganda tactics devised by one of the party's most effective leaders, Joseph Goebbels. The use of rallies, speeches, lectures and 'aeroplane campaigns' in certain areas were effective in raising the profile of the party and increasing the vote at elections. In particular, the tactics of identifying and then targeting certain groups within regions brought rich electoral rewards. For example, in the local election in Saxony in 1930 in which the poorer farmers were targeted, 14.4 per cent of the votes were received, which was a significant improvement on the 1929 election.

- The Nazis were successful at attracting the support of the young, particularly students; in 1930 over two-thirds of the party's members were under 40 years old.

- Without electoral success in the early 1930s the Nazis would not have been in a position to challenge for power, nor would that power had been offered to them.

Growing national exposure

Such organisation and discipline meant that the party was able to take advantage of the opportunity presented by the campaign against the Young Plan. As explained in the previous unit, the Reich Committee for a Referendum was formed by the leader of the DNVP, Alfred Hugenberg, to oppose the Young Plan, and it included respected national political figures of the right such as Franz Seldte of the Stahlhelm movement (the foremost nationalist ex-servicemen's organisation). Hugenberg also invited the NSDAP to join the committee, which Hitler accepted but only after prolonged negotiations on finance and guarantees of Nazi independence. The subsequent referendum in December 1929 on the so-called 'Freedom Law' resulted in humiliation for the coalition, only 13.8 per cent voting in favour. The campaign, though, had given considerable national exposure to both Hitler and the spectacular Nazi rallies, such as the rally of 200,000 party members and supporters at Nuremberg in August 1929. The impact at the ballot box was immediate. Local council elections in November 1929 saw a significant rise in the Nazi vote, and in the state election in Thuringia in December they polled 11.3 per cent. With the extra resources provided by the Reich Committee for a German Referendum and the national exposure via Hugenberg's newspapers, the Nazis were able to present themselves as a national party of significance. Despite the failure of the Freedom Law campaign, the Nazi Party was able to take greater advantage of the increasing polarisation of German politics because of their previous institutional and organisational reforms. This was a highly significant development.

The Wall Street Crash

The roots of Hitler's appointment as Chancellor in January 1933 lie in the disaster of the economic crash of 1929 and the subsequent Depression.

The Wall Street Crash of October and the rise in unemployment had the important effect of further polarising German politics. Worldwide bankruptcies and the closure of businesses hit German industry hard, partly due to the fact that its growth in the 1920s had been funded in part by American capital that was now withdrawn. The Depression and the economic crisis did not in themselves bring the Nazis to power. What they did was create the possibility, the opportunity and the context in which Nazi propaganda would not fall on deaf ears. They also acted as triggers for the undermining of democracy in Germany.

Unemployment

One should not underestimate the psychological effects of the wholesale collapse of the German economy from 1929 onwards, especially with the problems of 1918–23 so fresh in the mind. It was unemployment and the consequential insecurity that so undermined confidence in the present structures. By 1933 over 6 million (or one in three) German workers were unemployed. It was not necessarily the unemployed who formed the bedrock of growing Nazi support but those who believed that without political change then they too might well suffer a collapse in living standards: the **Mittelstand**, a peasantry threatened with worsening economic conditions, and so on. What the Depression did was polarise opinion and increase the popularity of those who offered radical solutions to the economic problems. This is why the intended authoritarianism of Hindenburg was widely accepted, why the vote for the KPD rose from 1928 onwards (from 3.2 million in 1928 to 5.9 million in November 1933). It also helps to explain why there was so little resistance to the coup in Prussia in 1932 – the SPD and the unions were significantly weakened by unemployment. The economic crisis was also sufficient to persuade a number of Germans to break with their voting habits of the past and vote for a political movement that, if seemingly violent and extremist in parts, was reassuringly familiar in its message, e.g. the need for the destruction of the Versailles treaty.

The use of Article 48

An important turning point in the demise of the Weimar Republic was the establishment of the Heinrich Brüning government in March 1930 in the wake of the collapse of Müller's 'grand coalition' government. Brüning's government was the first to be based on presidential and not parliamentary power. Brüning was the leader of the Centre Party but he did not hold a parliamentary majority. Reichspresident Hindenburg made it very clear from the start that if Brüning's minority government was defeated or lost a vote of no confidence at the hands of the Reichstag, the Reichstag would be dissolved and he would use Article 48 of the constitution to rule by decree. Achieving the support of the majority of the Reichstag was difficult for Brüning, and his government was defeated comprehensively in July 1930 over part of its Financial Bill. As a result, the government attempted to pass the legislation by decree using Article 48. A motion was immediately

Definition

Mittelstand

The lower middle class.

Biography

Heinrich Brüning

Chancellor of the Weimar Republic from 1930 to 1932. As a member of the Centre Party, he increasingly used Article 48 as the means by which he could govern. Brüning failed to deal with the worsening economic situation of the time. He did, however, end reparations in 1932. He fled from Germany in 1934 and settled in the United States.

passed in the Reichstag by 236 to 221 votes condemning this tactic and demanding the withdrawal of the decree as it had a right to do in the constitution as defined by a sub-section of Article 48. The President's response was to dissolve the Reichstag and call an election for September 1930 (the Finance Bill finally being introduced by decree). This dissolution of the Reichstag showed the contempt in which the President and his advisers held the Reichstag and the Weimar democracy. It also marked a significant shift from parliamentary government to presidential government.

Electoral success, 1930

This period of economic and political turmoil in national politics saw significant changes in voting patterns at local level. In June 1930, the Nazis won 14.4 per cent of the vote in elections for the Saxony *Landtag* (regional assembly), which was over 9 per cent higher than the previous year. The previous spring, Joseph Goebbels had been appointed to lead the party's propaganda unit and was instrumental in the planning and execution of the comprehensive electioneering programme not only in Saxony but also in the nationwide polls.

- The result in the September 1930 election was a triumph for the Nazis. Not only did their representation in the Reichstag increase from 12 to 107 seats but the vote they captured increased from 800,000 in 1928 to 6.4 million in 1930. In consequence the reformed Brüning cabinet governed with even less support and had to rely on the 'toleration' of the SPD and, ever increasingly, the use of Article 48.

- The election victory of 1930 acted as an important stimulus to Nazi party membership. Between September and the end of the year nearly 100,000 new members joined up, and the period saw spectacular growth in sectional party organisations. Of particular note was the expansion of the National Socialist Agrarpolitischer Apparat (AA). Created with the expressed aims of extending Nazi influence in the countryside, creating a vibrant rural organisation and infiltrating existing farmers' organisations, the organisation was highly successful. Similar campaign tactics to those used at national level meant that the momentum of election success was maintained throughout 1931, the Nazis averaging around 40 per cent in local elections.

However, the debate over 'legality' within the party, and in particular the SA, persisted. In March 1931 the leader of the Berlin SA, Stennes, and some of his members rebelled against the orders of Hitler to obey a decree requiring police permission for rallies. The revolt failed to win the support of the majority of SA troopers although it highlighted the inherent tensions within the movement. This should also be placed in the context of the crackdown in 1931 on the SA in Prussia on the orders of the Prussian Prime Minister and socialist Otto Brann. The fact that the leadership was seen to be dealing effectively with the revolts of the more radical party members such as Strasser or Stennes was important in securing confidence in Hitler's leadership and his commitment to 'legal' means of gaining power.

Economic collapse, 1931

From late 1930, Brüning's government had the tacit support of the SPD. However, after the constitutional crisis in the summer, Chancellor Brüning saw himself as responsible to the President rather than the Reichstag. This can be seen in the figures in Table 6.1.

Table 6.1 The decline in the Reichstag, 1930–32

	1930	*1931*	*1932*
Days the Reichstag sat	94	42	13
Laws passed by the Reichstag	98	34	5
Emergency decrees issued using Article 48	5	44	66

Because Brüning governed by virtue of the President's authority, the primary aim of Brüning's economic and financial policy was not to reduce unemployment but to remove the burden of reparations. It was not until June 1932 that he moved to stimulate economic growth artificially by such methods as labour schemes. But as Table 6.2, on economic statistics, shows, the economy was collapsing. As a result of Brüning's lack of initiative, the economy lurched into a crisis that resulted in the banking collapse of 1931. A combination of an impending freeze on payments and the possibility of an Austro-German customs union prompted a flight of foreign capital out of Germany. The result in July 1931 was the collapse of the Austrian Creditanstalt bank to be followed by financial panic and the closure of all German banks for a three week period. The government was forced to make available 1,000 million Reichsmarks to prop up the banking system.

Table 6.2 Economic statistics 1929–32

	1929	*1930*	*1931*	*1932*
German exports (1913=100)	98.0	92.2	82.7	55.6
Industrial production (1928=100)	100	87	70	58
Unemployment (in millions)	1.89	3.07	4.52	5.57

There is a strong link between the years of Brüning's economic stewardship and the rising fortunes of the Nazis in elections. While the economic conditions were not created by the establishment, their role in perpetuating the crisis for their own political ends was to have a real influence on the rise of Nazi popularity. The banking crisis of the summer of 1931 crystallised the concerns of those who feared social collapse and disorder. The resultant political confusion and a further rise in unemployment led Hugenberg to attempt to re-form a 'National Opposition' of the right with the aim of bringing down Brüning's government. The so-called 'Harzburg Front' of Stahlhelm, DNVP and the Nazis met in October 1931 but collapsed after internal wrangling.

Table 6.3 Elections to the Reichstag, 1930–33

Party	September 1930			July 1932			November 1932			March 1933		
	Votes (million)	Percentage of votes	No. of seats	Votes (million)	Percentage of votes	No. of seats	Votes (million)	Percentage of votes	No. of seats	Votes (million)	Percentage of votes	No. of seats
DNVP	2.6	7.0	41	2.2	5.9	37	3.0	8.3	52	3.1	8.0	52
DVP	1.6	4.5	30	0.4	1.2	7	0.7	1.9	11	0.4	1.1	2
Centre	4.1	11.8	68	4.6	12.5	75	4.2	11.9	70	4.4	11.2	74
BVP	1.0	3.0	19	1.2	3.2	22	1.09	3.1	20	1.07	2.7	18
DDP	1.3	3.8	20	0.37	1.0	4	0.34	1.0	2	0.33	0.9	5
SPD	8.6	24.5	143	8.0	21.6	133	7.2	20.4	121	7.18	18.3	120
KPD	4.6	13.1	77	5.3	14.3	89	5.98	16.9	100	4.8	12.3	81
NSDAP	6.4	18.3	107	13.7	37.3	230	11.7	33.1	196	17.3	43.9	288

End of reparations

The issue of reparations was taken seriously by US President Hoover who proposed a suspension of payments for a year. The international commission formed to further investigate the problem recommended the ending of payments, which was agreed at the Lausanne Conference in the summer of 1932.

SKILLS BUILDER

Study the contents of Table 6.3 closely. Identify and try to explain the main voting trends between the September 1930 election and the November 1932 election.

Further Nazi electoral success

The presidential election of March/April 1932 saw Hindenburg returned to office, but the significance was in the vote registered for Hitler. Despite saturation electioneering, the Nazi leader managed to poll only 30.1 per cent on the first ballot and 36.8 per cent on the second as opposed to Hindenburg's 49.6 per cent and 53 per cent. Yet the Nazis were still able to present such a defeat as a success, as their vote had more than doubled from the Reichstag election. Defeat in the presidential election, however, resulted in the Emergency Decree of April 1932, which banned the SA and SS (Hitler's bodyguard), mainly in response to the growing street violence and evidence that the Nazis had been formulating plans to stage a coup if Hitler had won the election. Such moves were taken against the background of intrigue among the President's ministers and advisers. The Minister of the Interior, General Groener, who had introduced the ban, was undermined by a whispering campaign led by General von Schleicher. His idea was to 'tame' the Nazis and to use elements of Hitler's mass movement to create a military dictatorship with populist backing. Schleicher met with Hitler on 8 May 1932. As a result of the meeting, Hitler agreed to accept a role in a new presidential cabinet in return for the removal of Brüning and the lifting of the ban on the SA/SS.

As the means by which Schleicher could influence the removal of Brüning and help bring about a more right wing government, it was successful; Groener resigned from the cabinet after being shouted down by Nazi deputies in the Reichstag on 10 May. Soon after, on 29 May, Hindenburg demanded Brüning's resignation, which he received the next day. A new cabinet was formed with Franz von Papen as Chancellor and Schleicher the new Minister of Defence. The date for new elections to the Reichstag was

Biographies

General von Schleicher

An increasingly important political figure in the last years of the Weimar Republic. As a leading army officer, he had some influence with President Hindenburg. In December 1932 he was made Chancellor. Schleicher then attempted to form a government with Nazi support but failed. The Nazis murdered him in June 1934 because Hitler was convinced that he was plotting against them.

Franz von Papen

A conservative politician who played a leading role in bringing Hitler to power. Chosen by Hindenburg to replace Brüning as Chancellor in June 1932, he was dismissed in December of the same year. To get his own back on von Schleicher (who had played a part in his dismissal) he persuaded Hindenburg to appoint Hitler as Chancellor in January 1933. Von Papen became Vice-Chancellor in Hindenburg's first cabinet.

set for the end of July, and the ban on the SA was lifted on 16 June. The subsequent street violence in the run-up to the election left over 100 dead and around 7,000 casualties.

Prussian coup d'état

The political establishment were set on a return to a more authoritarian form of rule, and the Nazi rise to power should be understood in this context. The process of the destruction of the democratic system started before Hitler became Chancellor in January 1933, and evidence for this can be seen in von Papen's coup d'état against the Prussian government in July 1932.

- The political violence in the run-up to the election was the perfect excuse for the removal of the SPD-dominated Prussian government, which was dismissed by von Papen on 20 July 1932 on the grounds that it had failed to keep the peace. Although the action to depose the government was done in the name of the constitution (Article 48) its legality was highly questionable.

- When it was questioned by the SPD leader Otto Braun, President Hindenburg ordered the army to seize control, and he appointed a Reich Commissioner to govern Prussia. The failure of the SPD and the trade unions to resist was fatal. The new regime in Prussia was created as an authoritarian one, with a political police that no longer served the Weimar state but obeyed the orders of von Papen and the Reich Commissioner.

The seizure of power under the pretence of 'legality' had set a precedent. By 1933 the emergency powers of the constitution had been used to effectively destroy that constitution.

> **Discussion point**
>
> *Turning points*
>
> The Prussian coup d'état is viewed by many historians as one of the most important turning points in the history of the Weimar Republic.
>
> - Why might this be the case?
> - In your groups, discuss what the other important turning points in the history of the Weimar Republic are – positive or negative.

Electoral success, 1932

The elections to the Reichstag in July saw the Nazi percentage of the vote increase to 37.3 per cent, which translated into 230 seats, making it the largest party in the Reichstag. This was a sensational breakthrough. Although this did not constitute a majority, it put the Nazis in a hugely advantageous position politically. As the largest political group in the Reichstag, they had a mandate from the German people to be involved in the government. This legitimacy was enhanced by von Schleicher and von Papen, who were prepared to ignore the violence and illegality of Nazism as its movement was a bulwark against the left. What made the NSDAP such an attractive ally was its nature as a mass movement and the broad base of its electoral support. This was unique in a party system where the other parties represented their own sectional interests.

- The established view is that the Nazi vote was primarily that of the middle class, the *Mittelstand* of civil servants, officials and others damaged by the economic instability of the Republic. Although the Nazis picked up a significant number of votes from those who had previously voted for the middle-class parties such as the DVP or DNVP, it is wrong to assume that the NSDAP lacked a broad social base.

- The Nazis failed to attract significant votes from the industrial working class, but the DNVP had gained over 2 million worker votes in the 1924 election, and it is to be assumed that the Nazis attracted these voters at the turn of the decade.

- The Nazi vote was weakest in urban areas, which were dominated by the working class. In Berlin in November 1932 the left (KPD and SPD) cornered 54.3 per cent of the vote. Despite this, by the early 1930s the NSDAP was the only party that could present itself as a national one that cut across class and interest lines. This was due to the attractions of the Nazis as a party of protest with lofty but ill-defined ideals such as **Volksgemeinschaft**. The Nazis offered a new Germany based on traditional values, economic revival and national salvation. It was a heady and popular mix in times of economic depression.

- Not all voted for the Nazis in large numbers. The city dweller, the unemployed and the Catholic were far less likely to vote for the Nazis than the rurally based Protestant because they tended to vote for the Catholic Centre Party.

- For significant swathes of the German population, a vote for the Nazis was primarily registered as a protest at the failures of the parties of the Weimar Republic and the political system itself. It was in this protest vote and the breadth of Nazi support that the foundations of the consensus and consent of the Nazi years can be found.

- As with many a successful electoral party, policy was vague but deliberately so, style being more important than substance. Yet it was this that made the Nazis successful electorally and, thereby, so attractive to the ruling establishment, which shared their critique of Weimar and the desire to destroy democracy.

Definition

Volksgemeinschaft

The ideal of a national community based on racial identity. All those of Aryan background would belong; all non-Aryans would not.

Discussion point

Here is a hypothesis for you to consider:

'Despite the fact that Hindenburg had virtually killed off democracy, electoral support was still of utmost importance in the Nazi rise to power.'

Working in groups, discuss whether you agree with this hypothesis, despite the fact that, at first reading, it seems to be contradictory.

Political intrigue and violence

Negotiations

The misjudgement of von Papen and Hindenburg in believing that they could control and use the Nazi movement is crucial in explaining the Nazi seizure of power, but it has to be put into the context of the time. From 1930 onwards, government was conducted by intrigue and deals such as those that led to the removal of Groener and Brüning from office in May 1932. Despite obvious popularity, the election results of July 1932 did not give the Nazis an outright majority or automatic power, and von Papen refused to hand over the Chancellorship to Hitler. Violence still had an impact on political developments, even the negotiations between Hitler, von Papen and von Hindenburg in 1932 took place against the backdrop of well-publicised acts of SA brutality. In August 1932, as Hitler opened discussions with von Papen about the conditions under which the Nazis would join any government (Hitler all along insisting that he would not accept any post other than Chancellor), a savage murder of a communist labourer called Konrad Pietzuch in Upper Silesia was reported in the press. Hitler's attitude towards political violence could not be clearer, as he openly supported the cause of the SA men who were found guilty of the murder. On hearing of the verdict of the court that the men should be executed, he sent a telegram to the men to pledge his 'unbounded loyalty to them'. He then persuaded von Papen to commute their sentences to life imprisonment and ordered their release shortly after becoming Chancellor. The violence that was such an integral part of Nazism was never far from the surface.

Election November 1932

As a result of the failure of negations between von Papen and Hitler, the Reichstag was dissolved on its first day (12 September), after the government lost a vote of no confidence by 512 votes to 42. The new election in November 1932 saw a fall in the Nazi vote of some 4 per cent (34 seats), but the Nazis were still the largest party. It has often been pointed out that the appointment of Hitler as Chancellor came at a time when the Nazis were declining electorally. Yet this misses the point, for by 1932 elections were not the sole means by which power was gained, such was the extent to which democratic politics had already been undermined. The November 1932 result simply reinforced the political stalemate:

- Hindenburg wished to continue presidential government but refused to appoint Hitler as Chancellor without him first achieving a majority in the Reichstag.
- The Nazi Party had the ability (in coalition with the Centre Party, for example) to vote down a government at will.

The only perceived alternative for the establishment was to rule without the Reichstag and suppress all opposition.

von Schleicher

In attempting a way out, Hindenburg sacked von Papen and appointed General von Schleicher as Chancellor on 3 December. His first act was to attempt to draw the Nazis into a coalition by offering the Vice-Chancellorship to Gregor Strasser. The leading Nazi's instinct was to accept such an offer as the only way the party was going to gain power, but he was forced to back down and resign after a fierce battle with Hitler. Without Nazi support, the von Schleicher government lacked credibility, a fact that soon became apparent when there was strong opposition to the economic policy he presented on 15 December. As a reaction to Schleicher's economic policy of late 1932, which was seen as far too conciliatory to the left, initiatives were undertaken to create a government of the right, which included the NSDAP. These initiatives were centred on von Papen, who had resented his treatment at the hands of von Schleicher the previous year.

Business input

Yet he was not acting alone. There were elements of the business community that disliked von Schleicher's reforms of September 1932 and were determined to see a return to a more authoritarian rule, whether under the Chancellorship of von Papen or Hitler.

While their role should not be exaggerated, industrialists such as Paul Reusch and financiers such as Kurt von Schröder helped pave the way for a Nazi takeover of power through their influence and obvious preference for authoritarian rule. Indeed, it was at Schröder's house in Cologne in January 1933 that Hitler and von Papen met and entered into negotiations that resulted in Hitler becoming Chancellor. Influential individuals, therefore, had an important role to play in creating the political circumstances in which it became desirable on their part to bring the Nazis into power.

Appointment

From 4 January 1933, von Papen and Hitler held talks about the composition of a future government based on a broad nationalist coalition very similar to the Harzburg Front (see page 122). Support for such a coalition came from a variety of sources, including the Agrarian League and industrialist organisations. This had an impact on Hindenburg, who turned to von Papen to form a viable government, particularly as it was clear that von Schleicher could command little support in the Reichstag. As negotiations between von Papen and Hitler progressed, the former conceded the role of Chancellor to the latter but in a cabinet that would be a coalition of the right. Hindenburg was ultimately swayed to appoint Hitler by the following logic: once the Weimar Republic had been undermined, a new, more authoritarian regime could be installed peacefully. This could take place only if it had a base of popular support, and it was this that only the NSDAP on the right of the political spectrum could provide. It was Hindenburg's understanding that Hitler was to be locked into a conservative-dominated cabinet in which von Papen would be Vice-Chancellor and General von Blomberg Minister of Defence. Hindenburg accepted von Schleicher's resignation on 27 January and Hitler was appointed as Chancellor on 30 January.

The consolidation of power, 1933

Limitations to power

The potential limits to Hitler's power were considerable. It must be remembered that Hitler was appointed as Chancellor of the Weimar Republic and as leader of a cross-party cabinet that included only three Nazis: Hitler as Chancellor, Wilhelm Frick as Minister for the Interior and Hermann Göring as Minister without Portfolio (which means that he was a member of the Cabinet without specific responsibility). The Vice-Chancellor was to be Franz von Papen and other parties of the right were well represented. Hugenberg of the DNVP was put in charge of the Economics Ministry and Franz Seldte of the Stahlhelm was made Minister of Labour.

The establishment that had brought Hitler to power held the reins of power and did not expect to lose control. The most powerful politician in Germany in 1933 was President Hindenburg, and Hitler had to work with a number of powerful establishment figures from the newly appointed Vice-Chancellor von Papen to the soon to be President of the Reichsbank and Economics Minister Hjalmar Schacht.

- Behind von Hindenburg's power was not just his prestige as President but the army, which, although still at the size set by the Versailles agreement, was highly influential.

- The new Chancellor's scope for action was also constrained by the power of institutions from the Reichstag to local government. The civil service, churches and press all stood as potential barriers to the Nazification of the political system.

- Hitler's sworn ideological enemies on the left wielded considerable power through the trade unions. In many urban areas, such as Berlin, the Nazi vote in the general election in November 1932 was as low as 22.5 per cent (as opposed to a national figure of 33.1 per cent).

- Just as the Nazis had risen from obscurity to power on the back of considerable discontent with the political system's inability to deal with Germany's economic problems, so the Nazis now had to deliver (or at least be seen to be delivering). As with nearly all governments, Hitler's regime would be primarily judged on the state of the economy.

- For many within Germany's politically important middle class, the violence and thuggery of elements of the Nazi movement was of deep concern. For the Hitlerite regime to establish broad political consensus, it needed to be perceived to be legitimate, law-abiding and respectable.

So the obstacles to the creation of a Nazi dictatorship were many, and, on first inspection, seemingly insurmountable. Even from within the Nazi

SKILLS BUILDER

1 Define 'political intrigue'.

2 On a spider chart, explain how political intrigue played its part in Hitler being appointed Chancellor in 1933.

3 Answer this question in writing:

'Why was Hitler appointed Chancellor of Germany in January 1933?'

SKILLS BUILDER

Identify what you think are the five most important obstacles to the advancement of a Nazi dictatorship in January 1933 and put them in order of importance.

movement, Hitler faced pressure from the SA and radicals to implement the Nazi revolution.

Enduring obstacles

Despite these significant obstacles, the Nazi regime had, to a considerable extent, consolidated power by the end of 1933. There were a number of reasons:

- There were high levels of collaboration of individuals and institutions with the regime because there were aspects of that government that they recognised and supported. This will be studied in greater detail in the next unit.

- The Nazis deployed propaganda effectively as a means of deceiving the political nation and beyond both of their real intentions and the significance of their actions.

- They managed to use terror and violence with efficient ruthlessness.

- The use of violence was balanced by the attempt to ensure that the consolidation of power had the veneer of legality. The Nazi leaders were pragmatic in their understanding that their revolution had to be achieved by legal means for it to be acceptable to the vast majority of the German population.

Those who believed that they had 'tamed' Hitler and his movement were to be proved very much mistaken. Although his 'Appeal to the German People' broadcast on 1 February was conservative in nature, the SA began to wreak revenge on the enemies of National Socialism. A decree in Prussia (which had fallen under the jurisdiction of Reich Commissioner Göring) 21 days later resulted in the police being reinforced by 'volunteers', i.e. the SA. The widely perceived threat of a communist seizure of power is the crucial factor in explaining how the Nazis were able to quickly undermine the constitution of the Weimar Republic. It also explains why so many non-Nazi groups were prepared to go along with the initial phase of *Gleichschaltung* (coordination). The national community promised by Hitler before and after becoming Chancellor in 1933 did not include communists. Despite the appointment of Hitler as Chancellor on 30 January 1933, the strength of the communist movement in Germany and its potential to challenge the Nazis was real.

- In the two elections of 1932, the Communist Party, the KPD, had seen its share of the vote increase from 14.3 per cent in July to 16.9 per cent in November. On the streets the Red Front Fighters' League matched the SA.

- The socialists were even stronger. Their paramilitary wing, the Reichsbanner, dominated the streets in a number of towns and cities in Germany. In the election of November 1932 the socialist SPD party received 20.4 per cent of the vote.

In his speech to the nation from the Sports Palace in Berlin on 10 February 1933, Hitler made it very clear that it was his intention to destroy the 'Marxist threat' of both communism and socialism.

Failure of the left

The failure of the communists and the socialist movement to challenge Hitler's chancellorship was due to their misreading of the situation. The communists believed that Hitler's government would not last. Their ideological beliefs led them to conclude that Hitler's appointment as Chancellor signified a crisis in the capitalist system that would inevitably lead to political and economic collapse and the victory of communism in Germany. Therefore, they concluded, the best tactic was to do nothing and wait. This was despite clear provocation:

- The appointment of 50,000 SA, SS and Stahlhelm (nationalist paramilitary) members as auxiliary policemen on 22 February led to a wave of violence against communists and socialists across Germany.

- On 24 February the police raided and ransacked the head office of the KPD. Hermann Göring claimed that evidence was discovered during the raid that pointed to a communist conspiracy to seize power through force.

The SPD leadership were unsure how to respond. To react violently would play into the hands of the Nazi leadership, which was clearly intent on undermining the ability of the socialists to function effectively as a political movement; the Nazis had already attempted to close down a number of socialist newspapers, and SA members frequently disrupted political meetings. Equally damaging to the ability of the left to effectively oppose the Nazis was the split between the communist and socialist parties. Although many on the left argued for the creation of a 'unity front', there was no agreement on how this should be formed. Indeed, the hatred the communists had for the socialists was only matched by the hatred they had for the fascists.

The Reichstag Fire and its aftermath

There is no doubt that Hitler believed his own propaganda that the communists aimed to stage a takeover of power. On the night of 27 February a young Dutchman, Marinus van der Lubbe, set fire to the Reichstag as a protest at the repression of the working class. Hitler and the Nazi leadership ignored the initial evidence that van der Lubbe had acted alone and concluded that the fire was the first act in the long awaited communist backlash. It gave the regime its opportunity to crush the communists and suspend a number of parts of the Weimar constitution. Most importantly, it gave the Nazis the opportunity to use legal means to begin the seizure of power. Crucial to the seizure of power was the issuing of the emergency decree 'For the Protection of People and State' on 28 February. Interestingly, the decree was first suggested by Ludwig Grauert, who was an adviser to Göring and as much a nationalist as a Nazi.

- The rights of freedom of speech, a free press and freedom of assembly enshrined in the Weimar constitution were suspended, and the police were given powers to detain suspects indefinitely without reference to the courts.

SKILLS BUILDER

Given the strength of the German communist movement at the start of 1933, it is remarkable that their opposition had been broken by the end of March. Answer the following question:

'Why were the Nazis able to destroy communist opposition so quickly at the start of 1933?'

- The important clause 2 of the decree allowed the cabinet to intervene in the government of the states (*Länder*) that, together, formed Germany. This power was previously the prerogative of the President, and the clause marked a significant shift in power.

Immediately Goebbels ensured that the Nazi propaganda machine portrayed the decree as a necessary step in the battle against communism, and, for that reason, it was widely welcomed. The decree is a very good example of how the Nazis were keen to ensure there was a legal front to their activities despite the fact that in reality the decree signalled the collapse of the rule of law. Indeed, Hitler stated explicitly in a cabinet meeting on 28 February that the struggle against the communists 'must not be made dependent on judicial considerations'. In the coming months his words were adhered to as the decree was used to justify the arrest, imprisonment and often torture of thousands of political opponents. The leader of the KPD, Ernst Thälmann, was arrested on 3 March, and 25,000 political prisoners were in custody in Prussia alone by the end of April.

General election, March 1933

Although it undermined the constitution, the decree was broadly welcomed, such was the fear of communism. It also paved the way for success in the election of March 1933. However, the success of the Nazis was not total. Despite the intimidation of rivals, the Nazis managed to get only 43.9 per cent of the votes, giving them 288 seats, which, even with the 52 seats of their nationalist allies, was way short of the two-thirds of seats needed to alter the constitution. But the Nazis had won, and the significance of clause 2 of the emergency decree of 28 February now became apparent. As all communist KPD deputies were barred from the Reichstag (despite gaining 4.8 million votes), the result gave Hitler a distinct political advantage.

Immediately the Nazis began the process of destroying political opposition in the regions of Germany. In Bavaria on 22 March, Heinrich Himmler (the leader of the SS) set up a concentration camp at Dachau to house political opponents in 'protective custody'.

Potsdam Day

The regime was still desperate to portray itself as respectable. The opportunity to turn the occasion of the opening of the Reichstag in Potsdam on 21 March 1933 into a propaganda triumph was seized by Goebbels with both hands. Hitler, wearing morning dress rather than party uniform, bowed deeply in front of Hindenburg and made a speech of impressive moderation. While many were reassured, the true nature of what was becoming a 'nationalist revolution' was more clearly discernable. To change the constitution he needed two-thirds of the seats in the Reichstag, which he did not have. He was keen to impress Hindenburg and the wider establishment that he could control the more radical elements in the Nazi movement. President Hindenburg, the son of Kaiser Wilhelm II and many leading generals witnessed Hitler's commitment to traditional German values. However, Hitler's intentions were more clearly seen in a piece of legislation introduced on the same day. The Malicious Practices Law banned criticism of the regime and its policies.

The Enabling Act, 1933

On 23 March Hitler presented the Enabling Act before an intimidated Reichstag. Brown-shirted SA men milled around outside the chamber and packed the public gallery. By the terms of the Act, the government gave the power to pass laws to the cabinet and allowed the government to alter the constitution as it saw fit. It granted Hitler four years of power as a dictator. Such a move needed a two-thirds majority vote in favour in the Reichstag and a two-thirds attendance. The communist deputies were barred (illegally) from the Reichstag and Göring, as speaker, simply reduced the required number of votes needed from 432 to 378. To achieve the required majority, the Nazis needed the support of the Catholic group in the Reichstag, the Centre Party, who, with 74 seats, constituted a significant voting bloc. Many within the Nazi movement saw organised religion to be as much of an enemy as the communist or socialist movements. In February 1933 there had been a number of attacks against churches and religious figures. The priority for the leadership of the Catholic Church was to protect its own interests. Therefore many Catholics were heartened by Hitler's reassurances to the leader of the Centre Party, Ludwig Cass, that the Enabling Act would not affect the Church's position in any way. They also supported it for the following reasons:

- Von Papen, a leading member of the Centre Party, was Vice-Chancellor and his influence was reassuring.
- Hitler promised that he would not restrict Catholic influence in education.
- Many Catholic deputies were intimidated by the threats of the SA and had no wish to suffer the same fate as the communists.

The Centre Party therefore promised its support, and the only party in the Reichstag to oppose the bill was the socialist SPD (the communists had been excluded from attending). The Enabling Act was passed by 444 votes to 94. Democracy in Germany had been killed off and the Reichstag's power and influence removed. The Weimar constitution was dead. Support for the Nazi proposal came from a wide cross-section of the country's political élite. This symbolises the alienation that the élite felt towards the Weimar democracy and the crucial part they played in its downfall.

Gleichschaltung (coordination)

As part of the consolidation of Nazi power, Hitler attempted to coordinate all aspects of German political and social life under Nazi control.

- The next step the Nazis took after the Enabling Act was the destruction of local state government. Every German region (such as Bavaria) had its own state government. On 31 March these were all dissolved by the

> **Discussion point**
>
> In pairs, discuss which of the following tools the Nazis used to best effect in the consolidation of power:
>
> - legality
> - violence
> - propaganda.
>
> Explain your answer fully.

Minister of the Interior Wilhelm Frick. They were ordered to reconvene but with a membership that reflected the recent elections from which communists had been barred.

- New state governors, *Reichsstatthalter*, were appointed with full powers to introduce Nazi policies.

- By the Law for the Restoration of the Professional Civil Service of 7 April 1933, Jews and political opponents of the Nazis were thrown out of the civil service. To bring the running of party and state closer together, the Nazis passed the Law to Ensure the Unity of Party and State on 1 December 1933.

- On 1 May, the trade unions enjoyed their traditional May Day celebrations. The following day the offices of the huge socialist trade union organisation the ADGB were stormed by SA members; the organisation was disbanded and its assets seized. Other trade unions, including the Christian trade unions, voluntarily disbanded. A committee under Dr Robert Ley was set up 'for the protection of German Labour'. On 10 May the German Labour Front (DAF) was established under Ley's leadership. Similarly, professional groups lost their independent organisations and were forced to join Nazi bodies.

- The violence and intimidation led many leaders of the socialist SPD to flee abroad, and on 22 June the party was officially banned and its assets seized. Around 3,000 of the more prominent socialists who had remained in Germany were promptly arrested, and a number were killed. In the Berlin suburb of Köpenich, a handful of socialists had the temerity to resist arrest, with the result that around 100 of them were murdered in cold blood. Intimidated and isolated, the other political parties took heed of events and voluntarily disbanded.

- On 14 July, the Nazi party was declared the only legal political party in Germany.

- The centralisation of the state was completed in January 1934 by the abolition of the upper house of the Reichstag (the Reichsrat). The provincial governments and the local governments were made completely subordinate to the central government.

The Church

The last party to voluntarily disband was the Centre Party on 4 July. Although a number of church people had been intimidated by the SA, the churches posed a greater obstacle to the acquisition of absolute power. Both Catholic and Protestant churches had large and loyal followings that could not be intimated out of their beliefs or even, at this stage, out of attending church. But, at a local level, action was being taken against prominent members of the Centre Party. For example, in June 1933 a number of prominent members of the Bavarian Centre Party were arrested on the orders of Himmler. Hitler's priority was to eliminate the political role of the Church, but he was prepared to compromise on its social functions for the time being. The result was the Concordat (agreed on 1 July although signed on 20 July) between the Catholic Church and the Nazi state, the road to which was smoothed by Hitler's Vice-Chancellor von Papen (who was a Catholic). By the terms of the Concordat the Catholic Church in Germany agreed to give up all political activity, but their right to congregate and worship was guaranteed.

Unit summary

What have you learned in this unit?

- The rise of the Nazi party must be placed in the context of economic crisis, in particular the aftermath of the collapse of 1929. The organisational and ideological flexibility of the NSDAP also added to its appeal, which was reinforced by the apparent 'legality' of the Nazi assault on power in the late 1920s and early 1930s in contrast to the attempted *putsch* of 1923.
- Without doubt the Nazi party's electoral success brought it to the brink of power. Hitler was appointed Chancellor as part of the establishment's desire to restore authoritarian government.
- The political transformation of Germany by the end of 1933 had been extraordinary. Not only had the Nazis destroyed much of the political opposition, they had become dominant ideologically.

What skills have you used in this unit?

You have prioritised, and you have made decisions. You have used your analytical skills to explain why Hitler became Chancellor of Germany.

Exam style question

This is the sort of question you will find appearing on the examination paper as a Section A question:

> 'Nazi consolidation of power in 1933 was primarily due to the use of terror and violence.'

> How far do you agree with this judgement?

Exam tips

You have read at the end of the previous two units how to approach these types of questions. To reiterate, planning is crucial, as is the structuring of your paragraphs, as was stressed at the end of Unit 1.

- To answer this specific question you should start by analysing how the regime used terror and violence to consolidate power.
- You should then weigh this against other factors, which include the use of legality, tactical alliances and the successful use of propaganda.

You are now ready to write up your answer.

SKILLS BUILDER

1 Hypothesis testing

Here is a hypothesis for you to consider:

'The appointment of Hitler as Chancellor in 1933 was primarily the result of Nazi electoral success'.

What are the arguments for and against this viewpoint?

2 What is your reaction?

In groups, identify different social and economic groups in Germany in 1933, e.g. the *Mittelstand* or the trade unionists. Try to think of as many groups as you can – you might want to trade ideas with the group next to you. Then try to explain how each group might have reacted to:

- Hitler's appointment as Chancellor
- the consolidation of power up to June 1934.

3 What if?

Let us now try one of those 'what if' exercises that we did at the end of Unit 3.

What if:

- Wall Street had not crashed in 1929?
- Brüning had launched a rescue package for the economy including labour schemes and work creation projects from the time when he took power in March 1930?
- von Papen had not launched the coup d'état against the Prussian state government in July 1932?
- An election had not been called in July 1932 (the Reichstag still had more than half of its term to run)?
- Communists and socialists had put aside their differences in early 1933 to oppose the new government?

7 Controversy: how popular was the Nazi regime in the years 1933–39?

What is this unit about?

This unit focuses on the nature of the **Third Reich** prior to the outbreak of war. It explores the popularity of the regime and the degree of consent it enjoyed. This unit explains the extent to which consent was based on terror and repression and how far it was the result of shared values, propaganda and indoctrination. This unit also explains how far the Nazi regime had built a 'Nazi consensus' by 1939 and which Germans opposed the regime.

You will:
- find out how the regime consolidated power and the levels of consent in Germany between 1933 and 1939
- work with source material to help weigh the various debates about why some Germans supported the regime and the extent and nature of opposition to it.

Key questions

- What were the reasons for, and extent of, consent shown towards the Nazi regime in Germany in the years 1933 to 1939?
- What was the extent and nature of opposition to the Nazi regime in the years 1933 to 1939?

Timeline

1933	March	Reich Ministry of Popular Enlightenment and Propaganda created, with Goebbels at its head
	May	Creation of the Women's Front (Frauenfront) by Robert Ley
	May	Sopade, the SPD movement in exile, founded
	September	Reich Food Estate created
	October	Editors' Law calls for 'racially pure' journalism
	November	Plebiscite held to confirm one-party rule in Germany
	November	*Schönheit der Arbeit* (Beauty of Labour) and *Kraft durch Freude* (Strength through Joy) set up
1934	June	Marburg speech, Night of the Long Knives
	July	By the Law Concerning Measures for the Defence of the State the government justifies its actions in the Night of the Long Knives
	August	President Hindenburg dies
	August	Plebiscite confirms Hitler as his successor and Führer (leader)
	September	Hjalmar Schacht introduces the 'New Plan'
1935	March	Regime makes public its rearmament programme

Definition

Third Reich

Reich means 'state'. The First Reich referred to the Holy Roman Empire, the Second Reich to the period from 1871 to 1918, and the Third Reich to the period from 1933 to 1945.

1936	June	Himmler placed in overall control of policing in Germany
	October	Hermann Göring put in charge of the Office of the Four Year Plan
1937	November	Hjalmar Schacht resigns as Minister of Economics
1938	January	Blomberg-Fritsch affair
1939	March	Hitler Youth Law makes membership of the Hitler Youth compulsory
	September	The Reich Security Head Office (RSHA) founded.

Source A

7.1 Photograph showing Adolf Hitler arriving at the 1933 Nuremburg Rally

SKILLS BUILDER

1 What impression does the photograph in Source A give of the popularity of Hitler in 1933?

2 Do you believe that this photograph has been staged? What are your reasons for believing this?

Consent and consensus

Source B

Although the regime deployed a formidable apparatus of terror, it is clear that it was based on a large measure of consent from broad sections of the population. First, the Nazis' success in creating a positive image of Hitler as 'Führer' and in identifying the regime with that Führer image was of crucial importance. In part this was the result of skilful propaganda by Goebbels and his Ministry who portrayed Hitler as a national leader above politics, selfless in his dedication to the service of the German people. Without concrete successes Hitler could not have sustained his positive image as Führer, the fact that he was associated with the solving of the unemployment problem and with the restoration of Germany's position as a European power appeared to confirm Goebbels's propaganda.

From J. Noakes and G. Pridham (editors), *Nazism 1919–1945*, Volume 2, published in 2000

Source C

The large spheres of consensus were undoubtedly much more important than the areas of dissent. A far-reaching consensus behind central elements of the National Socialist regime which – with the great exception of the former Left, of course – lasted until deep in the war was, further, able to neutralise dissent and to compensate for the particular rejection of particular aspects of National Socialism. The underlying consensus was rooted not only in an emotional concordance [agreement] with fundamental aspects of National Socialist ideology but in the ability of the regime before the war to improve considerably the living standards of almost all sections of the population in comparison to the period of the world economic crisis – or to at least raise hopes of an imminent improvement.

From Ian Kershaw, *Resistance without the People?*, published in 1985

Problems of evidence

Before we explore the ways by which the Nazi regime built a consensus, it is worth pointing out the fact that the debate about the relative popularity of the Nazi regime between 1933 and 1939 has in part been clouded by the absence of evidence. While the regime presented itself through propaganda as highly popular with the mass of the German people, there was no means through which popular opinion could be expressed, as Jeremy Noakes and Geoffrey Pridham have explained.

Source D

The image of German society conveyed by Nazi propaganda in newsreels and the press was of mass enthusiasm and commitment. However, in trying to understand what Germans really felt during these years the historian is faced with serious problems. Not only were there no opinion polls but it was impossible for people to express their views in public with any freedom; the results of elections were rigged; the media were strictly controlled. Newspapers are of limited value as a source, since the editors were subject to detailed instructions from the Propaganda Ministry on what to print and were severely disciplined if they stepped out of line. In short, an independent public opinion did not exist in the Third Reich.

From J. Noakes and G. Pridham (editors), *Nazism 1919–1945*, Volume 2, published in 2000

The removal of the communist 'threat'

The widely perceived threat of a communist seizure of power is a crucial factor in explaining why so many non-Nazi groups were prepared to go

SKILLS BUILDER

1 After reading Sources B and C, how would you define consent and consensus?

2 What is the impression given in Sources B and C of the extent of consent and consensus in Nazi Germany between 1933 and 1939?

3 What explanation is given in both sources as to why there was such consent and consensus?

4 What are the differences between Sources B and C?

SKILLS BUILDER

1 What, according to Source D, are the problems for the historian in finding out about public opinion in the Third Reich?

2 Where might historians find information about people's opinions in Germany in the years 1933 to 1939? How reliable might this information be?

Definition

Gleichschaltung

The coordination – the bringing into line – of different elements of German life.

Biography

Joseph Goebbels

Joseph Goebbels joined the Nazi party after university and was appointed *Gauleiter* (regional leader) of Berlin in 1925. As Minister of Propaganda from 1933 he was one of Hitler's leading lieutenants. Close to Hitler ideologically and as a friend, he committed suicide in the Führer's bunker in April 1945 after first murdering his own children.

along with the initial phase of *Gleichschaltung*, i.e. why they were willing to fall into line with the regime. The new national community promised by Hitler before and after becoming Chancellor in 1933 did not include communists. Despite the appointment of Hitler as Chancellor on 30 January 1933, the strength of the communist movement in Germany and its potential to challenge the Nazis was real. In the two elections of 1932, the Communist Party, the KPD, had seen its share of the vote increase from 14.3 per cent in July to 16.9 per cent in November. On the streets the Red Front Fighters' League matched the SA. In his speech to the nation from the Sports Palace in Berlin on 10 February 1933, Hitler made it very clear that it was his intention to destroy the 'Marxist threat' of both communism and socialism, and on 24 February the police raided and ransacked the head office of the KPD. The Reichstag Fire gave the Nazis the opportunity to use legal means to begin the seizure of power.

Opposition crushed

The introduction of the Emergency Decree for the Protection of People and State of 28 February paved the way for success in the election of March 1933, and the significance of clause 2 of the Emergency Decree also became apparent. With the excuse that they were restoring order the Nazis destroyed the power of the *Länder* within the space of a few days at the beginning of March. In Bavaria, Heinrich Himmler (the leader of the SS) set up a concentration camp at Dachau on 22 March to house political opponents in 'protective custody'. The other states fell into line, and by early April the Nazis controlled the parliamentary assemblies of all regions and had appointed Reich Governors to rule the states (Göring became the Reich Governor in Prussia). The public reaction is explained by two historians.

Source E

The violence and repression were widely popular. The 'emergency decree' that took away all personal liberties and established the platform for dictatorship was warmly welcomed. A provincial newspaper from the alpine outreaches of Bavaria – though long sympathetic towards the Nazis almost certainly reflecting feelings extending beyond the immediate support for the NSDAP – declared that the 'Emergency Decree' had 'finally got to the centre of the German disease, the ulcer which had for years poisoned and infected the German blood, Bolshevism, the deadly enemy of Germany.'

From Ian Kershaw, *Hubris*, published in 1998

Source F

Perhaps the greatest benefit the Nazis reaped from the Reichstag fire was of a psychological nature, for they succeeded in spreading a wave of fear and resentment against communism in all social classes, with the exception of the urban proletariat. Since 1918, newspapers, journals and the entire multifaceted print media of the Weimar Republic had been publishing detailed reports of horrors perpetrated in the Soviet Union since the Revolution, reports that were confirmed by tales of Russian emigrants who had found temporary exile in Berlin and other German cities. As far as average Germans were concerned, anything was preferable to communist rule in their own country.

From Hermann Beck, *The Fateful Alliance*, published in 2008

Source G

Germany was well on its way to becoming a dictatorship even before the Reichstag fire decree and the elections of March 1933. But these two events undoubtedly speeded it up and provided it with the appearance, however threadbare, of legal and political legitimation. After his election victory, Hitler told the cabinet on 7 March that he would seek a further legal sanction in the form of an amendment to the constitution that would allow the cabinet to bypass both the Reichstag and President and **promulgate** laws on its own.

From Richard Evans, *The Coming of the Third Reich*, published in 2003

Definition

Promulgate

To issue or to pass into the public domain.

SKILLS BUILDER

1 To what extent do these sources agree in their analysis of the aftermath of the Reichstag Fire?

2 How might the Reichstag Fire and its aftermath have strengthened the Nazi consensus?

Gleichschaltung

In order to maintain a general consensus, the regime went out of its way to portray itself as respectable. For most Germans, opposition to what was the legitimate state was unthinkable, and propaganda was instrumental in projecting the image of a legal seizure of power in 1933, which did much to allay conservative misgivings. Hitler, as much as any German politician, understood the importance of legality in German society. The significance of Potsdam Day and the Enabling Act was to underline the legitimacy of the regime, thereby making any opposition harder to justify.

What followed in the rest of 1933 was a process of political and cultural *Gleichschaltung*, which was in essence the Nazification of German society. In reality *Gleichschaltung* was a two-way process, with the Nazi movement encouraging coordination from their end. On the other hand, considerable numbers of Germans were happy to disband their institutions voluntarily or reform them under the Nazi banner. From January to May 1933, over 1.6 million Germans joined the Nazi Party, many for the purpose of securing career enhancement.

- Considerable numbers of civil servants joined the party in the immediate wake of the Law for the Restoration of the Professional Civil Service of April 1933, which cleared the way for the purge of the civil service of 'unreliable' political elements.

- The business community rapidly disbanded its representative institutions and created the Reich Corporation of German Industry, which immediately pledged its loyalty to the regime.

- Women's groups were dissolved and reformed as chapters of the Nazi Women's Front. From choirs to bowls clubs, veterans' associations to scouts, all independent organisations were either dissolved or voluntarily joined to the equivalent Nazi group. In this way the regime eliminated the possibility of rival organisations or dissent.

As Hitler came to power by a 'legal revolution' the support of the courts was of paramount importance at least in the first year of the dictatorship.

Most judges and lawyers in Germany were instinctively conservative in philosophy. There was no protest when all lawyers were 'coordinated' into the Nazi Lawyers Association in 1933. For example, Bumke, the President of the Supreme Court at Leipzig, was immediately converted despite his belief that the SS were murderers. The Law for the Protection of State and People of February 1933, which suspended civil liberties and placed Germany under a permanent state of emergency, was given full legal endorsement. Lawyers also served to extend the scope of Nazi policies and indeed to radicalise through their eagerness to please the regime.

The process of *Gleichschaltung* took place with such ease because of the fear of many but also because of the fact that many wished to be identified with the new regime. A number of leading intellectuals and cultural figures openly supported the movement – from the writer Gerhart Hauptmann to the composers Richard Strauss and William Furtwängler. Few German intellectuals dissented despite the fact that the law purging the civil service applied to academics, and from April 1933 a number of German intellectuals were forced out of their jobs and into exile. On 10 May the Nazis burned the books of now 'forbidden' authors in Berlin. It should be noted, however, that the action was not initiated by the Nazi German Student Federation (NSDStB) but by the rival German Students' Association (DS), which was attempting to outflank its rivals by following the ideology of the regime in such dramatic fashion. But the Nazis also used violence to enforce *Gleichschaltung* when necessary.

The use of propaganda

From 1933 Goebbels's propaganda was powerful and became not just a message but the means by which the *Volksgemeinschaft* would be formed. The Nazis deployed propaganda to denigrate their opponents, to indoctrinate, to enforce conformity, and also to project their ideology and to convert all Germans to the historical task of regeneration.

- In March 1933 the Reich Ministry of Popular Enlightenment and Propaganda was created, with Goebbels at its head. As part of the consolidation of power, in 1933 Goebbels moved quickly to seize control of all forms of communication. Central to the effectiveness of Nazi propaganda was the fact that, by the end of 1933, the Nazis had complete control of the media.

- In June 1933 the association of German publishers (VDZV) was purged of non-Nazis and Max Amann, the head of Eher Verlag (the Nazi publishing house), was appointed its chairman. Amann was to play a crucial role in controlling what was published. The Editors' Law of October 1933 called for 'racially pure journalism', and subsequently Jewish, communist and socialist journalists were dismissed. The law also really ended the possibility of independent journalism by heavily restricting the freedom of editors to publish what they wanted. It was essential for the consolidation regime that it performed an effective *Gleichschaltung* of the newspaper world.

Discussion point

Why were so many Germans prepared to fall into line with the new Nazi regime in 1933?

How far had the regime secured power by 1933?

The political transformation of Germany by the end of 1933 had been extraordinary. Not only had the Nazis destroyed much of the political opposition, they had become dominant ideologically. The speed with which the Weimar constitution had been dismantled and the opposition of the left crushed meant that no one was in doubt as to the power of the Chancellor. The Reichstag plebiscite held on 12 November 1933, in which Germany's voters were offered the choice of just one party to vote for, was a triumph for Hitler and his party, with 88 per cent of voters approving of the measure. However, even by the end of 1933, the power of the dictatorship was not complete. The churches, although compromised, remained independent. While business was generally supportive, Hitler still needed to court its leaders, especially while the German economy was still recovering from the Depression. Above all, the German army, the Reichswehr, stood outside *Gleichschaltung*. The leaders of the army owed their loyalty not to Hitler but to the ageing President von Hindenburg. For them, the greatest potential threat was the military ambitions of the ever-growing SA.

What were the tensions between the armed forces and the state?

While many generals welcomed Hitler's denunciation of the Versailles treaty and his promise to restore the army to its former political and military status, the aristocratic generals disliked Hitler because they saw him as an upstart. However, they shared Hindenburg's view that the Nazis' mass movement could be harnessed and tamed within a conservative dominated coalition. The army agreed, therefore, with the arming of the SS in 1930 and stood aside when Hitler was appointed Chancellor in January 1933. General von Blomberg was appointed Defence Minister in the government, and the pro-Nazi Von Reichenau became his calculating Chief of Staff. Any doubters within the army were calmed by the apparent legality of Hitler's revolution and by the flattery in his speech to top generals in February. Further collaboration was encouraged by the commemoration day at Potsdam on 21 March 1933.

Much of the Nazi propaganda in 1933 spoke in terms of a 'Nazi Revolution'. However, there were significant differences in understanding within the ranks of the Nazi movement as to what the concept of a 'Nazi Revolution' actually meant.

- To Hitler, the 'Nazi Revolution' meant the acquisition and consolidation of power as a means to bring about cultural change based on the concept of race. To Hitler, the 'Revolution' involved the destruction of democratic institutions, *Gleichschaltung* and adherence to the central points of his world view. Hitler was a radical, even within the Nazi Party, but his radicalism was tempered by pragmatism and the dominant instinct held by most politicians to hold onto power, even if it meant making short-term compromises.

- Röhm and his brown-shirted SA supporters, on the other hand, were not prepared to make such sacrifices. Having spearheaded the assault on the enemies of Nazism on the streets of Germany's towns and villages, they now agitated for a '**second revolution**', with no compromise with business and the establishment and the immediate purging of those considered 'enemies of the nation'. Where Röhm differed fundamentally from Hitler was over the idea of a social revolution as set out in the Party Programme of 1920. The problem for many within the SA rank and file was that the changes that had taken place in Germany since January 1933 had not challenged the economic power of the middle classes or the establishment. To put it bluntly, their standard of living had not improved.

In a newspaper article published in June 1933, Röhm threatened that 'the struggle' for a National Socialist Revolution would continue whether it had the support of the establishment or not. This was a challenge to Hitler's leadership of the movement and the political leadership of the nation. But Hitler was not yet prepared to face up to Röhm. Instead, in a speech to the Reich Governors on 6 July Hitler formally called for an end to the revolution, and at the end of 1933 Röhm was brought into the cabinet with the post of Reich Minister without Portfolio.

The SA threat to the Nazi consensus

Such a move did little to dispel the growing unease among the establishment about the seemingly growing presence and menace of the SA. In the regions of Germany, the SA acted virtually as a law unto itself; for example, it had its own police force, the Feldjäger, which acted independently of the **Gestapo**. The increasing size of the SA was intimidating: by 1934 it numbered over 2.5 million members. Above all, Röhm's ambition to turn the SA into a militia earned the mistrust of the army. At the beginning of February 1934, Röhm contacted the Defence Minister General Werner von Blomberg with the demand that the SA be allowed to take over national defence. Such a move placed Hitler in the position of having to choose to support the armed forces or the SA. In January 1934, Hitler had made a speech stressing the importance of the armed forces in the National Socialists' state. At a meeting on 28 February 1934, Hitler clarified to Röhm his belief that the SA's function was political not military.

It was not just the army that Röhm and the SA had upset. The Security Service (SD) of the SS formed in 1931 under Reinhard Heydrich was in increasing competition with the SA to run state security. While the SS had enjoyed a growing influence and expanding power base throughout 1933 and early 1934 it was clear to Heinrich Himmler and Reinhard Heydrich that their ambition to turn the SS into the most powerful Nazi organisation within the state relied on the destruction of the power of the SA (despite the fact that they were, at least nominally, a part of the SA organisation).

Röhm's contempt for the party organisation made enemies of the Führer's Deputy Rudolf Hess, while SA excesses in Prussia upset the region's Governor Hermann Göring. It was in all of their interests that Röhm's power was curtailed. With their encouragement, Hitler suspended SA military exercises in May 1934.

The Marburg speech

The opposition of the conservative élites to the Nazi regime was very much limited by their complicity in its coming to power and its consolidation of power. In their desire, as a political and economic class, to destroy democracy and the influence of communism and to create an authoritarian state, they very much 'worked towards the Führer'. Even as the regime shook off the shackles of its alliance with conservatives and nationalists, most conservatives were willing to continue to work within the regime. Few chose the path of resistance and active opposition. Those who did choose this path did so out of conscience and often with considerable bravery. Often their motive for opposition was to reverse the breakdown in the rule of law that they felt was undermining and morally corrupting Germany.

By mid-1934 the political outlook for Hitler was relatively uncertain. Added to the tension generated by the SA was the growing unease among conservative circles. Although not large in number, many of those who began to express unease about the Nazi regime had links with the army and were influential. Those such as von Papen's speechwriter, Edgar Jung, and his press secretary, Herbert von Bose, sounded out the possibility of replacing von Hindenburg as President with a conservative member of the establishment, so blocking Hitler's ambitions to seize the office himself (which would significantly increase his power). A group of Catholic conservatives in Vice-Chancellor von Papen's office, including Herbert von Bose, Edgar Jung and Baron Wilhelm von Ketteler formed an opposition cell whose most striking moment was the Marberg speech of June 1934. Delivered by von Papen and written by Jung, the speech was the most direct challenge to the regime thus far. While praising certain aspects of the regime in his speech, von Papen warned against the 'Second Revolution'. The speech was potentially a rallying call to the army to act, especially in the light of the menace of the SA, and it clarified for Hitler the level of discontent and unease in conservative circles. For the regime to consolidate effectively it needed continued economic growth and for this he needed the collaboration of the establishment. Hitler decided to act.

Operation Hummingbird

The purge of 30 June was code-named Operation Hummingbird. It was directed primarily at the SA leadership but was also undertaken to ensure that there would not be a concerted attempt by the conservatives to prevent his succeeding Hindenburg. Rumours of an SA plot had been fed to Hitler, primarily by Himmler, and he was prepared to believe them. Hitler and a detachment of the SS travelled to Tegernsee near Munich,

SKILLS BUILDER

Given your understanding of the events of 1933, explain the threat posed to the Nazi regime by:

a) the army

b) the SA.

Biography

Heinrich Himmler

The head of Hitler's bodyguard, the Schutzstaffel (SS), Himmler was to emerge as one of the most powerful men in the Third Reich. In 1934 the SS played a central part in the Night of the Long Knives. In 1936 Himmler was given overall control of the police, and his influence grew as he was well placed to realise the Führer's will. Himmler was a fanatical believer in racial theory, and his SS was to run the concentration camp system. In 1943 he was made Minister of the Interior.

where Röhm and his entourage were staying, and had Röhm arrested. Across the country a number of named enemies were murdered, including ex-Chancellor von Schleicher, von Bose (the author of the Marburg speech) and the Nazi radical Gregor Strasser. In all perhaps as many as 200 people were killed.

On 3 July the state made its actions legal with the introduction of the Law Concerning Measures for the Defence of the State. The Law made legal any action undertaken by the state, however murderous, as long as it was taken in 'self-defence'. This is another excellent example of how power was consolidated using illegal actions that were then justified by a distorted and false legality. The only Catholic left in the cabinet, the Minister of Justice Franz Gürtner, signed the law as did all his cabinet colleagues. Hitler moved to quell disquiet in the ranks of the SA by appointing the loyal Viktor Lutze to the leadership of the organisation. He immediately began a purge of Röhm supporters. The SA was finished as an influential political group. Hitler justified the murder of so many leading political figures to the Reichstag on 13 July. It was clear to all that the rule of law no longer applied in Germany.

Army and Führer

The army had played a critical role in the creation of Hitler's dictatorship and in so doing had condemned itself as an institution to complicity and subordination. The murderous events of June 1934 became known as the Night of the Long Knives. They fundamentally changed the relationship between Hitler and the German armed forces.

- There were some within the higher ranks of the army who were disgusted by the events of June 1934, and for a few, such as Hans Oster in the *Abwehr* (military intelligence), it was the turning point in his support for the regime. The removal of the SA diminished the threat posed to the army but, by helping Hitler purge his party, the leaders of the armed forces tied themselves closer to the regime.

- What happened next was crucial in understanding how the regime maintained support from the armed forces. On 2 August, Hindenburg died and Hitler declared himself 'Führer and Reich Chancellor'. But Defence Minister Blomberg and his close adviser Colonel von Reichenau decided to go one step further. They ordered every member of the armed forces to take an oath of unconditional loyalty to the Führer (rather than to the constitution as had previously been the case). The move was an attempt to bring Hitler even more closely into the orbit of the armed forces. Through the oath, the armed forces attempted to establish influence over Hitler. As it worked out, it tied the armed forces to Hitler's ambitions.

- On 19 August, 89.9 per cent of Germans voted *Ja* in approval to the suggestions that Hitler become Führer. The Night of the Long Knives – and its immediate aftermath – was perhaps the crucial turning point in the creation of the National Socialist consensus.

The terror state

The consensus was reinforced by the use of terror. Before the Night of the Long Knives, the SS had been accumulating police powers.

- In April 1933, Göring incorporated the Prussian political police into the state secret police, the Gestapo, and set them up in their new offices on Prinz Albrecht Strasse in Berlin. At the same time, Himmler was placed in control of the police in Bavaria.

- On 30 November, Göring reorganised the state secret police into the Gestapo, and in April 1934 he appointed Himmler 'Inspector of the Gestapo'. This was important as it gave Himmler and the SS some control over the state police. The SS created a huge concentration camp system in which enemies of the Nazis could be imprisoned and their labour exploited.

- The SS assumed complete command over the running of the camp system after the Night of the Long Knives in 1934. The camps were filled with those the Nazis considered undesirable or 'asocial'. This included political opponents, gypsies, homosexuals and Jews. In 1938 the German Quarrying Company (DEST) was set up to exploit the labour of the camps' prisoners.

- After the Night of the Long Knives in June 1934, the SS became the main police arm of the Nazi party with the aim of eliminating all

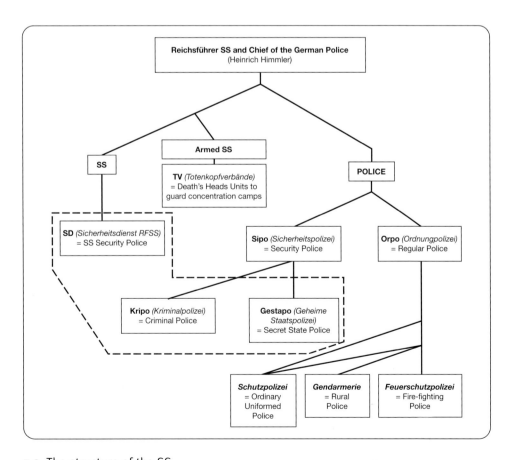

7.2 The structure of the SS

opposition within the state. This task became the specific responsibility of the SS Security Service (SD) and the Gestapo.

- The SD was reformed by Himmler in June 1934 under the command of Richard Heydrich. It was the intelligence arm of the SS with the special task of maintaining the security of the Führer, the party leadership, the Nazi Party and the Reich. Although the SD was supposed to operate under the authority of the Minister of the Interior, Frick, in reality it was controlled entirely by Heydrich and Himmler.

- In June 1936 any confusion over who was in charge was resolved. Hitler appointed Himmler head of the German police. He now controlled both the security service (Sipo) and the regular police (Orpo). Hitler's aim in appointing Himmler to such a post was to unite the police under the ideological control of the SS. In addition to the Sipo and the Orpo, Himmler controlled the security police (SD), which incorporated the Gestapo. From his sprawling headquarters on Prinz Albrecht Strasse, Himmler controlled an army of deskbound bureaucrats, torturers, policeman, spies and informers who spread far into every town, factory, school and house in Germany. The dominance of this terror state helps explain why so many Germans were willing, at least nominally, to 'work towards the Führer' at a local level. Countless thousands of Germans were interrogated, tortured and imprisoned.

- In 1939 the running of all security and police organisations was centralised through the creation of the Reich Security Head Office (RSHA).

Source H

The truth is that far from being levelled exclusively against small and despised minorities, the threat of arrest, prosecution and incarceration in increasingly brutal and violent conditions loomed over everyone in the Third Reich. The regime intimidated Germans into acquiescence, visiting a whole range of sanctions upon those who dared oppose it, systematically disorientating people, and depriving them of their traditional social and cultural milieux such as the pub or club or the voluntary association, above all where these could be seen as a potential source of resistance, as in the case of the labour movement. Fear and terror were integral parts of the Nazis' armoury of political weapons from the very beginning . . . Everything that happened in the Third Reich took place in this pervasive atmosphere of fear and terror, which never slackened.

Adapted from Richard Evans, *The Third Reich in Power*, published in 2005

Source I

Never before in no other land and at no other time, had an organisation attained such a comprehensive penetration (of society), possessed such power and reached such a degree of 'completeness' in its ability to arouse terror and horror, as well as in its actual effectiveness. [The Gestapo] spotted or overheard every German's slightest movement.

From Jacques Delarue, *The History of the Gestapo*, published in 1964

SKILLS BUILDER

What impression do these two sources give of the extent and role of the Gestapo and the use of terror in German society?

Denunciations

The impression of the Gestapo given in Source I has been questioned by a number of historians. Research by Professor Robert Gellately has suggested that the all-pervasive and intrusive images of the Gestapo deliberately projected by the regime and imitated by Hollywood needs to be corrected.

- The Gestapo was only 32,000 strong and in many cities it was short-staffed and over-administered. In the city of Hanover in 1935 there were only 42 officers; the large town of Würzburg had only 21.

- Gellately has also questioned the significance of the informer network. It has been suggested that Gestapo was fed information by an extensive network of informers; however, in Saarbrücken in 1939 there were only 50 informers.

- According to Gellately most prosecutions were the result of reporting from hostile or jealous neighbours rather than the scrupulous investigations of leather-clad agents; in Saarbrücken 87.5 per cent of cases of 'slander against the regime' were as a result of denunciations, while 8 per cent of cases were as a result of the activities of the Gestapo.

Nonetheless the Gestapo did strike real fear into all sections of society. Early protestations and challenges by brave lawyers and judges to its injustices won a few, though temporary, victories. By 1935 the courts deemed that all police actions carrying out the will of the leadership must be legal.

SKILLS BUILDER

1 To what extent do Sources J and K agree about the ways in which the Gestapo operated?

2 How far do the interpretations given by these two sources agree with that given in Sources H and I?

Source J

It seems justified to suggest that denunciations from the population constituted the single most important cause for the initiation of [Gestapo] proceedings of all kinds. The regime's dreaded enforcer [the Gestapo] would have been seriously hampered without a considerable degree of public co-operation. This behaviour has hitherto been largely ignored or not fully understood. Popular participation by provision of information was one of the most important factors in making the terror system work. That conclusion suggests rethinking the notion of the Gestapo as an 'instrument of domination': if it was an instrument it was one which was constructed within German society and whose functioning was structurally dependent on the continuing co-operation of German citizens. The motives for offering information to the authorities ranged across the spectrum from base, selfish, personal to lofty and 'idealistic'.

From Robert Gellately, *The Gestapo and German Society: Enforcing Racial Policy 1933–1945*, published in 1990

Source K

Much of the modern literature on the Gestapo has conveyed the impression of desk-bound policemen, almost buried under the avalanche of denunciations from ordinary citizens, particularly regarding violations of racial legislation. This may be so. But this approach has its own limitations. The Gestapo's primary task was to destroy political and clerical opposition. It was clearly effective for the communist underground was smashed in waves of arrests, before sinking without trace. The Gestapo did not simply stumble across communist networks. Apart from opening mail and tapping telephones, the most effective resources were contact agents or *V Leute*, as distinct from casual denouncers, informants and *agent provocateurs*.

From Michael Burleigh, *The Third Reich: A New History*, published in 2000

What is *Resistenz*?

Whereas Professor Gellately has given the impression of a population willing to denounce neighbours to the Gestapo, others have focused on those who did not fall into line with the regime. After the aftermath of the Night of the Long Knives the extent of significant opposition to the Nazi regime was limited. However, before this statement is explained, it is important to define what is actually meant by opposition. It is most appropriate to define opposition as active resistance to a regime. A number of historians have attempted to include passive resistance within the broader concept of opposition. Women wearing make-up and young people listening to jazz have been held up as examples of how Germans dissented from the regime without necessarily provoking a reaction from the security forces. A number of contemporary observers commented on the level of grumbling throughout the 1930s, which some historians have tried to interpret as showing indifference to the regime and, thereby, the making of a political statement. In the 1970s the historian Martin Broszat termed dissent and non-conformity as *Resistenz*. In a detailed study of Bavaria, he and his historian colleagues highlighted those Germans who were indifferent to the regime. They argued that this indifference, this *Resistenz*, limited the authority and impact of the regime. Broszat's ideas have provoked considerable debate.

SKILLS BUILDER

How does Martin Broszat define *Resistenz*?

Discussion point

Discuss in groups your initial reactions to the idea of *Resistenz*; do you find the concept convincing?

Source L

Such *Resistenz* could be grounded in the continued existence of relatively independent institutions (churches, bureaucracy, armed forces), in the assertion of ethical and religious norms or legal, spiritual or artistic standards which ran counter to National Socialism; effective *Resistenz* could find its expression in active counteraction by individuals or groups (in the forbidden factory strike, in the criticisms of National Socialist measures from the pulpit), in civil disobedience (non participation in National Socialist gatherings, refusal to give the Hitler salute, ignoring the ban on contact with Jews, prisoners of war, etc.), in the maintenance of communities of sentiment outside the of the coordinated National Socialist organisations (in anti-Hitler youth cliques, in church communities, in social gatherings of former members of the SPD or such like), or purely in the preservation of anti-National Socialist principles. The only precondition for these different forms of attitude fulfilling the concept of *Resistenz* is that they played an actual role in curtailing the impact of the national socialist regime and National Socialist ideology.

From Martin Broszat, *Resistenz and Resistance*, published in 1981

What was 'loyal reluctance'?

The concept of *Resistenz* has been questioned by some historians. Whereas the historian might wish to read into individual actions a rejection of Nazi ideology or discontent with the regime, the reality was probably different.

The ideal Nazi woman did not wear make-up. That many German women did wear make-up was not inspired by a desire to dissent from the regime but more that they wished to look good. The vast majority of those who were indifferent to the Nazi regime were so because they were generally indifferent to politics. The existence of indifference shows the inability of the Nazi regime to control people's lives totally. But this is not surprising, given the short period of time the regime had been in power. It is important to remember that Hitler and the Nazi leadership saw their project as lasting a thousand years; that they received such consent and so little active opposition in the early years was a considerable political achievement.

The idea of unqualified and widespread consent has been qualified by the use of the concept of 'loyal reluctance'. This term was coined by the historians Klaus-Michael Mallmann and Gerhard Paul who also challenged the idea of *Resistenz* in their study of the Saarland during the Nazi period. The crucial point is that indifference, non-conformity or even explicit complaints did not challenge the consensus or mean disloyalty to the regime. There is a range of examples to choose from to illustrate this concept. By 1939, the SD was reporting that there was widespread unrest among the German peasantry about low food prices (which were fixed by the state) and the shortage of labour (many peasants had migrated to the towns and cities because of better employment prospects and wages). At the same time, growing discontent was reported among the working class in the Ruhr due to poor working conditions and housing. However, such discontent did not manifest itself in rebellion but in the reluctance mentioned above. The peasants and workers were primarily interested in day-to-day economic issues.

SKILLS BUILDER

1 How do the points made in Source N differ from the points made in Source M and how do they challenge Source L?

2 What are the arguments for and against the concept of *Resistenz*? How convincing are those arguments?

Source M

The limited political reach of various kinds of *Resistenz* is easily visible, the fact that workers used their favourite position in the labour market during the labour boom and also grumbled when their daily living conditions were affected does not enable us to form a judgement on their political views. In the Bavarian countryside *Resistenz* signified more the desire to protect customary habits against the challenges of the regime than any political criticism; to the contrary, common political ground, for example in relation to National Socialist terror against the hated Left, probably predominated in the countryside.

From Klaus Tenefelde, *The Social Bases of Resistenz and Resistance*, published in 1985

Source N

To find a more suitable expression for those patterns of behaviour hitherto categorised under the concept of *Resistenz* we would like to suggest the concept of 'loyal reluctance'. [This term] makes clear the difference from the idea of resistance and the closeness to loyalty of such behaviour. These forms of behaviour did not call into question the political and fundamental consensus, the (partial) loyalty underpinning the National Socialist regime; it was an issue of forms of behaviour which at most caused the National Socialist regime peripheral trouble but did not otherwise impinge on its ability to function.

From Klaus-Michael Mallmann and Gerhard Paul, *Resistance or Loyal Reluctance?*, published in 1993

Opposition from the left

Historians are divided over the impact of the Nazi regime on the working class. Those who have argued that the impact was minimal stress that much of Nazi ideology was empty rhetoric and that far from loosening social hierarchy, the regime tended to strengthen class divisions by favouring the interests of big business. On the other hand, it is argued that the Nazi dictatorship did dislocate the existing class structure and ignite fundamental social change that can be described as revolutionary. It is difficult to gauge the response and mood of the working classes given the nature of the dictatorial regime.

- Some workers had always been ideologically hostile and remained implacably, but impotently, opposed. Others were more pragmatic but became disillusioned as their wages stagnated, regimentation increased and working hours lengthened. Industrial accidents, illness and absenteeism doubled between 1936 and 1939.

- Moreover there is evidence of dissent and opposition from the workers. The repressive state meant that organised opposition from even early in 1933 was nearly impossible. However, the communist and socialist movements had both been strong in Germany in the early 1930s. The weakness of the left in opposing the Nazi dictatorship was not helped by divisions between communist and socialist that meant that the left were unable to put up a concerted front.

- The communist response to the Nazi seizure of power was that the rise of the Nazis was a signal of the imminent collapse of capitalism. This attitude led the communist movement to the conclusion that nothing should be done to prevent the Nazi consolidation of power. It was a fatal error, for in the wake of the Reichstag Fire in 1933 some 10,000 communists were arrested. When, in 1934, the international communist leadership in Moscow decided for a reversal of stance, it was too late; the communist movement in Germany had been crushed.

Communist opposition to the regime did not disappear entirely. Exiles produced leaflets that were smuggled into Germany.

- In 1934 alone the authorities seized some 1.25 million communist leaflets. Gestapo figures suggest that there were still 5,000 active communists in Berlin in 1935. Their scope for active opposition was limited because attempts to infiltrate Nazi organisations such as the German Labour Front (DAF) were not successful, mainly because of the high levels of denunciation.

- Communists who remained politically committed to opposition in Germany in the 1930s were restricted to the distribution of anti-Nazi material. The newspaper *Rote Fahne* ('Red Flag') was still distributed up to 1935.

- There were strikes in 1936 at Rüsselsheim and Berlin and a Report of the Defence Industry Inspectorate from Nuremberg on 15 June 1936 found insubordination, sabotage and go-slows.

The lack of more overt opposition is hardly surprising and does not suggest any real enthusiasm for the regime. The working classes had been demoralised by the impact of mass unemployment after 1929 and were quickly emasculated by the abolition of their trade unions and arrest of their leaders.

- The Social Democratic Party leadership fled to Prague where they set up Sopade to keep links with socialists in Germany. In a few companies, such as AG Weser in Bremen, socialists continued to keep some group solidarity.

- Most socialists remaining in Germany kept their heads down. An SPD report of 1936 claimed that the abolition of collective bargaining had 'atomised' the work force and destroyed worker solidarity. Workers felt increasingly isolated and vulnerable, cowed by spies, informers and constant political interference. Another SPD report of 1938 claimed that 'everyone is afraid of saying a word too many and landing oneself in a spot'. Many workers became fatalistic to their plight, bored by regimentation and numbed by the relentless propaganda. They grumbled quietly or were silently apathetic.

- At the same time some workers, especially skilled workers, or those with little union tradition, were enthusiasts or became converted to the regime. SPD reports often complain about the compliance of the workers and their desertion of the class struggle. In exasperation one such report of 1935 claimed that the positive response of the working class to the regime was 'the real mystery in Germany'. This allegiance was naturally bolstered by the restoration of national prestige in the 1930s but also by economic recovery and state paternalism.

Propaganda and the cult of the Führer

Support for the regime was very much reinforced by the cult of the Führer. After achieving power in 1933, Joseph Goebbels's aim was to develop a Führer cult alongside the feeling for national rebirth and the creation of the New Germany. His success was, through propaganda, to identify them together. To this end, control of the media was essential. In March 1933, Goebbels was made Reich Minister of Popular Enlightenment and Propaganda.

At the heart of the Führer cult was uncompromising loyalty to the regime and Führer. Goebbels's propaganda linked directly to Hitler the perceived successes of the regime, the reduction in unemployment and economic improvement, the restoration of order and the destruction of the Versailles treaty. To challenge the regime would potentially put at risk such achievements. Goebbels skilfully used the Führer sparingly so as to preserve his god-like mystique. Propaganda was, therefore, to a certain extent responsible for swathes of German society following the regime unquestioningly. Most Germans blamed the system or work of extremists for their problems or the shortcomings of the regime – rarely the Führer. Cinema was used to propagate the myth. The gifted director

SKILLS BUILDER

From what you have just read, explain why organised opposition to the Nazi regime from the left was minimal.

Leni Riefenstahl was employed by Hitler to produce some of the most powerful propagandist films. In her *Triumph of the Will* (1935), featuring the Nuremberg Rally, and *Olympia* (1938), celebrating the Olympic Games, Riefenstahl took film-making to new heights, devising the technique of using a camera on a track within the audience to create the impression of being present at such awe-inspiring dramas. Goebbels insisted that the Führer himself featured only sparingly in the film so as to sustain his myth of a man of destiny removed from the real world.

The regime enjoyed a monopoly of all means of propaganda and deployed each to its maximum effect:

- The state press agency, the DNB, was set up in December 1933 to monitor all news material, and daily press conferences were held to manipulate and embellish information.

- Overt Nazi propaganda was relentlessly expounded by the regime's own papers controlled by the Amann press empire. The *Völkischer Beobachter*, edited by Wilhelm Weiss and published simultaneously in Munich, Berlin and Vienna, sold almost 2 million copies an edition, while *Der Stürmer*, the rabidly anti-Semitic tabloid of Julius Streicher achieved a circulation of half a million. Goebbels himself produced his own paper, *Der Angriff*.

- The Nazi regime was quick to harness the new technology of radio as a propaganda weapon. Germany had the largest radio audience in Europe in the 1930s; 4.5 million out of 20 million households possessed a radio and by 1939 the regime could broadcast to 16 million Germans. To sustain the widest possible audience the government produced the 'People's Radio' costing 35 marks, which was little more than the weekly wage of a factory worker.

- The Nazis exploited the techniques of enforced communal listening in factories, schools, offices and shops. Loudspeaker pillars were erected in public places and at larger gatherings. Apart from censored information, the principal output was a combination of sentimental propaganda such as the 1935 series *German Nation on German Soil* and light classical pieces as featured on *Treasure Trove*.

- A masterpiece of Nazi propaganda was the success of the Olympic Games in 1936. The regime suspended its anti-Semitic programme, and the games were held in an atmosphere of political stability and growing prosperity, which impressed thousands of foreign visitors and their governments. Germany, it appeared, was a civilised, tolerant and peaceful regime.

- The aim was to cultivate a positive or at least an uncritical reaction to the dictatorship by weaving Nazi ideas and symbols within the fabric of the popular routine. Holy days were transplanted by a series of festival or celebration days such as that to commemorate the Seizure of Power or the anniversary of the Munich Putsch. This new annual cycle not only marginalised traditional Christian practice, it became so commonplace that it was no longer identified as propaganda but simply as part of a new, almost natural, social and political order. This routine of events was supplemented by stage-managed events such as the Nuremburg Rally of 1934.

What was the extent of economic recovery?

Support from the working class was very much conditional on an improvement in the economic situation. The most important challenge facing the Nazis on taking office was to reduce unemployment. Within the first year, legislation and initiatives were introduced that dealt effectively with the numbers of Germans out of work.

- The work schemes first used by Chancellors von Papen and Schleicher in 1932–33 were extended by the Law to Reduce Unemployment of June 1933. These so called *Arbeitdienst* (work schemes) were part of an overall job creation plan that included the building of new roads, the *autobahnen*. The so-called 'Battle for Work' was extended by the government lending money to private companies so that they could create jobs.

- Initial state investment was poured into work creation schemes – between 1932 and 1935, in all some 5 billion Reichsmarks. In June 1933, the first law was passed releasing the money for the building of the first *autobahn*. The nature of the work creation projects reveals much about the regime's priorities. The Labour Service and Emergency Relief Schemes that put thousands back to work were labour intensive.

Unemployment was not the only problem facing the new regime. The desperate state of the peasantry, who had suffered from the collapse of agricultural prices between 1929 and 1933, was dealt with in a number of ways.

- The Reich Food Estate, created in September 1933, took control of the overall planning and organisation of agriculture.

- In the same month, the Reich Entailed Farm Law attempted to enhance the security of peasant ownership of land.

- Because Germany did not have much foreign currency to pay for imports of food, the regime launched a 'Battle for Production' in 1934 and 1935 to increase the production of grain. However, the drive to increase production was not successful because of the lack of new machinery and labour, and the poor harvests.

- In 1935 the regime reintroduced conscription, which had a significant impact in reducing the numbers unemployed.

- There was significant expansion in training schemes for the unskilled and in apprenticeships for working class school leavers.

In May 1933, Hitler appointed Hjalmar Schacht as President of the Reichsbank. One of the main reasons for the depth of the German depression between 1929 and 1933 was the over-reliance on foreign capital. It is not surprising, therefore, that one of Schacht's first acts was to increase state control of foreign trade and make it independent of the international currency system. In the summer of 1934 Schacht was made

Minister of Economics. He promptly introduced the 'New Plan' in September 1934, which gave the government extensive powers to regulate trade and currency transactions.

- In 1934 Schacht also proceeded to negotiate a series of bilateral trade agreements with countries in South America and south-east Europe that were aimed at preventing Germany running up a huge foreign currency deficit while still be able to procure essential raw materials. Those countries involved would be paid for their goods in Reichsmarks.

- Schacht also created the policy that was aimed at encouraging the growth in demand in the economy. This was done by the introduction of Mefo Bills. These were bills issued by the government as payment for goods. They were then held by investors or banks and could either be exchanged for cash or held for up to five years, earning 4 per cent interest a year.

The regime's attempts to reduce unemployment were successful. The economic recovery after 1933 and the creation of around 6 million jobs were vital in attracting working class support to the regime. In 1933 the percentage of the working population unemployed was 25.9 per cent. This figure had fallen to 7.4 per cent by 1936. This fall was partly helped by an improvement in the world economy as a whole. However, one should not underestimate the impact that economic recovery had on providing support for the regime.

As the regime consolidated its power, so it became more radical in its policy. In 1933 Hjalmar Schacht was an important conservative influence and a break on the radicalisation of the regime. His concerns to protect the economic recovery led him to advise caution on anti-Semitic policy for fear of an international backlash that might damage trade; in April 1933 he persuaded Hitler to restrict a boycott of Jewish shops and businesses to one day. But Schacht had little impact on the passing of the Nuremburg Laws in 1935 (see pages 190–191), which separated Jew and Aryan. From 1936, Schacht's influence diminished, with the creation of the Four Year Plan and the growing influence in economic affairs of Göring. In 1937 Schacht resigned and another important constraint on the radicalism of regime was gone.

How effective was state paternalism?

Hitler wanted a disciplined work force that would not challenge his dictatorship or threaten his plans for disarmament with excessive wage demands. On the day after the May Day holiday in 1933, i.e. on 2 May, the offices of the trade unions were ransacked. Within a few days, 169 trade unions were under Nazi control. Independent unions were abolished to be replaced on 10 May by the German Labour Front (DAF) led by Robert Ley. In many factories radical Nazi organisations, NSBOs, were set up. Their main objective was to spread Nazi propaganda in the workplace. The regime attempted to win the support of the workers by a combination of material improvement and state welfare. Workers were compensated for the loss of political rights and wage freezes by state paternalism.

- In November 1933 Robert Ley established two new organisations. Schönheit der Arbeit (Beauty of Labour) was set up to persuade employers to improve working conditions in factories. This was done by promoting schemes highlighting the benefits of better lighting, ventilation and cleanliness, and the potential benefits of giving workers wholesome meals. Kraft durch Freude (Strength through Joy) offered to reward loyal workers with evening classes, recitals and art exhibitions, theatre trips, sporting competitions and package holidays. By 1938 around 180,000 workers had been on a Kraft durch Freude-sponsored cruise, and 10 million (one-third of the workforce) had enjoyed a state-financed holiday.

- Winterhelp organised annual collections (in part financed by the payments made by participants in the obligatory 'one pot' meals – communal meals in which bankers and workers sat side by side to eat a basic meal) and offered charity to the unemployed and the destitute.

- These initiatives were enforced by occasional 'Days of National Solidarity' on which leading party members would collect money on behalf of the party. A generous contribution was perceived to be one way in which the average German could, in his or her way, 'work towards the Führer'.

- The promotion of cheap housing and the production of mass-produced consumer goods, including a 'people's radio' and a 'people's car' (Volkswagen) also demonstrated the regime's attempt to embrace all classes in the growing prosperity and camaraderie of the nation.

Case study: to what extent did the Nazis win the support of the working class?

Source O

7.3 Photograph of coalminers from Penzberg in Bavaria in regional costume. Their lack of enthusiasm for the Nazi salute is in marked contrast to the salutes of the Hitler Youth standing behind them. How representative is this apparent apathy?

Source P

Continuing discontent about social and economic conditions – much of it presumably expressed, not least in the working class, by those who had never wholly been won over to Nazism – was perfectly compatible with recognition of other 'achievements' of the regime, in particular those attributed to Hitler himself. Everyday grievances based on material dissatisfaction, important though they were in forming popular attitudes, by no means necessarily signified total rejection of Nazism or of the Führer who stood in every sense above and outside the system, detached from the everyday sphere of dismal normality.

From Ian Kershaw, *The Hitler Myth: Image and Reality in the Third Reich*, published in 1994

Source Q

The longer the regime lasted, the less people believed in its slogans about the new solidarity of the 'works community' and the 'national community'. Workers disapproved and criticism related primarily to practical everyday matters, and to the social achievements and failures of the regime. The personal figure of Hitler, as SOPADE reports confirm, was largely exempt from criticism. When analysing the popular mood in general 'grumbling' can be taken as an indication of a certain basic consent to the regime, or at least of a passive adjustment to a situation which could not be changed.

From D. J. K. Peukert, *Inside Nazi Germany: Conformity, Opposition and Racism in Everyday Life*, published in 1989

Source R

Whatever the Nazis' egalitarian [all are equal] rhetoric working class people persisted in a 'them and us' mentality. Their bosses remained exploitative 'capitalists' while the Social Democrat and union leaders of the Weimar period were replaced by an army of 'Brown' placement who were regarded with universal loathing. Economic recovery was regionally and sectorally patchy with unemployment in consumer industries and mining lingering for several years. Hours of grinding work increased, while the range of consumption goods diminished. However, there were enough compensations, including Nazi foreign policy, for working class resistance – as distinct from the enormous bravery of individual workers and others – to remain sufficiently chimerical [unrealistic].

From Michael Burleigh, *The Third Reich: A New History*, published in 2000

Source S

Frustration and disappointment with the realities of everyday life under National Socialism led ordinary Germans to grumble and complain, but seldom engage in behaviour that can be appropriately termed 'resistance'. Why? Organised terror played a central role. But the most important mechanism promoting unity and social integration in Nazi Germany was Hitler's charismatic leadership. The 'Hitler myth' secured the loyalty to the regime even of those who opposed the Nazi movement. Millions of ordinary Germans believed that the Führer would certainly right all wrongs in Nazi Germany.

From Ian Kershaw, 'The Hitler Myth: Image and Reality in the Third Reich', in David Crew (editor) *Nazism and German Society 1933–45*, published in 1994

SKILLS BUILDER

1 To what extent did the Nazi regime have the support of the working classes between 1933 and 1939?

2 Use Sources P, Q, S and T to explain the significance of the cult of the Führer.

3 What are the similarities and differences between Sources P and Q and between Sources R and T?

4 Which two sources agree most closely with each other and which two sources disagree most with each other?

Source T

The main reason for positive support was the personal popularity of Hitler. To many he was a direct successor to the populist vision of the Kaiser during the Second Reich . . . he had, of course, the considerable advantage of a monopoly of the media which was used for the process of indoctrination and propaganda. But in a sense Hitler transcended the image created by Goebbels. The main reason for his popularity, and this may seem surprising, was that he was seen as a moderate. After all, he made sure that his political changes were technically constitutional; he emphasised that he was upholding traditional virtues. He gained considerable ground in his quest for revisionism; the population compared with the rather slow developments of the Stresemann era Hitler's success in remilitarising the Rhineland in 1936 and annexing Austria and the Sudetenland in 1938, all without recourse to war. Not all Germans were taken in by the Führer cult; many saw through the projection of his image as an apparent moderate. Yet for those who were not swept along in professed support for the system, there were too many negatives constraints on action.

From Stephen Lee, *Hitler and Nazi Germany*, published in 1998

Hossbach Conference

The conference of Hitler's leading military leaders was called by the Führer for 5 November 1937. It is named the 'Hossbach Conference' after the minute taker, Colonel Friedrich Hossbach, who left historians a very full account of events.

How did the regime curtail the army?

There were more practical reasons why, particularly among the junior officers, the regime enjoyed some popularity during the 1930s. Law and order had been restored, the communist threat destroyed, and prosperity had been growing as unemployment was reduced. Hitler had proclaimed a vast rearmament programme in 1935 and an expansion of the army to 500,000. The Saar Plebiscite of 1935 and the reoccupation of the Rhineland in 1936 had undermined the Versailles settlement and appeared to vindicate Hitler's diplomatic skills. However, tensions remained:

- It had become evident to the more conservative elements within the Reichswehr that they were to be the junior partners in the state, and there were particular fears about the growth and militarization of the SS that threatened the Reichswehr's right to be the sole bearer of arms.

- Hitler, for his part, recognised that his ideological ambitions could not be achieved without the support of the armed forces. As a result he went out of his way to reassure the armed forces of his support. As tension grew between the armed forces and the Nazi movement (and most specifically the SS) in late 1934, Hitler called an extraordinary

Biography

Ludwig Beck

From 1935 Beck was Chief of the General Staff of the army. He opposed Hitler's war plans and resigned during the Sudeten crisis of 1938. He then joined the resistance movement. The conspirators of the July Plot planned to make him provisional head of state if successful. Beck committed suicide on hearing of the failure of the plot in 1944.

meeting of the German leadership in the Berlin's State Opera House in January 1935. At the meeting he promised that 'my faith in the *Wehrmacht* is unshakable' to the grateful applause of the military leadership.

Alarms were particularly raised by the adventurism of Hitler's foreign policy as clarified by the Hossbach Conference in November 1937. At this meeting Hitler made clear that his aim was not merely the revision of the Versailles settlement but unlimited expansion eastwards to win *Lebensraum*. It was clear at the Hossbach Conference in November 1937, however, that a number of leading members of the armed forces, including the Reich War Minister Werner von Blomberg and the Commander-in-Chief of the Army, Werner von Fritsch, were sceptical about his plans. In their view, Germany was not ready to go to war against Britain and France at this point. But they were not prepared to challenge Hitler openly and most generals embraced his plans. Although all members of the armed forces had sworn an oath of personal allegiance to Hitler, the head of the armed services did not report directly to Hitler but to the War Minister. This meant that there was the potential for important decisions to be made by individuals who were less than enthusiastic Nazis, such as the Chief of Staff General Beck. So by the beginning of 1938, Hitler's control over the armed forces was considerable but not total. A strange set of circumstances was to change all of that.

What was the significance of the Blomberg-Fritsch Affair?

In January 1938, Hitler attended the wedding of Reich War Minister Werner von Blomberg and his young bride Margarethe Gruhn. By the end of the month, the Gestapo had been tipped off that the new Frau Blomberg had been a prostitute. This was unacceptable to Hitler, who sacked Blomberg. He then remembered that there had been rumours two years before that the head of the army, Colonel-General Fritsch, had been involved with a rent boy. Himmler presented Hitler with the file, and after a few days the Führer decided that Fritsch should face a military trial. The downfall of Blomberg and Fritsch allowed Hitler to restructure the leadership of the armed forces.

- On 27 January, Hitler took over the leadership of the army himself. He also decided not to appoint a successor to Blomberg.

- At the start of February, Hitler took the opportunity to remove from post those within the armed forces who were not considered to be completely loyal, including 12 generals. The army was now under the complete control of the Führer.

The Blomberg-Fritsch affair and its aftermath was a significant turning point in the history of the Nazi regime. At the start of February, Hitler held his last ever cabinet meeting. He now had free rein to wage war, the armed forces being docile and obedient.

Source U

Although the crisis was unforeseen, not manufactured, the Blomberg-Fritsch affair engendered a key shift in relations between Hitler and the most powerful non-Nazi élite, the army. At precisely the moment when Hitler's adventurism was starting to cause shivers of alarm, the army had demonstrated its weakness and without a murmur of protest swallowed his outright dominance even in the immediate domain of the *Wehrmacht*. The outcome of the Blomberg-Fritsch affair amounted to the third stepping stone, after the Reichstag Fire and the Röhm Putsch, cementing Hitler's absolute power and, quite especially, his dominance over the army.

From Ian Kershaw, *Nemesis*, published in 2000

SKILLS BUILDER

Compare the line of argument in Source U with that in Source T. How do they compare in their analysis of the means by which the regime was able to secure its position?

The last flickers of opposition in peacetime

Hitler was born in Austria. In March 1938, he fulfilled a long-cherished personal ambition by invading Austria and proclaiming *Anschluss* (union) between Germany and Austria. German demands for a similar union with the German-speaking Sudetenland in Czechoslovakia threatened to provoke a war. The final attempt by the old guard within the army to avoid war during the Czech crisis occurred in September 1938. A handful of generals led by General Ludwig Beck and General Franz Halder plotted to oust Hitler before troops were mobilised to occupy the Sudetenland. However, the plot dissolved amid dithering among the conspirators and qualms among many officers about the oath of allegiance. In any case, the peaceful surrender of the Sudetenland by British Prime Minister Chamberlain and the French leader Daladier at the Munich Conference cut the ground from beneath the plotters' feet. In August 1938 Beck resigned his command, although he continued to keep in consultation with Carl Friedrich Goerdeler, who was by now the leading figure in the conservative resistance. A small group of officers on the staff of Admiral Canaris in the department of Counter Intelligence (OKW) who were opposed to the regime formed around Hans Oster and Hans von Dohnanyi.

For other conservatives, their path to opposition began with full support for the regime. One of the most significant conservative opposition figures to the regime was Carl Goerdeler, Mayor of Leipzig from 1930 to 1937 and Reich Commissioner for Price Control in the government from November 1934. However, he stood at odds with the narrow economic policy of the time, based on ever-growing autarky and diminishing international cooperation. In 1935 he resigned from the government, and in 1937 he gave up his post of Mayor of Leipzig in protest at the removal of a statue of the Jewish composer Mendelssohn. From 1937, Goerdeler built connections with other dissidents. He was, however, very much an exception; by the mid-1930s the conservative establishment were tied to the fortunes of the regime.

What was the extent of opposition from the churches?

Many of the leaders of Germany's Christian churches welcomed the Nazi seizure of power and, despite increasing doubts and tensions, continued to offer the regime a degree of moral respectability. Protestant and Catholic leaders were alienated from the Weimar Republic by the secular liberalism that had prevailed since 1918. Church leaders feared the spread of atheistic Bolshevism and so regarded Hitler's revolution as both a spiritual and moral salvation. Nazi anti-Semitism posed moral problems for some church leaders, but most believed that the Jews had become too dominant within society and politics and saw no objection to their constraint by legal means. In any case, leaders from both Catholic and Protestant churches believed that accommodation with the dictatorship would secure more benefits than open confrontation. Like all the forces of the old order, the churches were seduced by the legality and conservatism of events such as the Commemoration Day at Potsdam in March 1933.

Protestant divisions

The Protestant *Mittelstand* formed the bedrock of Nazi electoral support. German Christians led by Hitler's adviser on religious affairs, Ludwig Müller, advocated the wholesale restructuring of German Protestantism to embrace Nazi ideology.

- In May 1933, Müller was elected National Bishop (he was Hitler's nomination) winning widespread support in Thuringia, Saxony, Mecklenburg, Hesse-Nassau and Schleswig-Holstein. In July 1933, he 'coordinated' 28 Protestant churches into a single Reich Church, and in December he incorporated 700,000 members of Protestant youth groups into the Hitler youth.

- Dissident Protestants who rejected Müller's church formed the Confessional Church led by Pastor Martin Niemöller and Karl Barth. There were bitter divisions within the Confessional Church between moderates who wished to remain loyal to Nazism and more radical opponents such as Martin Niemöller, Dietrich Bonhöffer and Karl Barth. Moreover the Confessional Church was not opposed ideologically to Nazism – only to the attempt to destroy its independence.

- In any case, leading dissidents were easily intimidated and imprisoned. In 1935, the regime set up the Ministry of Church Affairs, which vigorously intimidated Christians. Over 700 Protestant priests throughout Prussia were arrested in 1935 for condemning the teaching of **paganism** in schools as part of the Nazi curriculum. In 1936, leaders of the Confessional Church sent a letter to Hitler complaining of the 'de-Christianisation of German life' under the Nazis. Most Protestants remained silent in the face of the intensification of anti-Semitic persecution while some believed that this was evidence of God's curse on the Jews. The reaction in Germany to the attack on the Jews in Kristallnacht in November 1938 (see pages 191–194) is instructive of the issues relating to the Protestant churches. Some individual churchmen

Definition

Paganism

In this context, the belief in ancient non-Christian gods.

objected: the Protestant Pastor Erich Klapproth wrote a letter of protest to Hitler and other Nazi leaders. But the churches as institutions remained silent and failed to object to the exclusion of Jews from public life.

Catholic Church

The continuing existence of the Catholic Church as an important institution within German society does not necessarily signify opposition to the regime. But the Catholic Church was more resilient to Nazi ideology. It was an international organisation led by the Pope and its control over its parishioners was more secure. Its leaders were assured by the Catholic Vice-Chancellor von Papen that their interests would be protected, and Bishop Bertram, President of the Conference of Bishops, advocated a policy of collaboration with the regime. The Centre Party led by Ludwig Kaas in the Reichstag was instrumental in giving Hitler the two-thirds majority he required to secure the Enabling Act in March 1933 that established his dictatorship. The Concordat that was signed in June 1933 promised to guarantee church control over education and youth groups in return for its political neutrality.

But the murder of the Catholic Minister Erich Klausener in June 1934, the banning of crucifixes from schools in 1935 and the increasingly pagan ideology championed by Nazi radicals alarmed leading Catholics. The banning of Catholic Youth Groups in 1936 and the undermining of denominational schools prompted the publication of the papal encyclical *With Burning Concern* in 1937, which was drafted in part by Cardinal Faulhaber (see page 205). As with the Protestant church, however, opposition to the regime was motivated more by an attempt to maintain independence and integrity within the system rather than by a philosophical objection to Nazism. Dissent was individual, not institutional. The reoccupation of the Rhineland, the *Anschluss* and the seizure of the Sudetenland were supported by Catholic leaders, as such gains transformed their church into the majority religion.

Indoctrination of youth and women

As part of its wish to build a Nazi consensus, the regime deliberately sought to capture German youth by appealing to its energy and anti-authoritarian spirit. Balder von Schirach was appointed 'Youth Leader of the Reich', empowered to educate young people 'physically, mentally and morally in the spirit of National Socialism'.

- Boys were to be trained as fearless soldiers and were organised in the 'German Young People' from 10 to 14, and the Hitler Youth from 14 to 16. By 1935 some 60 per cent of all German youth belonged to the Hitler Youth, and it was made compulsory by the Hitler Youth Law of 25 March 1939.

- Girls were taught to be loyal, submissive and prolific mothers. They joined the 'League of Young Girls' at 10 and the 'League of German

Discussion points

1 As historians, should we expect more opposition from the churches to the regime?
2 Why was the opposition to the regime from the churches restricted to the actions of individuals?

Girls' at 14. Membership of these organisations became compulsory in 1936, and an oath of allegiance to Hitler had to be sworn from 1939.

In February 1933 Hitler appointed Bernard Rust as Prussian Minister of Education and Minister of Culture. A year later he promoted him to the post of Reich Minister for Science, Education and Culture. It was Rust's task to begin the purge of the teaching profession that would make the Nazification of education possible.

- Jewish teachers were fired immediately, as were all those of suspect politics.
- The party tightened its control of teachers by encouraging membership of the National Socialist Teachers' Alliance (NSLB). By 1937 some 97 per cent or 320,000 teachers had joined.
- This organisation took specific responsibility for indoctrinating teachers in Nazi ideology. By 1939 nearly two-thirds of the NSLB membership had been on Nazi courses. The curriculum was amended to place an emphasis on racial theory, physical education and history.
- In 1937 the regime also set up an élite school system. The Adolf Hitler Schools were established to train the political leaders of the next generation. *Napolas* were Nazi military academies. Graduates of the *Napolas* would usually be expected to join the Waffen SS. *Ordensburgen* were for the élite students chosen from the other types of schools. The students were given military and political instruction to prepare them for leadership in the Third Reich.

A minority of young people, repelled by the brutality of the dictatorship, actively opposed the regime. Working-class dissidents formed 'Pirate' groups such as the **Edelweiss Pirates**, while disillusioned middle class youths joined 'Swing groups' to celebrate American-style culture. Nonetheless, a majority of Germany's youth remained loyal to the dictatorship.

Nazi ideology stressed that women should be confined to a purely domestic role in society. Their duty was to produce healthy Aryan children, uphold conservative principles and comfort their husbands in their service to the state. These ideas were advertised by the Nazi slogan of *Kinder, Küche, Kirche* (children, kitchen, church). The first step taken by the regime to bring women into line with Nazi ideology was the creation of the Women's Front (Frauenfront) by Robert Ley on 10 May 1933. All 230 women's organisations in Germany were to expel their Jewish members and integrate into the Women's Front or face being disbanded. Most organisations happily obliged, pleased to support a regime they saw as nationalistic and supportive of the traditional role of women. The new regime lost no time in shaping their negative policy towards women. Particularly under attack were educated women in professional jobs.

In 1933, nearly all the 19,000 female civil servants in regional and local government lost their jobs, as did around 15 per cent of women teachers.

Definition

Edelweiss Pirates

A diverse group that emerged on the outbreak of war. They were essentially dissenters who rejected the regimentation of the Hitler Youth. There was no national movement; the Pirates were based on local groups from the Navajos of Cologne to the Kittelbach Pirates of Oberhausen.

- By early 1934 there were no women left working in the Prussian civil service. The 3 per cent of lawyers who were women faced a decline in their status.

- From 1936 no woman could serve as a judge and women were no longer accepted for jury duty.

- However, the regime was careful not to upset the women's organisations that had so willingly joined the Women's Front. In 1934 the Minister of the Interior William Frick responded to widespread unease about the sacking of women teachers by reversing the policy at least temporarily.

- As the economic situation improved and as unemployment fell, so the situation of women in most professions (apart from the law) improved despite the regime's official line on women in work. In 1930 5 per cent of all doctors were women; by 1939 this figure had risen to 7 per cent.

The number of women in employment generally remained low in the first years of the regime. The economic improvement after 1933 was at first felt in the rearmament-based industries and therefore did not have too much of an effect on women in work. In 1936 still only 5.63 million women were employed. However, rearmament created a labour shortage, which meant that the regime began to try to persuade women to go back to work. By July 1939 the number of women in employment had risen to 7.41 million. This shows a contradiction between Nazi propaganda and reality.

How successful was Nazi indoctrination?

In such a dictatorial regime as Nazi Germany it is difficult to be certain about the effectiveness of indoctrination. Many Germans were enthusiastic Nazi supporters who did not require any indoctrination; others accepted the system through fear, ignorance, lethargy or indifference – 'loyal reluctance'. It is clear that the effectiveness of propaganda depended upon the issue, the audience and the year. Nazi propaganda was effective in that it stirred the fears and reinforced the prejudices of millions of Germans.

At the same time, there were limits to the power of indoctrination. It is clear that on issues of morality the regime was unable to overcome the Christian values or the innate decency of most Germans. For on the central issues of expansionism, war and racial persecution the dictatorship failed to carry public opinion; few Germans wanted war.

Source V

The test of the success of this indoctrination was the concrete danger of war. When a European war seemed imminent in the Sudeten crisis of September 1938, the German people showed themselves dismayed and displayed no readiness, not to mention enthusiasm, to go to war. In a secret speech to the press on 10 November 1938, Hitler was forced to take this into account when he admitted how regrettable it had been that 'circumstances' had forced him to 'mouth a pacifist line' for years. But it was not possible to create enthusiasm for a war. When the policy of extreme risk did actually unleash a war, in September 1939, the prevalent mood in Germany was one of anxiety; there was no war euphoria such as had marked the outbreak of hostilities in 1914.

From Jost Dülffer, *Nazi Germany 1933–1945: Faith and Annihilation*, published in 1996

Source W

Most young people in Germany from 1933 to 1945 were loyal members of the Hitler Youth . . . However, it would be wrong to believe the Nazi regime succeeded in winning over the entire youth of Germany. There were some young people who strongly objected to the rigid indoctrination and discipline, preferring instead to form nonconformist youth groups and gangs who engaged in acts of protest and defiance towards the Nazi regime. The two most significant youth groups in Germany during the Nazi era were the 'Edelweiss Pirates' and the 'Swing Youth'.

From Frank McDonough, *Opposition and Resistance in Nazi Germany*,
published in 2001

Source X

The evidence seems to suggest that the Nazi ideas had indeed an impact upon the German working class, and particularly on the younger generation, as they had on German youth on the whole. This in no way means that those same workers did not hope to improve their economic condition, or protect those gains they had already made. But it does indicate there was a large pool of nationalist phobias and racial prejudices among the working class on which the regime could draw, just as there is evidence of quite a powerful admiration for the Führer, whatever may have been thought of the party.

From Omer Bartov, *The Missing Years: German Workers, German Soldiers*,
published in 1990

SKILLS BUILDER

1 According to Sources V, W and X, how effective was Nazi indoctrination from 1933 to 1939?

2 To what extent does Source X agree with Source V?

Unit summary

What have you learned in this unit?

The Nazi regime consolidated its power in stages during the period 1933 to 1939. The regime won support for its anti-communist stance and because it was the legitimate government of the day. The main process by which the regime absorbed different groups was through *Gleichschaltung*. Throughout the 1930s a terror state emerged although the extent to which public participation drove the dynamic of this state is open to interpretation. The potential opposition within the conservative élites and SA was destroyed in the Night of the Long Knives, and the armed forces were compromised by their involvement with the regime and its foreign policy successes up to 1939. While formal opposition was minimal, there was widespread grumbling. How much this should be interpreted as being politically driven is open to debate.

What skills have you used in this unit?

Through your work with the source material you have developed your understanding of consent and opposition in Nazi Germany between 1933 and 1939. You have cross-referenced and interpreted the sources in the light of their content and the wider historical debate. Most importantly, you have learned about controversies and the different stances taken by different historians.

Source Y

The symbolic payments of the state, special contributions of industry, as well as 'Strength through Joy' trips and events stabilised relations to the Hitler state to a not inconsiderable degree. In 1938, every third worker took part in 'Strength through Joy' holidays. The regime skilfully nurtured the yearning of the labour force for middle class status and lifestyle. In weekly programmes, the district office in Munich was offering not only holidays but also theatre and concert visits plus courses in such sports as riding, sailing, tennis and skiing – which had earlier been the preserve of the higher social strata. Political problems were mostly ignored in the lecture events. Topics included the crossing of the Atlantic in a sailing boat and colour photography. It has long been overlooked that advancement in the Third Reich did not only occur symbolically.

From Hans Dieter Schäfer, *Split Consciousness: German Consciousness and the Reality of Life*, published in 1981

Source Z

While the new holders of power did not carry out a single 'socialist' measure in their party programme, comprehensive welfare schemes served to organize the workers by means of holiday trips, sports festivals, factory celebrations, folk dancing, evening entertainment and political education. At the same time, alongside the avowed aims of the 'Strength through Joy' and 'Beauty through Labour' movements, these schemes performed the functions of control and pacification. The benefits to the individual scarcely concealed the true nature of these entertainments, which were merely compensations for a considerable deprivation of political rights. They reflected a contemptuous attitude towards the workers who, in Hitler's words, demanded nothing more than bread and circuses and had 'no understanding of any ideal'.

From Joachim Fest, *The Face of the Third Reich*, published in 1963

Source AA

The people who travelled with 'Strength Through Joy' obstinately refused to do so in the spirit in which the regime intended. Concerned at the possible influx of ex-Social Democrats who participated in the tours, the regime sent along undercover agents disguised as tourists to spy on the participants. The picture their reports revealed almost as soon as they started work, in March 1936, was a disturbing one . . . The behaviour of many participants on the tours often signally failed to match up to the standards set by the organisers. Like tourists everywhere, what most of them really wanted to do was let their hair down. Gestapo agents reported frequent mass drunkenness and riotous behaviour . . . Yet while it largely failed to achieve its ideological aims, 'Strength Through Joy' was still one of the most popular of the regime's cultural innovations. By providing holidays and other activities that otherwise would have been beyond the means of many of the participants, the organisation became widely appreciated amongst the workers.

From Richard Evans, *The Third Reich in Power*, published in 2005

Exam style question

This is the sort of question you will find appearing on the examination paper as a Section B question:

'The Nazi regime enjoyed broad consent brought about by popular policies.'

How far do you agree with this opinion? Explain your answer using the evidence of Sources Y, Z and AA and your own knowledge of the issues relating to the controversy.

Before you start, please read the advice on page 166.

Exam tips

- Plan your answer before you start.
- Be very sure you know what 'view' is being expressed in all three sources.
- Analyse and interpret Sources Z and AA so as to establish points that support and challenge the view given in Source Y.
- Cross-reference between the sources by focusing on support and challenge.
- Use your wider knowledge both to reinforce and to challenge the points derived from the sources.
- Combine the points into arguments for and against the view given in the question.
- Evaluate the conflicting arguments by considering the quality of the evidence used, involving a consideration of provenance (where appropriate) and the weight of evidence and range of supporting knowledge you can find in support.
- Present a substantiated judgement as to the validity of the stated view and/or any alternatives in the light of your understanding of the issues of interpretation and controversy.

SKILLS BUILDER

1 Go back to your definition of consent, which you made at the start of this unit. Which groups gave their consent to the Nazi regime in the period 1933 to 1939 and why?

2 Form yourselves into discussion groups and answer the following question:

'Why was opposition to the Nazi regime in the years 1933–39 so limited?'

This is a difficult and complex question that cannot be answered from information in this unit alone. In your discussion groups, you need to come up with at least seven points, which you should place on a spider chart. Prioritise these points in order of importance.

3 Debate time: using the information in this unit, debate which of the following is the more convincing in explaining the reaction of the German people to the Nazi regime between 1933 and 1939:

- *Resistenz*
- loyal reluctance.

RESEARCH TOPIC

Opposition individuals

In the course of this unit a number of individuals have been mentioned as significant figures. Here is your opportunity to find out more about the role the following played in opposition to the regime. This is a suggested list of people:

- Herbert von Bose
- Carl Goerdeler
- Martin Niemöller
- Hans Oster
- Dietrich Bonhöffer

8 Controversy: how effectively did the Nazi state operate from 1933 to 1939?

What is this unit about?

This unit focuses on the operation of the Nazi state and, in particular, its effectiveness. Since the end of the Second World War in 1945, historians have been attempting to explain the destructive nature of the Nazi state. Part of the explanation has been found in Nazi ideology. But other historians have looked to explain events in terms of the dynamic nature of the state. Central to the exploration of the workings of the Nazi state is the role of the Führer.

You will:

- explore the controversy over how the Nazi state functioned
- work with secondary source material.

Key questions

- Was the Nazi state a chaotic polycracy or a state efficiently answering to the Führer's will?
- How was policy made in the Third Reich?

Timeline

1933	April	Anti-Jewish boycott
	October	Germany withdraws from the League of Nations
1934	August	Law on the Head of State of the German Reich proclaims Hitler to be Führer
1935	January	Reich Local Government Law gives local Nazi officials, the *Kreisleiter*, more power
	April	Anti-German Stresa Front formed
	June	Anglo-German naval agreement
	September	Nuremberg rally and passing of the Nuremberg Laws
1936	March	German remilitarisation of the Rhineland
	June	Hitler appoints SS leader Heinrich Himmler as chief of the German police
1937	November	Hossbach Conference
1938	March	*Anschluss* with Austria
	June	Decree forbidding Jewish doctors from treating Aryan patients
	September	Czech crisis meetings in Germany – Sudetenland given to Germany
	November	Kristallnacht

1939	January	Göring sets up the Reich Central Office for Jewish Emigration and places Heydrich at its head
	March	Germany invades the rest of Czechoslovakia
	May	Pact of Steel with Italy signed
	August	The Ministerial Council for the Defence of the Reich
	September	Leading *Gauleiter* become Reich Defence Commissioners

The central role of Hitler

After the end of the Second World War, it was common for historians writing about the Third Reich to focus on Adolf Hitler. The argument put forward by many historians was, and is, that at the heart of the Nazi state was the ideology, personality and leadership of Adolf Hitler. Historians such as Andreas Hillgruber and Karl Dietrich Bracher stressed that the domestic and foreign policy of the Third Reich could only be understood in the context of Hitler's '*Weltanschauung*' (world view) and the systematic and intentional implementation of his ideological aims. Hitler's ideological aims were defined in *Mein Kampf* (1924) and remained consistent throughout his political life. They included:

- the creation of a New Germany and a *Volksgemeinschaft* (national community) reorganised on racial lines and cleansed of all of those considered racially impure, most especially the Jews
- the creation of a Thousand Year Reich
- the concept of a struggle through which the German nation and the Aryan race would be saved from communism and through which Bolshevism would be destroyed
- the restoration of Germany as a great military nation and central European power and the destruction of the Treaty of Versailles
- *Lebensraum* (living space) for Germans in the east.

To these so-called **intentionalist historians**, there were moments in the history of the Third Reich when there was deviation from Hitler's 'programme', but this was often for pragmatic reasons. To the intentionalists there was no doubt as to the centrality of Hitler in any interpretation of the events of 1933 to 1945. Hitler was **omnipotent**.

Definitions

Omnipotent

All powerful.

Intentionalist historians

Historians who stress the importance of the intentions of individuals such as Hitler.

Source A

The antagonisms of power were only resolved in the key position of the omnipotent Führer. This state of affairs, and not the efficient functioning of the state as such, was the ultimate object of the co-ordination (*Gleichschaltung*) of authority, which was by no means perfect. For the dictator held a key position precisely because of the confusion of conflicting power groups and personal connections.

From Karl Dietrich Bracher, *The Reinforcement of the National Socialist Domination*, published in 1956

Source B

It was Hitler who laid down the broad, general principles that policy had to follow. These were simple, clear and easy to grasp, and they had been drummed into the minds and hearts of Nazi activists since the 1920s through his book *Mein Kampf*, through his speeches and through the Propaganda Ministry after that. Hitler's underlings did not have to imagine what he would want in any given situation: the principles that guided their conduct were there for all to grasp; all they had to do was fill in the small print. Beyond this, at decisive moments, such as the boycott action of 1 April 1933 or the pogrom of 9–10 November 1938, Hitler personally ordered action to be taken, in terms that necessarily, from his point of view, avoided specifics, but were nonetheless unmistakable in their thrust.

From Richard Evans, *The Third Reich in Power*, published in 2005

The area in which Hitler took the most consistent and most detailed interest, however, was undeniably that of foreign policy and preparation for war. It was without question Hitler who personally drove Germany towards war from the moment he became Reich Chancellor, subordinating every other aspect of policy to this overriding aim and creating a growing number of stresses and strains in the economy, society and political system as a result.

Source C

Hitler's originality lay not in his idea, but in the terrifying literal way in which he set to work to translate these ideas into reality, and his unequalled grasp of the means by which to do this. To underestimate Hitler as a politician, to dismiss him as an ignorant demagogue, is to make precisely the same mistake that so many Germans made in the early 1930s. It was not a mistake which those who worked closely with him made. Whatever they felt about the man, however much they disagreed with the rightness of this or that decision, they never underestimated the ascendancy which he was able to establish over all who came into frequent contact with him.

From Alan Bullock, *Hitler: A Study in Tyranny*, published in 1952

Source D

One of the most remarkable features of the history of Germany under National Socialism was the extent to which Hitler imposed his personal authority on the German people and state. The point cannot be stressed too strongly. Hitler was master in the Third Reich.

From Norman Rich, *Hitler's War Aims*, published in 1973

SKILLS BUILDER

1 How would you summarise the arguments in Sources A, B, C and D about the central importance of Hitler and his ideology in the Third Reich?

2 From what you know about the history of Nazi Germany, have you any examples that could back up this interpretation of how the Nazi state worked?

3 To what extent do Sources A, B and C agree with each other?

Definition

Definition

Monocratic state

A state that is governed by one person.

Divide and rule

This view of the omnipotence of Hitler was further developed by Eberhard Jäckel and Klaus Hildebrand. Jäckel suggested that the Nazi state could be described as *Alleinherrschaft* (sole rule), in which all essential political decisions were made by Hitler. The Nazi state was therefore a **monocratic state**. However, as has been hinted at in Source A, there was a fair degree of infighting and competition between different power blocs within the Third Reich, such as between the Economics Ministry and Office of the Four Year Plan (as is explained in greater detail on page 171). To intentionalist historians such chaos was a result of Hitler's deliberate policy of divide and rule. An important source of evidence for such a conclusion came from the memoirs of Otto Dietrich, Hitler's Press Secretary, which has provided a rich source of information for historians.

Source E

In the twelve years of his rule in Germany Hitler produced the biggest confusion in government that has ever existed in a civilised state. During his period of government, he removed from the organisation of the state all clarity of leadership and produced a completely opaque network of competencies. It was not laziness or an excessive degree of tolerance which led the otherwise so energetic and forceful Hitler to tolerate this witch's cauldron of struggles for position and conflicts. It was intentional. With this technique he systematically disorganised the upper echelons of the Reich leadership in order to develop and further his own will until it became a despotic tyranny.

From Otto Dietrich, *Hitler*, published in 1955

Source F

Hitler deliberately destroyed the state's ability to function in favour of his personal omnipotence and irreplaceability, and he did so right from the start . . . [He] brought about a state of affairs in which the most various autonomous authorities were ranged alongside and against one another, without defined boundaries, in competition and overlapping – and only he was at the head of them . . . For he had the entire proper understanding that . . . absolute rule was not possible in an intact state organism but only amid controlled chaos. That was why, from the outset, he replaced the state by chaos – and one has to hand it to him that, while he was alive, he knew how to control it.

From Sebastian Haffner, *The Meaning of Hitler*, published in 1979

SKILLS BUILDER

1 To what extent does Source F support the claim in Source E about Hitler's intention to divide and rule?

2 Otto Dietrich's book *Hitler* (1955) provided significant insight into the operation of the Third Reich. Given the fact that he was Hitler's Press Secretary, can he be relied upon to give an accurate historical account?

Divide and rule, the economic sphere

The evidence for such a 'divide and rule' policy can be found where more than one agency was given responsibility for the same area or where there was a blurring of responsibilities. Indeed, there are many examples of Hitler giving different agencies conflicting responsibilities. One conflict was between the traditional civil service and judicial system and the emergence of new agencies with a more radical agenda. A good case study can be found in the economic sphere.

- From 1933 to 1936 Hitler allowed Hjalmar Schacht free rein, first as President of the Reichsbank (March 1933 to August 1934) and then as Minister of Economics (August 1934 to November 1937). The introduction of the New Plan, the increase in government investment and the introduction of work creation schemes all satisfied the Führer's political need to reduce unemployment and to lay the foundations of a self-sufficient (autarkic) economy.

- However, Hitler was willing to overrule, and thereby undermine, Schacht in 1936 when he sanctioned the launching of the Four Year Plan sponsored by Göring. The Office of the Four Year Plan assumed control of a number of important areas of the German economy including the production of raw materials and direction of the labour force. It recruited officials from outside the civil service, most noticeably Carl Krauch of IG Farben, who shifted the focus of the Four Year Plan to the production of the raw materials necessary for war: oil, rubber and metals.

- Göring undermined the traditional civil service to the point that Hjalmar Schacht resigned from his post as Minister of Economics in November 1937. This was a very important turning point in the radicalisation of the regime, Schacht being an important conservative working within the state. His replacement as Economics Minister, the Nazi Walter Funk, was willing to subordinate the Ministry of Economics to the Plan. Göring also undermined other ministries such as those for agriculture and labour by appointing civil servants from within these ministries to work in the Four Year Plan. The strongest, Göring and the Four Year Plan, had survived, ultimately because it had the patronage of the Führer.

Historians should be wary of taking Otto Dietrich's and Sebastian Haffner's views at face value. To suggest that Hitler practised an intentional policy of divide and rule is to misunderstand how he, as Führer, perceived government and the role of the state. Hitler did not believe in systems or structures; rather, he believed that the laws of politics were shaped by the laws of nature and that essentially the strongest would survive. Hitler therefore avoided regulating and interfering in disputes whenever possible. Instead, he preferred to allow structures to develop on their own, organically rather than imposed from above, although this did not prevent him interfering from time to time.

The case for a *polycratic* state

In the 1970s and 1980s there emerged a group of historians who challenged the 'intentionalist' or 'programmatist' interpretation of the Nazi state as being simplistic. These historians argued that the key to explaining

Definition

Polycratic

When a system is multi-centred and power is decentralised.

Definition

Structuralist historians

Historians who place a greater emphasis on structures such as the structures of the state when explaining what has happened in the past.

domestic and foreign policy developments in Nazi Germany from 1933 onwards was the context in which Hitler and other decision makers operated – notably the agencies, power blocs and individuals competing in a chaotic structure. Such historians suggested that the workings of the state were essentially chaotic because Hitler was unwilling to regulate or create an ordered system of government and because there was a lack of clear planning and direction from Hitler. These so-called **structuralist historians** argue that it is only through understanding the chaotic competition of these agencies that the radicalisation of policy up until 1945 can be explained. This line of thought does not dismiss the role of Hitler but places his significance into the wider context of how other government structures developed and operated. Foremost among these structuralist historians are Martin Broszat and Hans Mommsen.

Source G

In various ways my work offers a corrective to the oversimplified picture of a monolithic system and of a well-oiled super state . . . Until about 1936/7 there existed a conflict-ridden balance between state and Party, between authoritarian forces of order and impulses coming from the party. Hitler practised no direct and systematic leadership but from time to time jolted the government or the party into action, supported one or another initiative of Party functionaries or department heads and thwarted others, ignored them or left them to carry on without a decision . . .

The characteristic conflict between rival forces in the Third Reich can by no means be understood merely in terms of a Machiavellian policy of 'divide and rule' deliberately instituted by Hitler to make himself indispensable. On the contrary, it was a largely unavoidable corollary [result] of the Führer's absolutism, and in practice was not conducive to the long-term survival of the regime . . . We can only explain why the Hitler regime ultimately fell prey to a policy of irrational destruction after years of astonishingly impressive success, against the background of ever changing structural circumstances.

From Martin Broszat, *The Hitler State*, published in 1983

Source H

Following the takeover of power the Nazi Party was faced with the problems of fulfilling the assurances which had been made to the professional civil service and which Hitler had repeated on the occasion of the Enabling Act. Two essentially different political directions immediately emerged whose fundamental incompatibility was a key cause of the fact that the Third Reich fell into a situation of institutional degeneration which in the long run reduced the effectiveness of the state apparatus and the system overall to a minimum. . . . The dualism from which the departmental and institutional pluralism of the National Socialist regime is not adequately described as 'party' or 'movement' against 'state' because the party with its organisations and 'associated formations', above all the SA, SS and DAF, was already by 1933 no longer a close, unitedly led organisation.

From Hans Mommsen, *The Civil Service in the Third Reich*, published in 1966

SKILLS BUILDER

1 What, according to Broszat, were the main features of how the Nazi state functioned?

2 How does Source G differ from Sources A, B and C?

Führer Adolf Hitler	The undisputed leader of the party
Reichsleitung der NSDAP (Reich leadership)	Several Reich leaders had specific responsibilities, such as the party treasurer, and the Führer's deputy in charge of party affairs
Landesinspekteur (regional inspector)	Originally there were nine regional inspectors, each with responsibility for a Gau, but they were eventually replaced by the Gauleiter
Gauleiter (district leader)	There were 36 leaders of Gaue or districts, such as Saxony or Swabia. The number grew with the inclusion of Austria, Sudetenland and Danzig
Kreisleiter (Circuit leader)	The next lower administrative unit, equivalent to a rural council
Ortsgruppenleiter (local group leader)	Leaders responsible for a town section
Zellenleiter (cell leader)	Based on a neighbourhood (4–5 blocks of households) or employment unit
Blockwart (block warden)	The lowest officials just above the ordinary member
PG-Parteigenosse (Party comrade)	The ordinary members

8.1 The organisation of the Nazi Party

Definition

Reichsleitung

Reich leaders with specific responsibilities, such as the NSDAP's treasurer.

The struggle between party and state

The last sentence of Source G is highly significant. Historians such as Broszat and Mommsen stressed that the power structures within the Nazi state evolved and changed partly because of the poorly defined roles of both agencies and individuals within the Nazi state. When Hitler became Chancellor in 1933, the state apparatus, including the traditional civil service, remained intact. As the regime consolidated its power, so the institutions of the Weimar Republic, Reichstag and regional government, were weakened. The civil service was increasingly challenged by the emergence of National Socialist agencies that ran in parallel to the traditional state.

One of the most important of these agencies was the NSDAP. From 1934 Hitler gave the Führer's Deputy for Party Affairs Rudolf Hess and indirectly his Chief of Staff Martin Bormann more political power and influence; for example, from 1934, Hess had the power to supervise new laws. Party and state clashed when in 1934, by the Law for the Reconstruction of the Reich, the Minister for the Interior Wilhelm Frick tried to put the newly created Reich Governors under the control of the Ministry of the Interior, thereby creating centralised state control. It did not work. Most of the Reich Governors were also *Gauleiter* of the party and they had already built up impressive local power bases. The *Gauleiter* were appointed as Hitler's personal representatives in the regions and they were not going to submit to Frick's authority without a struggle. In the end, although Hitler agreed to place the Reich Governors nominally under Frick's control, in reality they could appeal directly to the Führer.

Throughout the 1930s, party representatives increased their power at a local level.

Definition

Kreisleiter

The administrative rank below the *Gauleiter*, equivalent to rural council.

- The district party leaders (***Kreisleiter***) also had political influence at a local level, especially after being given the right to choose local mayors by the Reich Local Government Law of January 1935.
- From 1935 Hess and Bormann succeeded in asserting the dominance of the party over the state civil service. Bormann set up his own party organisation, which rivalled that of the Reich Chancellery. There were two main departments of Bormann's organisation: Department II ran party affairs and Department III managed party–state relations.
- From 1937 all state officials were made directly responsible to Hitler, and by 1939 party membership had become compulsory for civil servants.
- The declaration of war saw this trend continue, with the party reaching new heights of power and influence. On 30 August 1939 the Ministerial Council for the Defence of the Reich was set up, and in September 1939 leading *Gauleiter* became Reich Defence Commissioners and began to assume total control in their regions.

Even though the 1930s saw the rise of party power at the expense of the traditional state, Hitler was not concerned to protect the interests of either state or party. He used the former as long as it continued to provide the legitimacy the regime needed through the support of the civil service, judiciary and the institutions of state that continued to operate. However, he was also prepared to allow other institutions such as the SS to emerge and develop their power to the point that they acted as a rival to the state and/or the party. One should see these groups as mini-states within the state, their influence growing or declining depending on access to the Führer and their ability to interpret his will. Although Hitler was prepared to allow agencies to fight between themselves until the strongest prevailed, he was also prepared to intervene and side with those who were, to his mind, working most effectively towards his world view. In June 1936, Hitler effectively ended the battle for the control of the police by appointing SS leader Heinrich Himmler as chief of the German police. There was an element of 'fudge' in his decision in that Himmler was nominally still under the jurisdiction of Frick as Minister of the Interior, but, in reality, Hitler signalled an important turning point with this decision. From now on the police were not to serve the state but the Führer and were to be part of the 'ideological struggle' against the enemies of the New Germany.

Hitler's lifestyle

Part of the structuralist argument is based on an analysis of Hitler's lifestyle. Hitler was by instincts an artist, and from 1935 he lived an increasingly **bohemian lifestyle**, spending next to no time on the administration of the government. When in Berlin he would take lunch and then meet with dignitaries for no more than an hour in the afternoon. He would then take a walk, eat supper and watch films (his favourites included Disney cartoons). Guests would often be subjected to a lengthy monologue on Hitler's favourite themes before he retired to bed, sometimes as late as 2.00 a.m. Hitler did not like Berlin, preferring the mountain air and the sensational views from his retreat at the Berghof at Obersalzberg near Berchtesgaden in Bavaria. There Hitler's routine was none too strenuous; he would emerge just before noon to read extracts from the newspapers. A lengthy vegetarian lunch would be followed by an afternoon walk down the hill for tea and cakes, before the same evening and night-time routine as in Berlin. During the day he would occasionally deal with matters that were brought to his attention, but they would often be trivial, for example deciding on the punishment of traffic offences. The importance of Hitler's lifestyle has often been commented on by historians.

Definition

Bohemian lifestyle

A way of living that does not conform to normal patterns.

Source I

Hitler's Bohemian lifestyle did not mean, however, that he was lazy or inactive, or that he withdrew from domestic politics after 1933. When the occasion demanded, he could intervene powerfully and decisively. Hitler was erratic rather than lazy in his work habits. He wrote his own speeches, and he frequently engaged in lengthy and exhausting tours around Germany, speaking, meeting officials and carrying out his ceremonial functions as head of state. In areas where he did take a real interest, he did not hesitate to give a direct lead, even on matters of detail. In art and culture, for instance, Hitler laid down the policy to be followed, and personally inspected the pictures selected for exhibition or suppression. His prejudices – against the composer Paul Hindemith, for example – invariably proved decisive. In racial policy, too, Hitler took a leading role pushing on or slowing down the implementation of anti-Semitic and other measures as he thought circumstances dictated. In areas such as this, Hitler was not merely reacting to initiatives from his subordinates, as some have suggested.

From Richard Evans, *The Third Reich in Power*, published in 2005

SKILLS BUILDER

To what extent does Evans agree with the structuralist view that Hitler's work habits limited his effectiveness as Führer?

Was Hitler a weak dictator?

The logical conclusion to the structuralist argument was that Hitler was not an all-powerful dictator as had been previously suggested.

Source J

Personally, Hitler had a preference for creating new organs of state to carry out specific projects. He had a preference, too, for choosing the 'right man for the job' and giving him the powers to carry it out, regardless; and there is no doubt that he carefully sought out men who were loyal to, and dependent upon, him for all top positions in the regime. More importantly his personal popularity was a source of power. However, while this shielded Hitler against ultimate contradictions by ministers and generals, it was not much help in the practical business of selecting goals, reaching decisions and making policy. Hitler's sense of dependence on his own popularity was so great that the cult of the Führer may well have contributed to government inaction in domestic affairs. Hitler was certainly careful not to associate himself with any measure that he thought might be unpopular. In this sense Hitler can be said to be a weak dictator.

From Tim Mason, *Nazism, Fascism and the Working Class*, published in 1995

Source K

Hitler was unwilling to take decisions, frequently uncertain, exclusively concerned with upholding his prestige and personal authority, influenced in the strongest fashion by his current entourage, in some respects a weak dictator.

From Hans Mommsen, *National Socialism*, published in 1971

SKILLS BUILDER

1 What are the main criticisms levelled against Hitler by Mason and Mommsen in Sources J and K?

2 How do these comments compare with the impression given in Source I?

3 Which lines of argument from Sources I, J and K do you instinctively agree with?

Hitler and the Gauleiter

The comment in Source K about Hitler's 'current entourage' referred in part to his relationship with the *Gauleiter*. As we have already seen, in 1934 Hitler was prepared to back the demands of his *Gauleiter* against his Minister of the Interior Frick. In his memorandum of December 1932, in which he reflected on the structure of the Nazi movement, Hitler wrote that 'the basis of the political organisation is loyalty', and he insisted on such loyalty in return for patronage and influence. The relationship that best exemplifies the importance of personal loyalty was that between Führer and *Gauleiter*. One of Hitler's acquaintances in the years up to 1934 was Hermann Rauschning who later became disillusioned with Hitler and, in 1938, published an account of conversations with the Führer titled *Hitler Speaks*. A number of historians have picked up on comments made by Rauschning about the nature of Hitler's dictatorship. To Rauschning, 'Hitler was no dictator' but a dependant on those about him. He describes Hitler as simply approving the views of the powerful: 'He always marched with the big battalions.' He was particularly damning of Hitler's relationship with the *Gauleiter*:

One thing, especially, Hitler never did – he never ran counter to the opinion of his *Gauleiter*, his district commissioners. Each one of these men was in his power, but together they held him in theirs; and accordingly, whenever differences arose, he so steered his course as to carry the overwhelming majority of them with him.

Rauschning goes on to highlight the power and the influence of the *Gauleiter*, and he summarises his view by writing that 'Hitler was at all times dependent on them, and not on them alone'. Writing in 1938, it is clear that Rauschning lacks hindsight and perspective in his analysis. His falling out of sympathy with the regime also clouded his views. The *Gauleiter* were Hitler's most trusted and loyal lieutenants, and they exercised considerable power in their localities in the name of the Führer. Joseph Goebbels's power base was strengthened by his appointment as *Gauleiter* of Berlin and others, such as Albert Forster of Danzig and West Prussia, relied on Hitler's personal patronage for their power.

The power of the *Gauleiter* was enhanced by the lack of any collective leadership during the Third Reich; the party was essentially a 'Führer party' and the *Gauleiter* were unquestioning in their allegiance to the Führer. The *Gauleiter* were virtually omnipotent in their regions, and many were able to use their local power base to ward off interference and competition from rival agencies. The *Gauleiter* were mainly 'old fighters' who became the guardians of Nazi faith, wielders of vast patronage and key agents in the rallying of morale. The power of the *Gauleiter* increased as the regime consolidated its power because their blind enthusiasm, local patronage and control of the district party leaders, the *Kreisleiter*, gave them control of the locality. Ian Kershaw has described the *Gauleiter* as being 'the backbone of his [Hitler's] power'. This is a far more convincing analysis of the relationship between Führer and *Gauleiter* than that given by Rauschning.

Hitler the decision maker

The suggestion made by Hans Mommsen that Hitler was 'unwilling to make decisions' shows a misunderstanding of Hitler's role and significance in the state. As Führer from 1934, Hitler showed little interest in the day-to-day decisions of government and distanced himself from them. Cabinet government declined from meeting 72 times in 1933 to not meeting at all in 1938. In July 1934, as President Hindenburg was dying, Hitler absorbed the powers of Chancellor and President as Führer of Germany. This constitutional change was confirmed by the Law on the Head of State of the German Reich signed on 1 August 1934 by Hitler's leading ministers. The following day the army, on the initiative of General Blomberg, swore an oath of personal allegiance to Hitler. On 19 August in a plebiscite of the German people, 89.9 per cent voted in support of the constitutional reform. Hitler's power as head of state, party and military was unassailable. That summer, Leni Riefenstahl filmed *The Triumph of the Will*, a record of the Nazi party rally at Nuremberg. The film represented the Führer as a demi-god, worshipped by the German people, and represents a coming of age of the political religion. It is in this context that we should judge Hitler's involvement in government. The nature of the dictatorship and the way in which the Führer was represented in propaganda acted to distance him from the mundane detail of government because he was now so powerful.

However, the crucial decisions during peacetime were made by Hitler. The decision to destroy the leadership of the SA and the 'Second Revolution' by the Night of the Long Knives in June 1934 was Hitler's and Hitler's alone. The need to resolve the tension between the army and SA was the significant factor in explaining why Hitler chose to destroy an important element of the **Nazi movement**. Although he had the support of Göring (who was keen to see the destruction of his over-powerful rival Röhm) and Himmler (who recognised that the only way to increase SS power was at the expense of the SA), the decision to act with such ruthlessness was Hitler's. Indeed, the years following the Night of the Long Knives saw the disappearance of collective government and the establishment of Führer rule that strengthened Hitler's power at the heart of the regime.

Lack of formal mechanisms

So Hitler's authority was unchallenged. The lack of formal mechanisms through which that authority was given by the Führer has caused problems for historians trying to explain how the Nazi state operated. Hitler rarely read important documents before making a decision and disliked signing official papers. Instead, officials and subordinates sought a verbal agreement for an initiative or even a nod of the Führer's head. This type of approval, known as 'Führer orders', carried the ultimate authority within the state. On occasions, Hitler issued contradictory orders, which led to confusion.

- At a meeting in November 1935 to discuss Jewish emigration, Rudolf Hess's interpretation of the Führer's wishes – that he wanted to see all of Germany's Jews emigrate as quickly as possible – was contradicted by an official from the Ministry of the Interior who insisted that Hitler wished the Jews to remain in Germany for the time being so that they could be used as hostages. The likelihood was that Hitler had given different impressions to different people, but whatever the reason, it did not make for clear government.

- On occasions, Führer orders were given prematurely, without consultation, and thereby provoked protest from within the party and state hierarchy. In October 1934 the head of the Labour Front, Robert Ley, gained the Führer's approval for a measure aimed at strengthening the power of the Labour Front at the expense of employers and state. Such a move was opposed by a number of leading figures including Rudolf Hess, the Minister of Economics Hjalmar Schacht and leading businessmen. In the face of such pressure, the Führer allowed the measure to strengthen the Labour Front to be shelved. This example does not prove that the dictatorship was weak but that, on occasions, Hitler needed to use his power pragmatically.

Definition

Nazi movement

Not just the leadership and political party, the NSDAP, but the SA, SS and all other organisations including those representing young people and women.

SKILLS BUILDER

1 Summarise the debate about Hitler's relationship with the *Gauleiter*.

2 How did confusion in government come about?

Case study: foreign policy

It is in the area of foreign policy that one can discern Hitler as very much the key decision maker.

Hitler's foreign policy aims

As is shown in the party programme of 1920 and his *Mein Kampf* (1924), Hitler's *Weltanschauung* revolved around a policy of unlimited territorial expansionism, which marked a significant shift from the Bismarckian, Wilhelmine and Weimar periods. It should be pointed out that the following ambitions were shared by considerable numbers of German politicians as well as the public at large.

- As a first stage, Hitler wished to destroy the Versailles settlement and create a 'Greater Germany' of all ethnic Germans that would dominate a 'Mittel Europe' (Central Europe).

- He also envisaged destroying the Soviet Union and winning *Lebensraum* by enslaving the peoples of eastern Europe as far as the Urals.

Diplomacy 1933–35

Given Germany's weaknesses in 1933, Hitler realised that he had to move cautiously. The German army had been limited to 100,000 by the Treaty of Versailles, the economy was still in depression, Germany had no allies and was surrounded by hostile alliances constructed by France. Hitler's short-term objectives were, therefore, to secure alliances, undermine his rivals, achieve more acceptable aims and, above all, give an appearance of moderation.

- He signed a Four Power Pact that sought to revise the Versailles treaty by diplomacy and in 1934 secured a non-aggression pact with Poland to last for 10 years.

- These moves in part were intended to distract reaction from Germany's withdrawal from the League of Nations in October 1933, which Hitler justified by the obvious weakness of the League and its failure to secure multi-national disarmament.

In 1935, Hitler ordered conscription and the beginning of rearmament. In July 1935, the Austrian Chancellor Dollfuss was assassinated and the Nazis threatened to intervene in Austria. In response, the Italian dictator, Benito Mussolini, moved his troops to the frontier with Austria at the Brenner Pass to prevent a German invasion of Austria. Hitler was not strong enough to call Mussolini's bluff and the latter's successful military threat to intervene if Hitler seized Austria underlined Germany isolation. The coup against Dollfuss increased fears about German ambitions and led to a reinforcement of defensive alliances against her. In 1935 Britain, France and Italy signed the Stresa Front, which condemned German rearmament, reaffirmed the Franco-German border fixed at Versailles, and defended Austrian independence. In addition, in May 1935 France allied with Russia against unprovoked aggression, and Russia promised to defend Czechoslovakia.

Rearmament and conscription

Despite such diplomatic hostility, Hitler had greatly strengthened Germany's position by 1935.

- First, rearmament and conscription were successfully introduced in direct flouting of the Versailles treaty.
- Second, the Saarland, placed under League of Nations control since 1918, voted for re-incorporation into Germany. The area, though small, was rich in coal and was an important symbolic triumph for Hitler.
- Third and most significant, Hitler secured the Anglo-German Naval Agreement in June 1935, which permitted Germany to build a fleet of 35 per cent of the strength of the British navy. This agreement undermined the Versailles treaty and destroyed the Stresa Front.

An unexpected boost to German fortunes was Mussolini's invasion of Abyssinia in October 1935. This adventure weakened the League of Nations and destroyed the anti-Nazi alliance. Both Britain and France condemned Mussolini's aggression while Germany offered support.

The reoccupation of the Rhineland 1936

It was Hitler's decision to exploit the crisis caused by Mussolini's invasion of Abyssinia by the remilitarization of the Rhineland in March 1936. German troops had been banned from the Rhineland by the Treaty of Versailles, and its reoccupation risked military intervention by France and Britain. Hitler instructed his troops to retreat in the face of any resistance, but rightly gambled that France would not retaliate. France was in no mood to fight, and the view in Britain was that Germany had some justification for occupying what was her own land. The need to retain Germany as an ally against Russia was the principal objective of British foreign policy. The League of Nations, paralysed by the Abyssinian crisis, remained inactive. The peaceful reoccupation of the Rhineland was celebrated by the Germans and helped to consolidate Hitler's dictatorship. It also marked an important turning point in the perceptions of Hitler's dictatorship. He was living up to his promises that he was a man of action who would destroy the Versailles treaty.

The Anschluss with Austria, 1938

By 1937 Hitler had rebuilt Germany's military and diplomatic strength. Germany's economy had recovered, the army had been increased to half a million, and some key alliances had been formed. The Spanish Civil War from July 1936 offered Hitler's army valuable training as they supported Franco's Nationalists against the Republicans. The Berlin–Rome Axis confirmed Germany's understanding with Fascist Italy in November, and this alliance was then bound with the Anti-Comintern Pact that Germany had signed with Japan (the Comintern being the international organisation for communism). By comparison, Britain and France appeared confused and submissive. In November 1937 Hitler felt confident enough to announce to his more conservative generals at the so-called Hossbach Conference that his aim was not merely to reverse the Versailles treaty but to seize *Lebensraum* to the east to 'guarantee the nation its daily bread'. A key stage in this expansionism was the union or *Anschluss* with Austria, which had been prohibited by the Treaty of Versailles. Opinion within Austria was deeply divided but renewed Nazi agitation in the spring of 1938 encouraged German ambitions. The Austrian Chancellor Kurt Schuschnigg was bullied by Hitler to accept union but resisted and planned to hold a plebiscite to demonstrate Austrian resistance. Hitler cancelled the plebiscite and ordered his army to march into Austria. It entered Vienna on 11 March amid widespread rejoicing, and Hitler proclaimed the union of Austria and Nazi Germany. The timetable for German expansion and the decision to annex Austria had been Hitler's.

The seizure of Czechoslovakia 1938–39

With the *Anschluss* with Austria the state of Czechoslovakia was vulnerable to German expansionism. Hitler despised the Czech state as an artificial creation of the Versailles settlement. He coveted its coal and iron resources and, most importantly, demanded the incorporation into Germany of the 3.5 million German speakers who lived in its northern and western borderlands, which were known as the Sudetenland. These mountainous lands had been given to the Czech state in 1919 as a protective barrier, and the Czechs had reinforced them by formidable frontier defences.

- Encouraged by the *Anschluss* and claiming economic discrimination by the majority Czechs, the Sudeten Germans led by Conrad Henlich agitated in March 1938 for union with the Reich.

- The Czechs partially mobilized their army in defence of the state, but a new rising on the 12 September re-ignited the Sudeten crisis.

- German intervention in support of the Sudeten Germans risked European war as the state was guaranteed by the Versailles settlement and the Czechs had alliances with Russia and France. Realising the dangers of the crisis, British Prime Minister Neville Chamberlain flew to meet Hitler at Berchtesgaden on 15 September. Here it was agreed that Germany could annex those German-speaking provinces who voted by plebiscite to join the Reich.

- At a second meeting in Bad Godesberg on 22 September, however, Hitler demanded the immediate occupation of the Sudetenland without a plebiscite and insisted that Polish and Hungarian claims on Czechoslovakia also be satisfied. The Czechs mobilized their army and European war appeared unavoidable. In Germany dissident generals plotted against Hitler to save the country from expected defeat. War was averted by Mussolini, who arranged a third meeting between Hitler,

Chamberlain and the French Prime Minister Daladier at Munich on 29 September. Britain and France appeased Hitler. Neither had the stomach for a fight nor felt strong enough to challenge Germany to another conflict when Russia was considered to be the greatest threat. Moreover, it was argued that the incorporation of the Sudetenland could be justified by the principle of national self-determination.

- Some in Europe even believed that this might be Hitler's 'last territorial demand'. The Sudetenland was seized by Germany in October, and Poland and Hungary each annexed land from the crippled Czech State. The Czech President Beneš claimed that 'we have been abandoned and betrayed'. Hitler was disappointed because he had hoped that the Czech crisis would lead to war. However, the episode tells us much about his centrality in the direction of German foreign policy.

The conquest of Poland 1939

In March 1939 Germany invaded the rest of Czechoslovakia without resistance. The western lands of Bohemia and Moravia were incorporated into the Reich, and Slovakia became a puppet state led by Dr Emil Hácha. It was clear after the invasion of Czechoslovakia in March 1939 that Hitler was not merely aiming to unite all Germans but was embarking on a policy of unlimited eastward expansionism. In response to this, Britain and France guaranteed the independence of Poland on 31 March.

- Hitler recognized that an attack on Poland would not be tolerated by Britain or France and sought to reinforce his alliance with Italy by the 'Pact of Steel' on 22 May 1939.

- More astonishingly Foreign Secretary von Ribbentrop and the Russian Foreign Minister Molotov secured a Nazi-Soviet pact on 23 August. By the pact Germany and Russia agreed to partition Poland and not to attack each other for at least two years. Stalin won the Baltic states and bought valuable time to complete his economic plans and rebuild his army after the Purges, which had seen most of the Soviet military leadership destroyed. Hitler won a free hand to seize half of Poland without fighting a war on two fronts.

- On 28 August Hitler demanded the return of those lands lost to Poland by the Treaty of Versailles, Silesia, the Polish Corridor and Danzig, claiming that German speakers were being persecuted by Poles and faking a Polish border raid. Germany invaded Poland on 1 September.

- Britain demanded that Germany withdraw and, when this was ignored, declared war on 3 September. Hitler unleashed a new form of warfare against Poland, by which rapidly advancing infantry and support units exploited devastating strikes by Stuka dive bombers and tightly packed formations of Panzer tanks. Against this attack, the brave but disorganized and old-fashioned Polish army, still using cavalry, was defenceless. Britain and France, as Hitler calculated, could do nothing to save Poland while Russia attacked in the east. After heroic resistance Poland surrendered on 27 September 1939.

Germany's foreign policy between 1933 and 1939 provides numerous examples that prove the ultimate executive power of the Führer. Perhaps most significant were the decisions to go to war in September 1939 against the advice of Göring, who feared that an invasion of Poland would provoke war with Britain and France. Although he was spurred on in his decision by Foreign Minister von Ribbentrop, the decision was ultimately Hitler's and was made on the back of a succession of foreign policy victories from the Rhineland to *Anschluss*.

Source L

Hitler's role in the creation of the Nazi regime and in steering towards a perpetually radical programme is an issue which has preoccupied historians. There is no consensus as to whether Hitler played a critical role in defining the Nazi regime's character, or whether he was merely a catalyst, bringing together pre-existing political ideas. Any attempt to understand the course of German foreign policy on the eve of the World War II will include a debate on the role of the Nazi leadership, the army, and a number of ministries. Hitler's foreign policy initiatives and plans for war were pursued with the complicity of these powerful groups and, as they proved to be successful, they strengthened the Nazi Party's grip on power and enhanced his authority.

From Anita J. Prazmowska, *Hitler and the Origins of World War II*, published in 2005

Source M

This was the hallmark of his [foreign policy] in his first years [as Chancellor and Führer]. While seeking to allay the suspicions of his neighbours, he was using the respite gained to carry out the process of *Gleichschaltung* and to make the first preparations for the all-out rearmament effort that was to come later. Simultaneously, he was looking for an opportunity to withdraw from engagements entered into by Stresemann and Brüning, which promised to be onerous. Finally, he was making his assessment of the attitude of the various [foreign] Powers would be likely to adopt when he began to move towards his real objectives.

From Gordon Craig, *Germany 1866–1945*, published in 1978

Source N

The popular notion of a Führer standing over and above the wrangles of everyday politics was not wholly mythical. From 1935–36 onwards, Hitler did in reality withdraw increasingly from involvement in domestic affairs of State, and did leave the ordinary business of government more and more to the overlapping and competing chancelleries, ministries, and special plenipotentiary organisations like that of the 'Four Year Plan', which turned internal government into administrative chaos, while concentrating himself in growing measure on matters of diplomacy and foreign policy.

From Ian Kershaw, *The Hitler Myth*, published in 1987

Source O

Successes and unending triumphs were indispensable for the regime, and for Hitler's own popularity and prestige on which, ultimately, the regime depended. Only through expansion – impossible without war – would Germany, and the National Socialist regime, survive. This was Hitler's thinking. The gamble for expansion was inescapable, it was not a matter of personal choice. The legacy of Munich was fatally to weaken those who might even have constrained Hitler. Any potential limits, external and internal, on his freedom of action instead disappeared. Hitler's drive to war was unabated. And next time he was determined he would not be blocked by last-minute diplomatic manoeuvres of the western powers, whose weakness he had seen with his own eyes at Munich.

From Ian Kershaw, *Nemesis*, published in 2000

Working towards the Führer

The historical debate has now moved on from the polarised stances of 'intentionalist' and 'structuralist'. What has followed has been a synthesis of ideas consisting of some of the following elements:

- a recognition of the importance of Hitler as arbiter between power blocs and leader

- an acceptance that the regime had chaotic characteristics

- a recognition that the Nazi evolved over time and the dynamic for change came from above and below

- an acceptance that the coherent element that held Nazi Germany together was an ideological belief that was understood by all and was identified with the Führer.

In his book *Hubris* (1998), Ian Kershaw addresses the extent to which Hitler shaped Nazi ideology. He argues:

- The strands of Nazi ideology existed before Hitler was heard of, but Hitler was indispensable to the rise and exercise of power of National Socialism. This is a very important distinction. The ideology of National Socialism, what Kershaw calls 'an amalgam of prejudices, phobias and utopian social expectations', emerged as part of the broader European political culture at the turn of the nineteenth century.

- Hitler defined the reality of National Socialism in power. His ability to do so comes from the stranglehold he had on the party from the assertion of the *Führerprinzip* (the principle that the Nazi movement was dominated by one leader, the Führer) at the Nazi conference at Bamberg in 1926 through to the demise of the left wing Nazi leader Gregor Strasser in 1932.

- His power over the Nazi movement was sealed by the Night of the Long Knives and the destruction of the power of the leadership of the SA in 1934. Hitler had asserted his world view as the sole source of Nazi ideology and power within the state.

- However, National Socialism became, through its quest for and success in achieving power in 1933, distilled into what we can call Hitlerism. Although individuals and groups within the Nazi movement and German society believed in their own variants of different aspects of Nazi ideology, these were tailored and refined from 1933 to 1945 to match the *Weltanschauung* (world view) of the Führer.

- The acquisition of power changed the emphasis of National Socialist ideology because the purpose of the ideology had changed. Before 1933 its purpose had been to gain power; after 1933 its purpose lay in bolstering the power of the Führer. Once power had been achieved by Hitler in 1933, the dynamic of the new state, its political system and Nazi society was for all within them to 'work towards the Führer'.

This source of the term 'work towards the Führer' comes from an otherwise little known bureaucrat in the Prussian Agriculture Ministry, Werner Willikens.

Source P

Everyone with opportunity to observe it knows that the Führer can only with great difficulty order from above everything that he intends to carry out sooner or later. On the contrary, up till now everyone with a post in the new Germany has worked best when he has, so to speak, worked towards the Führer. Very often and in many spheres it has been the case – in previous years as well – that individuals have simply waited for orders and instructions. Unfortunately, the same will be true in the future; but in fact it is the duty of everyone to try to work towards the Führer along the lines he would wish.

From a speech on 21 February 1934 by Werner Willikens, State Secretary in the Prussian Agriculture Ministry, quoted in Ian Kershaw, *Hubris*, published in 1998

There are two central and important themes identifiable in this short quote:

- First, the idea of a New Germany was central to the inclusive nature of National Socialism.
- Second, Willikens and others believed that a New Germany could be realised was by 'working towards the Führer'.

Kershaw's impact on the historiography of Nazi Germany has been profound. The concept of 'working towards the Führer' as the central dynamic of how Nazi Germany worked has been accepted by most historians.

Cumulative radicalisation

The dynamic of the Nazi state revolved around the successful interpretation of Hitler's world view. At the centre of power in the Nazi state was the authority of the Führer. Hitler hated bureaucracy, preferring to leave administrative matters to others. As Führer, he saw himself above day-to-day politics, preferring to focus on broad themes. But the Führer was also head of the government, and in failing to focus on routine matters, he left a vacuum for others to fill. Therefore power and influence were up for grabs. In the Nazi state, access to Hitler and the ability to

Definition

Cumulative radicalisation

In this context, the way in which state policy gradually became ever more extreme.

successfully work towards the Führer dictated the relative power of those around him. Indeed, the two factors were related: those who were able to best interpret the will of the Führer were accorded access and influence.

One of Hans Mommsen's many significant contributions to the debate about how the Nazi state worked has been his idea of **cumulative radicalisation**.

Source Q

The assumption that the fragmentation of politics arose from a deliberate divide-and-rule strategy on Hitler's part is, however, misleading. Rather, this was a reflection of the social-Darwinist conviction that the best man would ultimately prevail. The consequent technique of operating through special emissaries promised short run efficiency, but meant in the long run that a great deal of energy was wasted in personal feuds and taken up by increasing inter-departmental rivalries as well as between party and state agencies. These mechanisms were, however, of the utmost importance for the internal development of the regime. The social-Darwinist struggle led to an escalating ruthlessness in pursuit of the extreme goals of the movement, and thus to a process of cumulative radicalisation. Owing to the lack of institutional guarantees, individual chieftains felt compelled to fight competitors with all means at their disposal. Each office holder tried to gain the special sympathies of the Führer by appearing as a fanatical fighter for the realisation of the visionary and extreme goals of the *Weltanschauung*.

From Hans Mommsen, 'Cumulative Radicalisation and Progressive Self-destruction as Structural Determinants of the Nazi Dictatorship', in Ian Kershaw and Moshe Lewin (editors), *Stalin and Nazism*, published in 1997

Source R

In the meantime, however, there were clear signs of what would become a lasting trait of the Third Reich: pressure from party radicals, encouraged and sanctioned at least in part by Hitler, resulting in the state bureaucracy reflecting the radicalism in legislation and the police channelling it into executive measures. The process of 'cumulative radicalization' was recognisable from the earliest weeks of the regime.

From Ian Kershaw, *Hubris*, published in 1998

SKILLS BUILDER

1 After reading Sources Q and R, explain how cumulative radicalisation works.

2 Using Source Q, explain the relationship between 'working towards the Führer and 'cumulative radicalisation'.

The critical point to make is that there was a 'push and pull' mechanism at work in 'cumulative radicalisation'. On the one hand was the 'push' factor of the leading individuals and agencies coming up with more and more radical policies as they worked towards the Führer. On the other hand was the 'pull' factor in that Hitler was by instinct one of the most radical of the Nazi leaders. When in power, Hitler attempted to portray himself as the personification of reason and respectability. In 1933 the Nazis stage-managed Potsdam Day exactly for that reason, and the purge of the SA was undertaken as a means of crushing the revolutionary wing of the movement. However, such actions should not disguise the fact that Hitler should be considered, especially on racial policy, one of the most radical of the leading Nazis. Perhaps Goebbels can be considered as radical in a number of policy areas, but it is instructive, therefore, that he was closer to Hitler than any of the other leading Nazis. The point about Hitler's standpoint is important because it helps explain the fact that 'working towards the Führer' automatically meant adopting a radical position.

Hitler's authority

The authority of the Führer was unquestioned and, indeed, was further strengthened by the lack of constraint. In most political systems, the power of a particular position is limited through being defined in a constitution. Such a restriction was not imposed on the Führer. Source S sets out how the most important constitutional thinker of the Third Reich, Ernst Rudolf Huber, defined the concept of Führer.

Source S

The office of Führer has developed out of the National Socialist movement. In its origins it is not a state office . . . The position of the Führer combines in itself all sovereign power of the Reich; all public power in the State as in the movement is derived from Führer power . . . For it is not the state as an impersonal entity which is the source of political power but rather political power is given to the Führer as the executor of the nation's common will . . . Führer power is not restricted by safeguards and controls . . . but rather it is free and independent, exclusive and unlimited.

From Ernst Huber, 1934, a constitutional theorist quoted in J. Noakes and G. Pridham (editors), *Nazism 1919–1945*, Volume 2, published in 2000

Source T

The Führer is the supreme judge of the nation. There is no position in the area of constitutional law in the Third Reich independent of this elemental will of the Führer . . . Constitutional Law in the Third Reich is the legal formulation of the historic will of the Führer.

From a speech in 1938 by Hans Frank, head of the Nazi Association of Lawyers and of the German Academy of Law, quoted in J. Noakes and G. Pridham (editors), *Nazism 1919–1945*, Volume 2, published in 2000

Hitler's power was absolute in theory and in practice. In 1938 Hans Frank (head of the Academy of German Law and the Nazi Lawyers Association) defined Hitler's power in a similar fashion to Huber by placing the emphasis on the role played by the Führer in interpreting the nation's will. Hitler's world view, therefore, was given central prominence. Frank's argument is given in Source T.

This historic will was clearly defined and broadly understood. The dynamic of the Nazi state ultimately revolved around the attempt of all associated with the regime, from Himmler's SS and Goebbels's propaganda machine to the military and business élites, to realise the Führer's historic will even if this ultimately drove Germany into a war of annihilation and destruction the like of which had never been seen before. So it is valid to point to the central importance of Hitler. This debate over whether Hitler was a strong or weak dictator has effectively been ended by the wide acceptance among historians of Ian Kershaw's model of the state in which all were 'working towards the Führer'. Therefore, according to Kershaw, Hitler did have a supreme role because all those below him in the power structure were attempting to interpret his world view. The structures of power were chaotic, but the position of the Führer and his world view as the ultimate source of authority remained unchallenged. This helps to explain how policies emerged and developed. Throughout the dictatorship, Hitler remained relatively distant from decision making, especially on domestic policy.

Source U

Decisive in this was the process, which we have followed, of the expansion of his power, relative to other agencies of power in the regime, to the point where, by spring 1938, it had freed itself from all institutional constraints and had established unchallenged supremacy over all sections of the 'power cartel'. The five years of Hitler's highly personalised form of rule had eroded all semblance of collective involvement in policy making. The fragmentation at one and the same time rendered the organisation of any opposition within the power-élite almost impossible and inordinately strengthened Hitler's own power. The scope for more cautious counsel to apply the brakes had sharply diminished. The constant Hobbesian 'war of all against all', the competing power fiefdoms that characterised the National Socialist regime, took place at the level below Hitler, enhancing his position as the fount of all authority and dividing both individual and sectional interests of the different power entities (the Movement, the state bureaucracy, the army, big business, the police, and the sub branches of each). Hitler, therefore, as the sole lynchpin, able internally to deal, as in foreign policy, through **bilateral relations** offering his support here, denying it there, remained the sole arbiter, even when he preferred to let matters ride and let his supporters battle it out for themselves. It was less a planned strategy of 'divide and rule' than an inevitable consequence of Führer authority.

From Ian Kershaw, *Nemesis*, published in 2000

Definition

Bilateral relations

Negotiation agreements between two countries.

SKILLS BUILDER

Identify five points in Source U about the Führer and his power by 1938. Support your comments with quotes from the source.

The dynamic for radicalisation

The dynamic for change within the Nazi movement can be found in a synthesis of initiatives taken from below and the work of Nazi leaders, officials and civil servants all developing policy 'working towards the Führer'. At a non-governmental level, ordinary Germans attempted to 'work towards the Führer' by accepting and shaping initiatives at a local level. The process of 'working towards' the Führer's *Weltanschauung* took place on two levels:

- *The decision makers within the regime* The party leadership, the bureaucracy, business and the military became more radical in their efforts to work towards the central themes of Hitler's world view, namely the 'removal of the Jews' and preparation for the conquest of Europe to provide *Lebensraum*.

- *Social consensus* Considerable numbers of Germans conformed to the regime and the Führer in their day-to-day lives by joining Nazi organisations, reporting anti-Nazi behaviour to the Gestapo, performing the Hitler salute, not buying goods in Jewish shops or through supporting the imprisonment of communists in concentration camps. Of course, not all Germans conformed, many grumbled, a few dissented and even fewer opposed. But from the majority there was 'loyal reluctance' and from many there was positive enthusiasm.

This created the dynamic for radicalisation that was such an important feature of the regime after 1934. Perhaps the most significant case study in support of Kershaw's model is the development of racial initiatives from 1933 to 1939. As has already been explained, racial policy stood at the heart of Hitler's *Weltanschauung*, notably a deep-seated anti-Semitism. The pressure for official anti-Semitic action came from above (via Hitler and all of those in the Nazi leadership who were working towards him) and from below. The pressure from below came from radical anti-Semites who saw the creation of a Nazi regime as the opportunity to attack Germany's Jews.

Case study 1: boycott 1933

Causes

Indeed, the assault began the moment that the Nazis came to power in January 1933. Driven by the thugs of the SA and groups such as the Fighting League of the Commercial Middle Class, the Jews were attacked on the streets, in synagogues and in their homes, with no attempt from the authorities to restrict the violence. In Breslau in early March 1933, Jewish lawyers and judges were attacked and expelled from the courthouse. The violence brought condemnation from abroad. In March 1933, Jewish groups in the United States of America and Europe pressed for a boycott of German goods in protest against the anti-Jewish violence.

Response

The response of Nazi radicals such as Julius Streicher was the demand for a boycott of Jewish businesses in Germany. The idea won favour with Hitler who was radical in his views when it came to Jewish affairs. At one level the boycott was a response to the growing violence and threat of foreign protest. On another level it reflected the desire of the Nazi leadership, even at this early stage, to flex its anti-Semitic muscles. In the end Hitler agreed to a more cautious approach and ordered that the boycott be limited to one day, 1 April.

Outcome

The real importance of the boycott was that it triggered a more radical response from the state. The unease about the impact of street violence resulted in the decision to introduce laws that discriminated against the Jews. The aim of the SA and the civil servants was the same: to remove

Jewish professionals from public life. The process of ministers framing laws to exclude Jews from their jobs, thereby reflecting the initiatives taken at a local level, was apparent, even at this early stage of the regime. The Minister of the Interior, Wilhelm Frick, framed the Law for the Restoration of the Professional Civil Service of 7 April, which included the 'Aryan Clause' preventing Jews from working in the civil service. The same day a decree was issued banning Jewish lawyers from practising. This is a clear example of how racial policy was made 'on the hoof' rather than following any predetermined plan.

The response of the Jewish community to state sponsored attacks was mixed. Many continued to believe that the Nazis were a storm that would soon blow over. Others were less sure, understanding that the attacks of 1933 were part of a process to exclude Jews from German life. By the end of 1933 over 37,000 Jews had left Germany, including 20 winners of the Nobel Prize, the most famous being the scientist Albert Einstein.

Case study 2: Nuremburg Laws 1935

Causes

In 1935 there was a resurgence of agitation that followed a similar pattern to the unrest of 1933: local violence stirred up by *Gauleiter* such as Streicher or Goebbels, an intensification of discrimination in the workplace followed by a 'working towards the Führer' at a policy level by the establishment and Nazi leadership. From early 1935, the propaganda against the Jews intensified in journals such as *Der Angriff* (which was edited by Goebbels). Although, as an organisation, the SA was politically weaker after the Night of the Long Knives purge, there were thousands of SA members still active and keen to implement the Nazi programme. But by 1935, many grass-root Nazis had become frustrated at the apparent lack of progress in implementing the Nazi revolution. In the summer of 1935, attacks against Jewish businesses and Jews intensified; in May there were anti-Jewish riots in Munich and in July Jews were attacked on the streets of Berlin.

Response

As the violence spread, the reaction among the wider population was mixed, many Germans disliking the hooliganism of the SA. Conservatives in the government, led by Hjalmar Schacht, argued that street violence was having a negative effect on Germany's image abroad and that a more systematic 'legal' approach to the 'Jewish Question' was preferable.

- A meeting of ministers held in August and chaired by Schacht agreed that the government needed to take the initiative on the 'Jewish Question'.
- Concerned about the apparent lawlessness of local attacks on the Jews, on 8 August 1935 Hitler ordered an end to random attacks. However, in order to placate the radicals in the party, the leadership moved to 'deal' with the issue of marital and sexual relations between Jews and Aryans.

- As the Nazi party assembled for their annual rally at Nuremberg on 10 September, there were no official plans for the passing of any law to deal with the issue of relationships between Jews and Aryans.

- On 12 September, the Reich Doctors' leader, Gerhard Wagner, made a speech indicating that a law banning mixed marriages was imminent. The next day, Hitler ordered his civil servants to draw up legislation to deal with this issue. Civil servants including the officer in charge of Jewish Affairs at the Interior Ministry, Bernhard Lösener, rushed to Nuremberg. Working under the watchful eye of Gerhard Wagner, they presented four drafts of the Law for the Protection of German Blood to Hitler. While choosing the most conservative version, Draft D (which made marriage and sexual relationships between Jew and Aryan illegal and punished them with harsh penalties), Hitler demanded that his civil servants also draw up a Reich Citizenship Law that would deprive Jews of German citizenship. Both Nuremberg Laws became law at the party rally.

Outcome

The Nuremberg Laws served their purposes. They ended, for the time being, the localised attacks on the Jews that were undermining the credibility of the government in the eyes of those Germans who found such violence distasteful. Those in the party who wanted radical action were pleased with the new levels of state discrimination against the Jews. The conservatives were satisfied that action against the Jews had been taken off the streets and had entered the statute book. For the next two years, the Jewish Question was 'placed on the back burner'. The Berlin Olympics of 1936 brought Germany into the world's spotlight, and the regime did not want a picture of discrimination and violence to dominate. However, the Nuremberg Laws ensured that discrimination against Germany's Jews was now considered not only acceptable but legal. They were, therefore, a very important turning point in the radicalisation of Nazi policy against the Jews.

Case study 3: Kristallnacht, 1938

Origins

It is in the origins of Kristallnacht that one can see a clear example of the dynamics of the state. There was no blueprint for a more radical approach to the Jewish Question. Initiatives emerged in response to events. Official sanction for a more radical anti-Semitic line was given by Hitler in his keynote address to the party's annual Nuremberg rally in September 1937. In his speech Hitler launched into an attack on the threat of 'Jewish Bolshevism'. This was not the first time in the year that Hitler had raised the issue of the Jewish Question; in April 1937 he informed a gathering of *Kreisleiter* of the need to move carefully in Jewish policy but without compromising their resolve to ultimately solve the Jewish Question.

- The dismissal of Schacht as Minister of Economics in November 1937 meant the removal of the most important restraining influence on a more radical anti-Semitic agenda. For the past four years, Schacht had counselled caution and restraint in official policy towards the Jews, fearing that open anti-Semitism would lead to international disapproval that might affect trade and Germany's economic revival. Schacht's departure from office and the growing influence of Göring in economic affairs resulted in a series of anti-Jewish decrees; for example, on 15 December 1937, Göring issued a decree limiting the ability of Jewish business to buy raw materials or deal in foreign currency. This further discrimination against Jewish business interests was part of a long-term strategy to 'Aryanise' Jewish business.

- The most significant turning point in the series of events that led to Kristallnacht was the *Anschluss* of Austria in March 1938. The annexation of the land of Hitler's birth meant the incorporation of another 195,000 Jews into the Reich. The incorporation of Austria into the Reich sparked an orgy of violence and discrimination against the Jews in Austria that outstripped anything yet seen in the rest of Germany. Jewish property was seized; by the end of 1938 the homes of 40,000 Austrian Jews had been stolen. The more direct and radical actions of the Austrian Nazis were to serve as an example to their northern counterparts that they were only too eager to copy. In April 1938, Göring issued the Decree for the Registration of Jewish Property, which demanded that all Jewish property be valued and registered with the state.

- In an atmosphere of official sanction for action against the Jews, a number of state ministries and party agencies competed with each other to prepare directives and decrees that would identify and isolate the Jews. All attempted to 'work towards the Führer'. The June 1938 decree forbidding Jewish doctors from treating Aryan patients was the idea of the Reich Doctors' leader Gerhard Wagner, who had been pressing for the exclusion of Jews from the medical profession since the Nazis had come to power.

- The staff of the Deputy Führer, Rudolf Hess, claimed the credit for the passing of the legislation of July 1938 that was aimed at identifying and isolating Germany's Jews. As a result, from 1 January 1939 all Jews were to adopt the names of Israel (for men) and Sarah (for women), and a separate decree insisted that the passports of all Jews be stamped with the red letter 'J'.

- The most diligent of all Nazis in radicalising anti-Semitic action was the leader of the party's Security Service (SD), Reinhard Heydrich. From 1936, the ability of the security services and the SD to act outside the law with impunity was an important stimulus to the growing lawlessness of anti-Semitic behaviour. Heydrich's interest in the Jewish Question gave those staffing the SD's Jewish Section (Section II/112), such as the ambitious Adolf Eichmann, growing influence within the regime. Their work focused on the dual role of removing Jews from the economy while encouraging and facilitating emigration. After the *Anschluss* in 1938, it was Eichmann who created the 'Central Office for the Emigration of Austrian Jewry' to encourage Jewish emigration from Austria and, thereby, facilitate '*Entjudung*' (de-Judaisation) of the Austrian economy. It is clear that, in 1938, Hitler and the leading Nazis envisaged the solution to the Jewish Question as being in emigration, be it to Madagascar or Palestine (Hitler's and Eichmann's preferred solution in 1938). In July 1938 Hitler told Goebbels that 'the Jews must be removed from Germany in ten years'. However, moves to force the Jews out of Germany were still restricted by the necessities of diplomacy.

- By 1938 the influence of Joseph Goebbels had been compromised by Hitler's patronage of the filmmaker Leni Riefenstahl and the success of rival Nazi leaders in interpreting the Führer's will, not least Himmler and Göring. Added to that was his uncertain position in the eyes of the Führer following the disclosure of his affair with the Czech actress Lida Baarova. So Goebbels used his position as *Gauleiter* of Berlin to agitate against the Jews of Germany's capital city, thereby winning the Führer's approval. In May and June 1938, Jewish shops in Berlin were attacked with such ferocity that Hitler, fearful of an international backlash, ordered Goebbels to restrain the mob. However, there was no general order to restrain anti-Semitic violence, and the summer of 1938 saw attacks in a number of towns and cities, including Frankfurt. This momentum for radical action from below was to have the effect of provoking a radicalisation of official policy and the organisation of a countrywide **pogrom**.

The trigger for Kristallnacht was the shooting on 7 November 1938 of Ernst von Rath, an official in the German Embassy in Paris, by a young Polish Jew, Herschel Grynszpan. The young Pole had hoped to assassinate the German Ambassador as an act of protest against the recent expulsion of 18,000 Jews from Germany. Immediately the press seized upon the story and inflamed tensions with the suggestions of a nationwide Jewish conspiracy. In towns across Germany, such as Dessau, there were spontaneous outbursts of anti-Semitic violence.

Response

Von Rath's death gave Goebbels the opportunity to seize the radical agenda. In a speech on 9 November to party leaders, Goebbels gave the green light for the radicalisation of the persecution of the Jews. Those *Gauleiter* who hesitated, such as Adolf Wagner in Munich, were prompted by Goebbels to act. The violence against the Jews on Kristallnacht was widespread and extreme. Hundreds of Jews were murdered, 8,000 business premises and thousands of synagogues were destroyed, and over 30,000 Jews were arrested and taken to concentration camps such as Dachau. The SS and SA were involved in Kristallnacht at a local level although neither Himmler nor Heydrich were aware of the pogrom until after it had started. The destruction of property and damage to the economy were not considered by Goebbels, to the fury of Hermann Göring, who was not

> **Definition**
>
> **Pogrom**
>
> An organised violent attack on an ethnic minority.

consulted before the pogrom was initiated. In theory, Jewish affairs and economic life were, in 1938, the responsibility of Göring. The rounding up and internment of Jews in camps was the responsibility of the SS. But Hitler's support for Goebbels's initiative meant that both Göring and Himmler had to accept that radicalisation of Jewish policy had taken place without their being consulted. This fact is highly significant: it shows how important initiatives could emerge from anywhere within the regime – the critically important fact was that they needed to have the approval of the Führer.

Outcome

Despite the influence of Goebbels in provoking the pogrom, Göring was instructed by Hitler to coordinate the next stage of discrimination. Although Kristallnacht was not of Göring's making he was quick to seize the opportunity that it presented and recognised that it was a significant turning point in the radicalisation of anti-Jewish action. In the aftermath of the violence a meeting was called on 12 November by Göring at which further measures against the Jews were discussed. Other leading Nazis to attend the meeting included Heydrich and Goebbels. In the light of the meeting a number of decrees were issued that reflected the cynical nature of the regime. The Jewish community was forced to pay a huge 1,000 million mark fine (again, the idea of Goebbels) and the decree excluding Jews from German economic life attempted to fulfil the promise of its title. In his diary Goebbels commented in understated fashion: 'The radical view had triumphed.' By working towards the Führer, he had given the economic campaign against the Jews significant impetus.

On 24 January 1939 Göring set up the Reich Central Office for Jewish Emigration and placed Heydrich at its head. He also created the Reich Association for the Jews in Germany, which was to supervise the process of emigration, again with Heydrich in overall control. The longer-term impact of Kristallnacht was to alter the focus of Jewish affairs from removing Jews from the economic life of Germany to removing them altogether. That the SS had control of that process was to have a profound impact on later events.

Case study 4: Bouhler and Aktion T4

Origins

In early 1939 the father of a severely disabled child from near Leipzig petitioned the Führer to allow his son to be killed. The petition was taken to Hitler by Hans Hefelmann, an official responsible to Philipp Bouhler in the Führer's Chancellery.

Response

Hitler allowed the killing to go ahead and out of this was born a policy of child 'euthanasia' under the direction of Bouhler. An organisation was set up with the code name of Aktion T4 to be responsible for the coordination of killing mentally and physically handicapped children in Germany. In August 1939 the medical authorities were obliged to inform a Reich committee of any children with serious abnormalities.

Outcome

The Aktion T4 initiative had taken place outside the usual government agencies but had the all-important support of the Führer. The result was the death of up to 90,000 children, who were murdered by doctors in asylums such as Hartheim or Bernburg using either injections of luminal or carbon monoxide poisoning before lying about the cause of death. The 'Aktion T4' programme happened because of the work of ambitions officials aiming to achieve the Führer's blessing for a policy initiative that mirrored his world view.

It is in the radicalisation of racial policy between 1933 and 1939 that one best sees the concept of 'working towards the Führer' operating in practice. There was no blueprint, no plan for the development of racial policy but there were clearly defined points of ideology. Many agencies and individuals within the regime jostled to gain the Führer's approval by initiating more radical policy, understanding that Hitler's deep anti-Semitism lay at the heart of his world view. This was how and why state anti-Semitic policy radicalised as it did.

Unit summary

What have you learned in this unit?

You have learned that the idea that the Nazi state was monolithic is too simplistic and hides a more complex reality. But the intentionalists' arguments have a number of important elements in them, likewise the work of the structuralists. Recent work to synthesise these standpoints has produced an interesting analysis. The Nazi state that ruled Germany from 1933 to 1945 should be seen to consist of a number of mini-states that drew their political identity from one or more strands of National Socialist thought whether it be anti-Semitism, racial superiority, class struggle, nationalism, militarism or the creation of a People's Community (the *Volksgemeinschaft*). The relative power and significance of these mini-states depended on how successfully their leaders were able to gain access to, and favour from, Adolf Hitler, leader of the National Socialist movement and, from 1934, Führer of Germany.

What skills have you used in this unit?

You have used secondary evidence to enhance your understanding of the workings of the Nazi state. You have extracted information from the sources and you have summarised meaning. You have also compared sources and have explained how they work. As part of working with the evidence, you have been asked to express an opinion as to the accuracy of historical interpretation and the reliability of the author.

SKILLS BUILDER

1 Explain in less than 300 words the dynamic of radicalisation in anti-Semitic policy in Germany between 1933 and 1939.

2 Which of these case studies do you feel gives the best example of 'working towards the Führer'? Explain your answer fully.

Exam style question

This is the sort of question you will find appearing on the examination paper as a Section B question:

'The government of the Nazi state was chaotic and lacked coherence in the years 1933 to 1939.'

How far do you agree with this opinion? Explain your answer, using the evidence of Sources V, W and X and your own knowledge of the issues related to this controversy.

Source V

As orthodox historical opinion tells us, government was characterised by multi-centred incoherence, with a war of all against all, bordering on chaos. But the exceptional nature of Nazi governmental chaos can be pushed too far. Democratic governments are riven with factional intrigues and personal rivalries; suffer duplication of functions; rely on outsiders to galvanise sluggish bureaucracies; and are constrained by innumerable external factors . . . In other words, what has been increasingly elevated into the explanatory master-key of Nazi rule, namely the mutual radicalising effects of competing agencies, may be both insufficient, and less remarkable, as an explanation for the single-mindedness with which the Nazis went about achieving their ideological goals. If what is said to be uniquely characteristic of Nazism also typifies many other modern governments and organisations, then this alone can hardly explain a regime of rare destructiveness.

From Michael Burleigh, *The Third Reich: A New History*, published in 2000

Source W

The whole structure of the government has been aptly dubbed 'authoritarian anarchy'. The popular picture of the Third Reich as a monolithic unity with all parts of the well-oiled machinery responsive to the Führer's will has long been discredited by historians . . . The administrative structure of Nazi Germany formed a complex mosaic of party and state agencies with ill-defined and over-lapping jurisdictions, sometime complementing each other, more often mutually antagonistic, all striving to obtain a monopoly of power in their own domain. A practice which permitted men such as Himmler and Göring to build up immensely powerful bases by combining government and party office was not, if course, without attendant dangers. Quite illogically, Hitler supposed that the strong, once they had survived the struggle by battle, would serve him loyally.

From William Carr, *Hitler: A Study in Personality and Politics*, published in 1978

Source X

Historians are in no fundamental disagreement over the fact that the government of Nazi Germany was chaotic in its structure. It is of course easy to exaggerate the 'ordered' character of any modern governmental system. However, it seems that the fragmentation and lack of co-ordination in the internal administration of the Third Reich existed to such an extreme degree that the overlapping, conflicting, and sometimes outrightly contradictory spheres of authority can be aptly depicted as 'chaotic'.

From Ian Kershaw, *The Nazi Dictatorship*, published in 1985

You tackled a Section B question at the end of the last section. Look back at the exam tips you were given there. Now is the time to build on and develop those tips.

SKILLS BUILDER

1 On a chart, outline the strengths and weaknesses of the structuralist and intentionalist approaches.

2 Set up a debate titled 'The intentionalist rather than the structuralist approach better explains the operation of the Nazi state.' Remember to use arguments for and against each approach.

3 What is the significance of ideology in the Nazi state 1933 to 1939?

RESEARCH TOPIC

Anti-Semitism

In this unit you have been given some detail of the main turning points in the radicalisation of anti-Semitic policy 1933 to 1939. Research these issues/events in greater detail:

- The Nuremburg Laws

- Kristallnacht

- Jewish emigration from Germany.

9 What was life like in wartime Germany, 1939–45?

What is this unit about?

This unit explores life in wartime Germany. It gives an outline of the events of the war that form the backdrop to the analysis of morale, dissent and opposition in the war years. The unit moves on to look at the war economy and how it changed in response to military developments. It explains how efficient the Nazi war economy was and what its main failings were. There is then an explanation of how the 'Final Solution' to the 'Jewish Question' came about.

Key questions

- To what extent did the war have an impact on morale in Germany and how extensive was opposition to the regime?
- How efficient was the Nazi war economy?
- Why did the Nazis undertake the 'Final Solution' to the 'Jewish Question'?

Timeline

1939	November	Georg Elser attempts to assassinate Hitler
1940	May	France invaded
1941	April	Order to remove crucifixes from walls in Catholic Bavaria meets opposition
	May	Deputy Führer Rudolf Hess flies to Scotland
	June	Invasion of the Soviet Union, Operation Barbarossa, begins
	August	Bishop von Galen publically challenges the T4 programme
	December	Germany declares war on the USA
1942	January	The Wannsee Conference
1943	January	German Sixth Army surrenders at Stalingrad
	February	Goebbels's 'Total War' speech
	February	Executions of Hans and Sophie Scholl
	March	Operation Flash fails to kill Hitler
	July	Bombing of Hamburg creates firestorm
	May	Axis armies surrender in North Africa
1944	June	D-Day
	July	Bomb Plot fails to kill Hitler
1945	February	Dresden destroyed
	April	Dietrich Bonhöffer executed

Figure 9.1 is taken from the front cover of a book for children that had the title *Der Giftpilz* (*The Poisonous Mushroom*). The propaganda was produced by Julius Streicher and was sometimes used in schools. What is the message for children?

9.1 Front cover of *Der Giftpilz* (*The Poisonous Mushroom*)

The events of the war

The information in this section of the unit is given to provide you with a backdrop to the Home Front in Germany between 1939 and 1945.

The outbreak of war

In September 1939, Poland was invaded and quickly conquered by the German armed forces. The declaration of war had brought Germany into conflict with Britain and France. However, Hitler was to show little restraint. By the end of 1940, France, Belgium, Holland, Denmark, Norway and Luxembourg had been invaded and overwhelmed. Not only had the Treaty of Versailles been avenged but European domination had been achieved. Only Britain managed to hold out. This was partly due to the defeat of the Luftwaffe in the Battle of Britain of 1940, but it was also because Hitler turned his attention to his main goal, the destruction of the Soviet Union. Temporarily distracted by the need to support their flagging ally Italy in the Balkans, German forces invaded Russia on 22 June 1941.

Operation Barbarossa

Despite the signing of the Nazi-Soviet Pact in August 1939, Hitler had always intended to invade the Soviet Union. For Hitler, Russia was not only a strategic threat to his European Empire but the birthplace of Bolshevism and international Judaism. By invading Russia Hitler intended to:

- win *Lebensraum* for German settlers
- use the large reservoir of Slav labour
- exploit oil reserves in the Caucasus and the grain supply from the Ukraine.

Operation Barbarossa began with a force of 3 million troops. They were mainly German but some were from her allies, including Italy, Hungary and Romania. The attack took place along three fronts: the northern was to capture Leningrad; the centre to capture Moscow; and the southern to overrun the Ukraine and the Crimea and drive on to the Caucasus. Hitler hoped to repeat the spectacular triumphs of his *Blitzkrieg* against Poland in 1939 and against France in 1940. The Germans made rapid advances along all three fronts. By November 1941, Leningrad and Moscow were under siege and 3 million Soviets had been taken prisoner. However, the vast distances, the poor roads, the partisan activity and the '**scorched earth policy**' of the retreating armies delayed the German

Definition

Scorched earth policy

The destruction by a retreating army of everything that might be used by an advancing army, such as food and raw materials.

advance. By December heavy snow and freezing temperatures brought the Germans to a standstill 30 miles west of Moscow. Hitler had sent his troops into Russia totally unprepared for such extreme conditions. He had also underestimated the strength and resistance of the Red Army. Even more decisive was the ability of the Soviets to uproot 1,500 key factories in 1941–42, transport them and their workforce thousands of miles east of the Urals and reassemble them to become more productive than the German economy by late 1943. On 6 December 1941 the Russians counter-attacked under General Zhukov, an action that at least halted the German advance.

Stalingrad

In June 1942 the Germans launched a huge summer offensive to capture the Caucusus oilfield. Hitler also ordered the Sixth Army to capture the strategically important city of Stalingrad, which guarded the river Volga. The city was besieged from September, and bitter street fighting continued throughout the autumn. Stalin was determined to hold on to the city that bore his name, and General Zhukov organised heroic resistance of the city. On 19 November, the Red Army launched a counteroffensive that trapped the Sixth Army in a giant pincer movement. Although Hitler ordered the Sixth Army's commander General von Paulus to fight to the death, on 31 January 1943 he surrendered. The Red Army captured some 92,000 men including 24 generals. The defeat at Stalingrad was one of the most important turning points of the war. The Russians exploited their success with a crushing victory in an enormous tank battle at Kursk in July 1943. This victory paved the way for the Red Army's liberation of Eastern Europe and entry into Germany.

North Africa

German troops led by General Erwin Rommel invaded North Africa in February 1941 in support of their defeated Italian allies. After a series of impressive victories, Rommel's Afrika Korps drove towards Egypt in May 1941, besieging the important town of Tobruk. The British led by General Auchinleck counter-attacked in November and forced Rommel back to El Agheila. As British forces were weakened by the need to reinforce the Far East campaign against Japan, Rommel was able to capture Tobruk and 30,000 prisoners on 21 June. However, the German advance was halted in October 1942 when the British Eighth Army led by General Montgomery inflicted a heavy defeat on Rommel at El Alamein. In November 1942 an Anglo-American force led by General Eisenhower landed behind Rommel in Morocco in Operation Torch. In May 1943, the remains of the **Axis** forces in North Africa surrendered.

Italy

Allied troops invaded Sicily in July 1943 and crossed to mainland Italy in September. In the same month the deposed Italian dictator Benito

Mussolini was rescued by German troops led by Captain Skorzeny and was taken to Berlin. As the new Italian government surrendered to the Allies, German troops led by Field Marshall Kesselring seized many important Italian cites and strategic points. The Allied advance was slow and was held up at Salerno, Anzio and Monte Cassino. Rome was captured by the Allies as late as June 1944, and German troops fought on in Italy until May 1945.

Defeat on the Western Front

British and American troops invaded France on 6 June in 'Operation Overlord'. Led by Generals Eisenhower and Montgomery, some 326,000 troops were landed along the five Normandy beaches. The Americans on Omaha beach encountered severe German resistance, but Hitler was slow to reinforce the Normandy sector. They captured Cherbourg and also broke out to the South East and cut off 50,000 crack German troops in the 'Falaise Pocket'. British troops suffered heavy casualties as they advanced through the difficult **bocage** countryside of Normandy. Outnumbered, the German troops fell back. Paris was liberated on 24 August, and Brussels and Antwerp in the first week of September. The Allied advance then slowed as supplies were exhausted and German troops rallied to defend German soil. In an attempt to accelerate Allied progress, General Montgomery launched the doomed 'Operation Market Garden' at Arnhem. Hitler hoped to repeat the victory of 1940 by launching an attack through the Ardennes Forest on 16 December 1944. In the 'Battle of the Bulge', the German advance was halted and the Allied advance resumed. American troops crossed the Rhine on 22 March 1945, and 320,000 German troops surrendered in the Ruhr in early April. On 25 April, American and Soviet troops met at Torgau on the River Elbe.

War in the east

Following the victory at the great tank battle at Kursk, Soviet forces drove the Germans back to the river Dnieper and cut off the units in the Crimea. In the north the Siege of Leningrad was finally broken in January 1944, and western Russia was liberated by July. By the end of 1944 the whole of Russia had been liberated and Germany's allies Romania and Bulgaria had surrendered. In 1945 the Red Army drove into Germany to be met with fierce resistance. Led by Zhukov, Soviet forces crossed the River Oder in March and began the final assault on Berlin. The Battle of Berlin was the greatest in the war and cost the Russians 300,000 men as they encircled Hitler's capital. On 25 April Russian and Allied forces met at Torgau, and on 30 April, as the Red Army closed in on his underground headquarters beneath the ruined Reich Chancellery, Hitler and his wife Eva Braun committed suicide. Although some units in Bavaria and the Tyrol continued fighting, Admiral Dönitz, the new Head of the Reich, surrendered to the Allies on 8 May.

Definition

Bocage

An area of pasture and woodland. It is typified by small fields, narrow side-roads and lanes with high banks and thick hedgerows either side.

Discussion point

With a work partner, choose what you think are the most significant turning points of the war that would:

- damage morale on the Home Front
- increase the possibility of opposition to the regime from some army officers
- give an impetus to greater war production.

You might find that some of your chosen turning points appear in all three categories. Do not worry about that – it will simply prove that the turning points that you have chosen are especially important.

Morale on the Home Front

The continuing importance of the consumer

As was pointed out in Unit 7, very few Germans wanted war. But there was a considerable bedrock of support for the regime in 1939, and this was to continue nearly to the end of the war. One reason for this continuing support was that the regime was highly sensitive to the issues of rationing and shortages on the Home Front. Before and during the war the Nazi leadership intended to avoid a repetition of the scarcities in basic foodstuffs and clothing that caused such widespread unrest during the 1914–18 war. Despite rationing, therefore, considerable sacrifices were not made by the consumer until 1942. The rationing system introduced in late 1939 was generally fair and sufficient, although the quality of the products declined. This was less a product of a shift in resources, however, than the cutting of vitally important imports. For a predominantly meat eating nation, the ration of 500 grammes a week was perceived as difficult but as the *Wehrmacht* conquered vast tracts of Europe, so there was an improvement in the supply of general foodstuffs as a whole. This was especially the case after the defeat of France in the summer of 1940. The most serious reduction in rations was in April 1942 when the meat ration was cut to 300 grammes per person. This caused considerable disquiet and the meat ration was increased by 50 grammes in October 1942.

There was greater flexibility in rationing in Germany than in Britain, with extra rations for those undertaking strenuous occupations. There were also Christmas bonuses, such as that in 1942 when every citizen received extra rations, including 200 grammes of meat. These were propaganda stunts that masked difficulties, but the ability of the regime to undertake such stunts demonstrates the importance the regime placed on maintaining adequate supplies. While clothing became scarce, particularly during 1941, this can in part be put down to the panic buying in the early months of the war, which reduced stocks considerably. That there were shortages thereafter was partly due to supply problems but also to inefficiency in distribution, the economy suffering a lack of the rationalisation that became such a feature later on (see pages 210–211). By 1942 there were shortages of soap; permits were introduced for furniture on 1 August 1942; and household goods were rationed from 20 January 1943. The German population faced difficulties and shortages, but at least until the very end of the war, they did not face the hardship or the levels of inflation seen in the 1914–18 war.

Early victories

During the war Germans fought patriotically for their fatherland and, of course, celebrated spectacular early victories in 1939. After the victory in Poland most hoped for peace and blamed the British for the continuation of the war because they had not come to the negotiating table. On 8 November 1939 Georg Elser, a carpenter, attempted to assassinate Hitler by exploding a bomb when the Führer was making a speech commemorating the Munich Putsch. The bomb exploded but not when Hitler was in the hall. Public opinion was relief, and the British were blamed for the bomb. The elation at the victory over France in June 1940 was replaced with frustration at Britain's refusal to submit. Morale was further damaged with the news in May 1941 that the Deputy Führer Rudolf Hess had flown to Scotland.

Greater concerns

The war against the Soviet Union launched in June 1941 provoked concern, especially when Goebbels appealed to the nation on 19 December 1941 for winter clothing for the troops. The failure to win outright victory in the east led many to question Nazi ideology for the first time. Even when German fortunes appeared bleak after Stalingrad, propaganda was still able to exploit patriotic defiance. Goebbels's 'Total War' speech in February 1943 rallied many but not all Germans to fight a war to the end. As German forces were defeated in North Africa, the Soviet Union, the Atlantic and Italy so there was greater contempt expressed for the leadership of the Nazi movement. Hitler's increasing isolation in his bunker in Berlin or at his headquarters in Rastenburg in eastern Prussia meant that the Führer was prone to greater criticism and jokes. The following one-liners were reported to the party chancellery in March and April 1943:

- What's the difference between the sun and Hitler? The sun rises in the east, Hitler goes down in the east.

- One can now get the book of the Germans, *Mein Kampf*, on points on the *Spinnstoffkarte* (literally means clothing ration card, but in slang it also meant the 'talking rubbish card').

- What is the difference between India and Germany? In India one person [Gandhi] starves for everyone, in Germany everyone starves for one person.

Of course, the reports did not necessarily mention the attitude of the silent and loyal majority, but the defeat at Stalingrad clearly marked a turning point in morale.

Bombing

The bombing campaign undertaken by the Royal Air Force (RAF) and United States Air Force (USAF) was partly aimed at destroying the German war industry but also at undermining morale on the Home Front. It is difficult to assess how successful it was in achieving the latter. Certainly it caused widespread death and destruction: 305,000 Germans were killed by Allied bombing, 780,000 were injured, and nearly 2 million homes were destroyed. Firestorms caused by the bombing of Hamburg in the summer of 1943 and Dresden in February 1945 killed at least 80,000 civilians between them. The state attempted to provide bomb victims with alternative accommodation and some financial compensation. But while a

1 What factors determined the state of morale of the German people on the Home Front during the Second World War?

2 Why, despite the jokes and the grumbling, did morale on the Home Front hold up for so long during the war?

'Blitz' spirit was sustained among many, by 1943 the population in areas such as the Rhineland, which was systematically bombed, had become demoralised. The sense of impending doom was made worse by knowledge of the advance of the Soviet armies. Goebbels more than any other Nazi leader continued to offer hope, either in the form of promises of a secret weapon that would turn the tide of war or in calls for *Ausharren* (perseverance), which generated a spirit of heroic resistance. Once it was clear that the Allies were not going to be thrown back into the sea and that weapons such as the V1 and V2 bombs launched at London and the south-east of England were not going to have the required impact, morale sank to a low ebb. Goebbels attempted to raise morale by commissioning blockbuster escapist films such as *The Adventures of Baron Munchausen* (1943) and epic tales of resistance such as *Kolberg* (1945), but they had minimal impact on the popular mood. As the reality of certain defeat dawned, so Nazi propaganda became ever less effective. That said, neither the bombing nor even the invasion of Germany caused a collapse of the Home Front in Germany.

Opposition

Church opposition

Crucifix crisis

Despite a decline in morale, especially from 1943 onwards, there were few signs of outward resistance. There were occasions when 'loyal reluctance' was pushed to the limit. Such an occasion involved the Bavarian Catholics. In April 1941, the *Gauleiter* of Munich and Upper Bavaria, Adolf Wagner, demanded that all crucifixes in Bavarian schools be removed. To committed Nazis such as Wagner, the presence of such crucifixes was a visible sign of the continuing strength of the Catholic Church in the region. Wagner's order met with a storm of protest. Meetings, letters, petitions and even demonstrations from angry Bavarians demanding that the crucifixes be restored forced Wagner to overturn his original order. Even though this incident was one of the few in which there was clearly expressed opposition to the regime, it is still clear that most Bavarians were not expressing a dislike of the regime. They were mostly defending their distinct regional culture, without challenging the authority of the Führer.

Bishop von Galen

The challenge made by Bishop von Galen in August 1941 to the Nazi policy of killing asylum patients as part of the T4 programme was perhaps one of the most courageous acts of the war. Galen, like many other Catholic leaders, had welcomed the 'crusade' against godless Bolshevism launched in June 1941. However, the closure of local monasteries moved Galen to attack the policy of 'so-called' euthanasia from the pulpit. Acting pragmatically, Hitler called off the campaign to close religious institutions and ended the T4 programme. Despite the attacks on its clergy and property, any opposition from the Catholic and Protestant churches towards the regime was motivated more by an attempt to maintain independence and integrity within the system than by a philosophical objection to Nazism. Dissent was individual, not institutional. Many individual priests such as Dietrich Bonhöffer went against the official policy of their churches and resisted or opposed the regime. Bonhöffer was arrested in 1943 and was executed in April 1945. The official policy of the churches as institutions remained one of pragmatic cooperation even to the extent of Cardinal Faulhaber's condemnation of the Bomb Plot in 1944. Even though the Catholic Church knew of the systematic extermination of the Jews as early as 1942, it failed to condemn it in public.

The left

Any communist opposition to the regime was completely undermined by the Nazi-Soviet Pact, which lasted from August 1939 to June 1941. Thereafter, rather than as a single united movement, opposition came from individuals and underground groups. The KPD (communists) and SPD (socialists) formed small groups, published reports and maintained contact with exiled leaders. Arvid Harnack from the Reich Economic Ministry and Harro Schulze-Boysen from the Air Ministry formed Rote Kapelle (Red Orchestra). Most important for the communists were the resistance cells set up in factories and coordinated by Robert Uhrig.

- In the summer of 1941 there were 89 factory cells of opposition in Berlin alone. There were communist resistance cells in other German cities including Hamburg and Mannheim.

- They produced papers and pamphlets attacking the regime and calling for acts of resistance. In 1942, the communist resistance united under the leadership of Wilhelm Knöchel.

The main weakness of the communist resistance was that it was vulnerable to Gestapo infiltration. In 1943 the communist resistance movement was devastated and Knöchel was arrested. Others carried out individual acts of defiance. Herbert Baum led a Jewish communist group that fire-bombed an anti-Russian exhibition in Berlin in 1942. Disillusioned by the inactivity of their leadership, the socialists began to form splinter groups, including 'Red Patrol', 'Socialist Front' and 'New Beginning', that championed a more assertive policy and worked for cooperation with other opposition groups.

Youth

Disillusionment set in by 1939 and accelerated as Germany's fortunes in war turned by 1942. Some young people had already become alienated by the regimentation of youth groups, and this mood increased as the focus on military training intensified. The absence or loss of a father encouraged delinquency, drinking, smoking and promiscuity among young people. A minority of young people, repelled by the brutality of the dictatorship, actively opposed the regime. Various youth groups attempted to resist the

Discussion point

In groups discuss the following question:

Should the Protestant and Catholic Churches have done more as institutions between 1933 and 1945 to oppose the Nazi regime?

You may need to re-visit material from pages 160 to 161 to be able to debate this point.

regime. Disaffected working class youths formed groups such as the Edelweiss Pirates who attacked members of the Hitler Youth. Hans and Sophie Scholl led Munich students in the White Rose group, which distributed anti-Nazi leaflets and sought to sabotage the German war effort. In 1943 the Scholls led an anti-Nazi demonstration in Munich. As a result they were arrested by the Gestapo, tried and executed in February 1943.

Conservative opposition

The early victories during the war limited the scope of action for opposition to the regime. From 1941, Carl Goerdeler had created links with the dissident General Beck and created a loose group that drew in a range of conservative and military opponents to the regime. Prominent in the group were officials in the Foreign Office such as Ulrich von Hassell and Adam von Trott. Von Hassell was a particularly senior diplomat who was disgusted by the discrimination and then systematic violence used against the Jews. Seeing the writing on the wall for Germany by early 1943, the group attempted to build diplomatic links with the Allies. Many were drawn to this circle out of conscience, and it is on this basis that most opposition to the Nazis was formed. Another significant centre of conservative opposition to the regime was the Kreisau Circle. Starting in earnest in 1941, it drew in those critical of the regime from a range of intellectual traditions and backgrounds. The leading lights of the Kreisau Circle were Helmuth Graf von Moltke and Peter Yorck von Wartenburg. Their aim was to discuss the political and social landscape after the Nazi regime had fallen. The significance of the Kreisau Circle was that it contained a range of members, from the socialist Theo Haubach to the Jesuit Augustin Rösch. The group set up contacts with other conservative and religious groups although relations with the Goerdeler circle were strained (which was as much the result of a generation gap between them). Although there were differences in the aims and aspirations of the Kreisau Circle and Goerdeler group, there was also common ground:

- All wished to see the restoration of human rights and freedoms denied by the Nazis. They wanted an end to the war and the restoration of the rule of law.

- The members of the Kreisau Circle wished to see a democratic Germany, based on the foundations of self-governing local communities and the *Länder*.

- Some conservative opponents of the regime did not share this view; many in the Goerdeler group rejected the idea of democracy in favour of an aristocratically governed society. The consent given to the Nazi regime in plebiscites led some to reject the rule of the masses.

- The conservatives looked for political consensus after the war, with a mixed economy of private and state ownership to ensure economic growth and social harmony, although Goerdeler wanted to see an end of state involvement in economic affairs.

- While Moltke wanted to see the emergence of a federal European Union, Goerdeler was more in favour of Germany retaining a role as an independent European power.

The Kreisau Circle was discovered by the Gestapo in 1944, and Moltke was arrested. However, both the Kreisau Circle and Goerdeler's group continued to meet throughout the year and were closely involved in Stauffenberg's plot to kill the Führer. As a result in the aftermath of the plot many were arrested, tortured and executed. Although the numbers of conservatives who opposed the regime was not great, there were individuals of great courage and conviction who were prepared to challenge the amorality of the regime.

Army

By 1939 the army had become a subordinate, ↗ respectful if not fully integrated, part of the Nazi regime. The oath of allegiance continued to enforce an unquestioning loyalty to Hitler. Most of the generals were ideologically committed to the regime, and the early years of the war galvanised allegiance as it did all sections of society. The stunning victories won by *Blitzkrieg* in Poland in 1939 and in western Europe in 1940 undermined the doubters and confirmed Hitler as a military genius. It was not until 1943 that a serious nationwide opposition movement led by dissident generals emerged. For a few this was the result of a long-term opposition to a regime they had despised on moral grounds from the outset. For the majority of dissident generals, opposition was more pragmatic:

- The increasing political interference of the SS had now become intolerable.
- Some generals from the Eastern Front were shocked by atrocities committed against partisans and Jews and by their realisation of the implementation of systematic extermination.
- For most generals, however, opposition was triggered by the growing belief that Germany was losing the war. US entry into the war in December 1941, the failure to defeat Russia, Montgomery's victory at El Alamein in 1942, and, most importantly, Germany's catastrophic defeat at Stalingrad in December 1942–January 1943 made it evident that the war had turned decisively against Germany.

In March 1943, the attempt to kill Hitler in Operation Flash failed because the bomb placed on the Führer's plane by Major General Henning von Tresckow failed to explode. In the autumn of 1943, those conspirators in the *Abwehr* (military intelligence), were arrested by the Gestapo.

The Bomb Plot 1944

Aims

The oath of allegiance and the 1918 myth of the 'stab in the back' deterred many would-be plotters from joining any conspiracy until Hitler was

SKILLS BUILDER

1 How serious a threat to the regime was posed by the conservative, youth, socialist and communist opposition groups?

2 What was the extent of their opposition?

assassinated. The deadlock was broken by the emergence of Count von Stauffenburg as a leading plotter in 1944. Linked to the Kreisau Circle and determined to achieve 'internal purification', Stauffenburg offered to assassinate Hitler by a bomb with a preset timing device. The Allied invasions in Normandy in June 1944 gave a greater sense of urgency to the conspiracy. Many generals wished to make a peace before Germany herself was invaded so that the myth of invincibility could, as in 1918, be preserved. Others, such as von Tresckow, advocated the plot because they wanted to demonstrate to posterity that not all Germans had been corrupted by Nazism. The plan to assassinate Hitler was code-named Operation Valkyrie. Its aim was to trigger a rising throughout the Reich and the occupied lands ousting the Nazi regime and replacing it by a new order with Beck as President and Carl Goerdeler as Chancellor. The new government would then make a peace with the Western Allies and end the war before the Russians invaded eastern Germany.

As Chief of Staff to General Fromm, Stauffenburg had access to the Führer's headquarters at Rastenburg. On 20 July 1944, he left his bomb in a briefcase by Hitler in a briefing room. Leaving the meeting to take a telephone call, he then left the **Wolf's Lair** to fly to Berlin. Hitler, though shaken, survived the bomb blast for three reasons:

- The briefcase was moved three places away from Hitler so he was no longer caught in the full blast.

- As the bomb exploded Hitler was leaning over a map on a heavy oak table that deflected much of the explosion.

- As the day was so hot the briefing took place in a wooden building, which allowed the full force of the explosion to dissipate.

In Berlin, the conspiracy was paralysed by indecision. Goebbels's broadcast that Hitler had survived undermined Stauffenburg's desperate efforts to ignite the conspiracy. By late afternoon loyalist troops led by Colonel Remer had surrounded the army headquarters in Berlin. Stauffenburg's superior, General Fromm, who had committed himself to the plot, now switched sides and arrested Stauffenburg and his fellow conspirators. In an attempt to conceal his own treachery, Fromm ordered the four to be shot in the courtyard of the Bendlerblock. General Beck, who had been unable to commit suicide, was executed in his own office.

Outcome

Hitler's revenge was severe. Hundreds of suspected conspirators were arrested, tortured and sentenced to death. Some, such as Rommel and von Tresckow, escaped by suicide. Many were executed by garrotting at Plötzensee prison in north Berlin.

- The army was now emasculated. The Hitler salute became compulsory in all ranks. Political officers were appointed to root out dissent, and Himmler became commander-in-chief of the Home Army.

Definition

Wolf's Lair

Hitler's military headquarters near what was Rastenburg in East Prussia. He spent a considerable amount of time there between June 1941 and November 1944.

- But only 22 out of 2,000 generals were executed for their parts in the conspiracy. Army resistance was therefore heroic but belated. It was confined to a few individuals. Its leadership was too naive and isolated to pose a sustained threat to the regime.

- The Bomb Plot partly restored a little dignity and self-respect to the army, but its futility and its belatedness did not succeed in rehabilitating the tarnished image of the army as an institution. Total defeat in 1945 finally shattered the myths of military invincibility and the 'stab in the back'.

The German war economy

War production

The outbreak of war in September 1939 saw the responsibility for the planning of the German war economy shared among competing agencies.

- At the Ministry of War, General Thomas led the economics section in charge of the armaments programme.

- Yet such was the overlap in the Nazi state that he had rivals for administrative supremacy of the war economy, chiefly the Ministry of Economics led by Walter Funk and the office of the Four Year Plan led by Hermann Göring.

- In March 1940, however, a Ministry of Munitions was created under Fritz Todt, and this went some way to ending the confusion in this area of production.

Early problems

Even though the first three years of war were, on the whole, successful, they created strains in the German economy. The main problem was that, until 1942, the German economy was not fully mobilised for war. Instead, it fought a series of quick wars, *Blitzkrieg* wars that did not place such great demands on economic production. Indeed, in the arms industry, output per head fell from 1939–40 by 12.5 per cent mainly because of the effects of conscription and the concentration on consumer industries, which in the same period saw output increase by nearly 16 per cent. However, Operation Barbarossa changed all of that. Military expenditure rose from 17.2 billion Reichsmarks in 1939 to 55.9 billion Reichsmarks in 1942. The demands of war resulted in a shift of labour, investment and priorities towards munitions; for example, the numbers working in aircraft manufacturing doubled between 1939 and 1941 but a shortage of labour became apparent even in the early days of the war.

- By May 1940 there were 3.5 million fewer workers in the workforce than one year before. This shortfall was partly made up by the use of French prisoners of war (some 800,000 by October 1940) and other nationals (mainly Poles), which made a total of around 2 million foreign workers in Germany by the end of the year. This was not enough to meet the

Discussion point

In groups discuss the following question:

To what extent was army opposition to the Nazi regime dictated by the course of the war?

After some discussion, get a member of your group to write some points down to give feedback to the rest of the class. Your points might stimulate some debate.

Biography

Fritz Sauckel

A party member from 1923, *Gauleiter* of Thüringia and a NSDAP member of the Reichstag, Sauckel was a committed Nazi. He was an important figure in the German war effort from 1942. As Plenipotentiary General of Labour Allocation until the end of the war, he directed the importing of foreign labour. He was executed by the Allies after the end of the war.

Albert Speer's rise to power and influence show how much power depended on access to the Führer and the ability to realise his vision. Speer was able to realise Hitler's vision most effectively in his role as Hitler's architect. Hitler had grandiose visions for the rebuilding of Germany's cities and Speer was able to turn these visions into plans. In January 1937, Hitler put Speer in charge of the re-building of Berlin and, from that moment on, his influence grew rapidly. From 1942 he had a central role in directing the war effort as Minister for Armaments and War Production. He managed to persuade Allied prosecutors at the Nuremburg Trials that he should not be executed, and he died in 1981.

growing demand, with 1.7 million workers drafted into the armed forces in 1941 and a further 1.4 million called up between May 1941 and May 1942.

- Such a shortage produced urgent measures. In February 1941, General Thomas had called for the use of more rational measures of production to increase efficiency. Yet even this would not be enough. Following on from a decree in the Netherlands in February 1942, the so-called Plenipotentiary General for Labour Allocation, Fritz Sauckel, issued a compulsory labour decree for all occupied countries in August of the same year. In September, the Vichy government in France established compulsory labour for men and women between the ages of 18 and 65. Such measures brought in around 2.5 million new workers, and by the end of 1942 there were some 6.4 million foreign workers in Germany toiling for the Reich.

Speer and total war

On 3 December 1941, Hitler issued the Führer Order on the 'Simplification and Increased Efficiency in Armaments Production', which demanded that Todt should rationalise the armaments industry. Thereafter there was a significant change in priorities. Industry accepted responsibility for raising levels of production, with central direction coming from Todt's ministry. In February 1942, Albert Speer was appointed Todt's successor in the post of Minister for Weapons and Munitions. Speer developed Todt's plans for the rationalisation of industry and the more efficient control of raw material distribution. Against the background of a more protracted struggle on the Eastern Front, a campaign of total war was launched by the regime. It was initiated in a speech by Goebbels at the Berlin Sportsplatz in February 1943 in which he called for universal labour service and the closure of all non-essential businesses. Such moves to improve production and productivity were reinforced by the appointment of Speer as Reich Minister for Armaments and Production in September 1943. This post gave Speer responsibility for all industrial output and raw materials.

Rationalisation

Almost immediately, Speer attempted to reorganise and rationalise these sectors of the economy. Many firms were still not working double shifts and production was dispersed. Speer's aim was to introduce labour, time and space saving measures thereby boosting production. As part of this rationalisation process, the Armaments Commission was set up in 1943 to standardise production, thereby allowing greater mass production. The results were impressive.

- The promotion of better use of floor space led to production of the Me109 plane at Messerschmitt increasing from 180 per month from seven factories to 1,000 per month from three factories.

- In 1944 the numbers of tank models were reduced from 18 to 7 and the types of different vehicles from 55 to 14. The result was greater productivity.

- Central control of raw materials, the reduction of handworking practices and more realistic contracts saw a rise in output per head in armaments so by 1943 the figure was 32 per cent higher than that in 1939. It must also be remembered that this was in the period when the workforce was in itself becoming less productive.

- Better processes cut the amount of precious raw materials used, e.g. each gun saw a reduction of 93 per cent in the aluminium used after rationalisation had taken place.

- The last years of the war saw a significant improvement in industrial production, despite Allied bombing. For example, the production of the BMW engine for planes increased by 200 per cent between 1941 and 1943 with an increase of only 12 per cent in the workforce.

- Production lines were introduced, with immediate effect. For example, in the manufacturing of the Panzer III tank in 1943 they cut the time required to assemble each tank by 50 per cent.

- In the manufacture of munitions, output per worker rose by 60 per cent from 1939 to 1944 despite the disruption caused by Allied bombing. Although the numbers in the industrial workforce increased by only 11 per cent between 1941 and 1943, the production of all weapons grew by 130 per cent in the same period.

Such growth was an important feature in an economy so hamstrung by labour and raw material problems. Changes in work methods, increased mechanisation, better distribution of materials, a more equitable wage structure for German workers and the introduction of mass production techniques resulted in significant increases in productivity. This was supported by a leap in military expenditure.

Continuing chaos

Despite the impressive improvement in the efficiency of the war economy under Speer's guidance, economic performance during the war was not coherently organised. The Nazi state was too chaotic, with too many competing agencies/power blocs for any consistent policy to be formulated. Often when clear direction was given from the centre, it countered economic logic. But much of Nazism as an ideology was both irrational and illogical, the 'Final Solution' being the clearest case in point, as you will soon read. Until the ideology was undermined by military failure, however, its aims were supported at least implicitly by large sections of the financial and industrial world.

- The looting of conquered countries was undertaken in a systematic way by sections of German business such as the chemicals giant IG Farben, which used its influence with Nazi officialdom to create a position as the largest chemical producer in Europe by 1942. (The profits of IG Farben had more than doubled from 1936 to a figure of 300 million Reichsmarks by 1940.)

- Other companies, such as the state-run Reichswerke, acquired ownership of large sections of conquered enterprises, in Reichswerke's case, in steel, mining and related industry. After the *Anschluss* with Austria and the takeover of Czechoslovakia in 1938, Reichswerke took over large sections of those countries' enterprises under Göring's instructions. This included companies such as Skoda and Steyr-Daimler-Puch. All acquisition of businesses in occupied lands was regulated by the state, which limited private involvement because of the desire to avoid direct competition with the state.

Following the Bomb Plot, Goebbels was appointed to the post of Reich Plenipotentiary for Total War. This gave him even greater control over production and allowed his ally Speer more scope for change. From January 1945 the German economy was in a state of collapse, partly as a consequence of invasion but also because of exhaustion and the effects of the Allied bombing programme. As it was apparent that defeat was inevitable, Hitler ordered the evacuation of all in the path of the advancing armies and a 'scorched earth' policy. However, this order was ignored by Speer who refused to destroy German industry in the west, understanding that it would be essential for German recovery after the end of the war.

Table 9.1 German military expenditure

Year	Million marks	Percentage of net domestic product
1938	22,000	25.3
1939	37,340	38.1
1940	66,445	60.4
1941	86,500	72.1
1942	110,400	88.3
1943	132,800	98.4
1944	149,800	115.2

Source: V. Berghagen, *Modern Germany, Society, Economy and Politics in the Twentieth Century*, 2nd edition, published in 1987.

Use of foreign workers

The improved figures in production are even more impressive when one considers that the German economy increasingly relied on foreign workers whose productivity was 60–80 per cent lower than that of the German worker, not surprising, given the appalling way most of the foreign workers were treated. Workers from the east, in particular, were treated with a contempt that acted to lower their productivity. From 1940 Polish workers suffered numerous restrictions, including being forced to wear a yellow badge marked with a P and not being able to use public transport. The use of foreign labour became of even greater importance once all able bodied German men were called to the front. From 1943 to the end of the war, 2.5 million extra foreign workers were employed.

- In an attempt to increase production, however, Fritz Sauckel, Plenipotentiary General for Labour Allocation, attempted to improve the situation of all workers with regard to pay and overtime. In March 1944, all eastern workers were given the same pay and benefits as other foreign labourers.

- But attempts to improve conditions were far too little, and too late. Thousands died on projects such as the V2 rocket production at Peenemünde in the Harz Mountains for want of basic food, shelter and sanitary provision.

As a result of such poor treatment, the recruitment of millions of forced labourers failed to solve Germany's foreign labour problems.

Raw materials

Iron ore

The factor that, more than any other, shaped Nazi war aims and plans was Germany's lack of the natural resources, iron, coal, oil and the other materials, that it needed for a sustained war effort. Perhaps above all else it lacked reserves of high-quality iron ore. The attempt to compensate for this led to the attempts at the huge Reichswerke Hermann Göring to develop the production of low grade ore for manufacturing purposes. Yet this could never meet the demands of the expanding military needs, thereby making Germany in part dependent on imports, in particular from Sweden.

- During the war the amount of ore imported from neutral Sweden remained constant: in 1940 it was 5.4 million tons and in 1943 it was 5.6 million tons.

- However, the annexations of Austria, Bohemia, Poland and Alsace-Lorraine by 1940 brought with them huge quantities of high-quality iron ore.

- In 1943 these areas alone produced 6.7 million tons for the Nazi war effort.

Overall, the supplies of iron ore to the German war economy increased from 13.4 million to 20.2 million tons between 1940 and 1943. Other areas of conquered Europe yielded raw materials that were vital for the war effort too: manganese ore from the Soviet Union, nickel from Norway and bauxite from France, for example.

Other raw materials

The important point to note is this: Germany needed to annex or have control over the natural resources of other nations in order to fight a major war. That this policy failed was due to the failure of the military *Blitzkreig* from 1942. The invasion of the Soviet Union had ideological causes, the destruction of Bolshevism being a central theme of *Mein Kampf*. Yet there were very strong economic considerations, not least the desire to control the oil fields in the Caucusus.

- German access to oil supplies was limited, the main supplier being Romania, which exported nearly 3 million tons to its ally in 1943. However, this was not enough to supply an economy and armed forces that from 1942 were engaged in total war. Even conquest did not ensure increased supply of needed materials.

- Despite the increase in ore and the acquisition of the steel industries of the Low Countries and France, there was a chronic shortage of steel throughout the war and particularly before 1942. In 1941 it was calculated that demand for steel exceeded supply by 30 per cent.

- This was mostly due to a shortage of coal despite Germany's large natural reserves and the acquisition of large mining reserves in the Soviet Union and Belgium. As with other industries, however, the Soviets had destroyed virtually all they had to leave behind. The extent of this destruction is clear when one considers that in 1942, the Donets Basin, which was rich in coal, only produced one-twentieth of its pre-war output. The production of German coal remained static throughout the war, output of hard coal increasing by 1.5 million tons or around 1 per cent. This was a factor that was crucial in limiting the growth of steel production. Coal from other areas such as Belgium was used to fuel indigenous industry.

The failure of the Nazis to fully exploit the raw materials of the countries they occupied was crucial in preventing the expansion of the German economy necessary to fight a major war.

SKILLS BUILDER

On a spider chart, outline the problems Germany had with the supply of raw materials during the war.

Female labour

Despite the labour shortage in Germany, between 1939 and 1944 only 200,000 extra women entered the workforce. In 1939 the number of women in employment was 14.6 million, a figure that actually declined to 14.2 million in 1941 and peaked at 14.9 million in 1944. The refusal of Hitler to allow conscription of women was ideologically based, the Nazi view of the role of women revolving around '*Kinder, Küche, Kirche*' (children, kitchen, church). Even with the move towards 'total war', the registration of women to work in January 1943 had little effect – in all, only some 400,000 women were recruited for work. Despite the shortfall of 4 million workers in the economy by 1944, there were still over 1,360,000 women in domestic service. Attempts by Speer to rectify this glaring anomaly in September of that year had little effect due to the number of exemptions allowed and the fact that Hitler still refused to countenance full-scale mobilisation. Yet there were other factors which prevented a greater proportion of women entering war work.

- As women had been very much encouraged to marry and raise families, so the numbers of women in such a situation had risen dramatically, nearly 1 million more children being born in Germany in 1939 than six years previously. Similarly, a far higher proportion of women were married by the eve of the war for the 25–30-year-old age group, the difference between 1933 and 1939 was 9.2 per cent. The benefits paid

to wives of soldiers were a great disincentive to work and meant that
wives could resist the temptation to supplement their husband's pay. All
of this made the conscription of women harder and further complicated
the labour crisis.

- The proportion of women in the workforce at the start of the war was
relatively high despite Nazi ideology. Of those between the ages of
15 and 60, 52 per cent of women were working and an astonishingly
high 88.7 per cent of single women were in employment. This meant
that there was not the slack in the employment market that was found
elsewhere, especially as Germany had been approaching full
employment as a consequence of the rearmament programme started
in the mid-1930s.

- The nature of women's employment also made it harder to redistribute
women into essential war industry. Large numbers of women worked in
agriculture – in 1939 they comprised 36.6 per cent of the workforce and
their importance grew with the conscription of men into the army. By
1944, 65.5 per cent of the agricultural workforce were women (this figure
applies to native-born Germans). Similarly, a high proportion of women
were employed in textiles in 1939 (58.2 per cent), and these women
could not be spared for other areas of war work such as munitions
because of the demands on the industry and the effects of male
conscription.

So Nazi ideology was not the sole reason why women were not fully
mobilised into essential war work from 1939. The fact was that the
proportion of women already in the workforce was significantly high.

War economy: conclusion

The German economy did not expand sufficiently to meet the demands
of 'total war'. This was due to many factors, primary among which were
the shortage of raw materials and the shortage of labour. The key to
economic failure was the fact that conquest did not make up the shortfall
in these two essential components of any economy. Yet economic
development was also influenced by factors that had a negative effect
on overall productivity. In the early years of the war, the consumer goods
sector of the economy shifted production to meet the demands of the
military but not wholly so. The slow growth in armaments and the lack
of restructuring of industry reflects the continuity with the pre-war period.
This was dictated by the political priorities of a regime brought to power
on the back of socio-economic turmoil and wishing to avoid its repetition
at all costs. As has been shown, there was a conflict between the impulses
of an ideologically destructive regime and one in need of economic growth
to survive. So from 1942 the economy, and industry in particular,
underwent a rationalisation process that made it more productive.
However, the fundamental problem was the lack of raw materials and
labour. It is the greatest irony of the Second World War that while the
Nazi regime scoured Europe looking for labour, it was in the process of
murdering six million Jews.

SKILLS BUILDER

In not more than 200
words, explain why
the labour shortage in
Germany in the war
years was not solved
by recruitment of
women workers.

SKILLS BUILDER

Using all of the
relevant information
in the unit thus far,
identify the strengths
and weakness of
the German war
economy. Write down
your ideas on a table
in points. You may
wish to work with
another member of
your group in the
completion of this
task.

The Final Solution

Introduction

The historian Joachin Fest wrote in his book about Nazi Germany *The Face of the Third Reich*, published in 1970:

> At the core of National Socialism, the foundation of its own belief and superiority and at the same time the 'state philosophy' of the Third Reich, lay the idea of race.

The creation of a racially 'pure' Germany lay at the heart of Hitler's world view and vision for a New Germany. That this 'vision' ultimately led to systematic mass murder on a scale hitherto unimaginable will be explained in this section of the unit. The central importance of racial policy means that it was a central theme in the process of the regime's radicalisation and increasingly dominated Nazi domestic policy. The manner in which racial policy initiatives emerged and were implemented give us the clearest examples of how the Nazi state operated (as was explained in Unit 8).

The prophecy

Central to Hitler's world view was the destruction of the power of **International Jewry** and a titanic military struggle to win the Aryan people living space. To Hitler, these themes were bound up with each other. On 30 January 1939, Hitler spoke to a packed and expectant Reichstag. In his speech he revealed the link that he made between war and racial struggle:

> I want today to be a prophet again: if international finance inside and outside Europe should succeed in plunging the nations once more into a world war, the result will not be the bolshevisation of the earth and thereby the victory of Jewry, but the annihilation of the Jewish race in Europe.

In his speech Hitler used the word *Vernichtung*, which translates into English as 'annihilation'. It should not be automatically assumed that, by this, Hitler had already planned the Final Solution. The conditions for the Final Solution, the circumstance of war, the invasion of Russia, the lawlessness of the conquered territories, local initiatives and population movement, did not yet exist. But the significance of this speech should not be overlooked; for Hitler the prophet, these words signalled the consequences of the ultimate struggle between International Jewry and the Aryan world. It was a struggle that he felt was inevitable and one for which he ultimately took responsibility.

However, there was never a plan, a blueprint for the annihilation of Germany's Jews. Nor was there a coherent policy to deal with the Jewish Question at any point in the 1930s. Indeed, policy was uneven and was often made in response to events. It also was framed in response to the demands of the rank and file Nazi party and SA members who constituted a radical impetus from below. As you read in Unit 8, pages 189–195,

Definition

International Jewry

The idea of anti-Semites such as Hitler that there was a worldwide conspiracy of Jews who wished to take over the world and destroy the Aryan people.

during the first few years of the regime, official anti-Semitism was limited by the need to ensure economic recovery and maintain the veneer of legality both at home and abroad. It is important to show how the murderous plan to wipe out the Jews of Europe emerged because the events show clearly how the Jewish policy of the Nazi state was made in an ad hoc fashion.

Persecution of Germany's Jews

The start of the war led to a further tightening of restrictions on the Jews. On 1 September a curfew was introduced for all Jews, and on 21 September Reinhard Heydrich ordered the concentration of Jews around railway junctions. At the same time, all radio sets were confiscated from Jews in Germany. The relentless policy of separating the Jews from mainstream German society continued. In January 1940 all ration books belonging to Jews were to be stamped with a capital 'J'. The aim was to identify Jews and ensure that they did not claim goods barred to Jews, such as leather. On 1 September 1941 all Jews were ordered to wear a Star of David badge; failure to do so would lead to immediate arrest and imprisonment. The Nazi obsession with identifying who was a Jew for purposes of persecution continued throughout the war. The persecution was relentless, often focusing on seemingly trivial issues; for example, in November 1942 a law was passed stating that Jews could no longer receive the Reich sports medal. All this was happening while mass murder had already begun in the East. The final humiliation for many German Jews was in April 1943 when they finally lost their German citizenship.

Case study: Victor Klemperer

On the outbreak of war, Victor Klemperer was a retired Jewish professor of French at the University of Dresden. Married to a non-Jew, Eva, Klemperer had been increasingly discriminated against since the Nazis took power in 1939. Victor kept a diary that, at regular intervals, he gave to a non-Jewish friend for safe keeping. These diaries have become the most vivid source of information about the day-to-day life of Jews in Nazi Germany. In 1940 Victor and Eve were forced from their home and made to share an overcrowded Jews' House (a house specially designated for Jews to live in). For carelessly forgetting to black out his window at night, Victor was imprisoned in June 1941. In September he and his wife were forced to put on the Star of David, and the following month his typewriter was confiscated. Jews started to be deported east, but Klemperer was saved by the fact that he had been awarded the Iron Cross First Class (Germany's highest military decoration) in the First World War and by the fact that his wife was not a Jew. However, by mid-1942 he and his wife were reduced to begging because the rations for Jews were so small, and the Jews' House in which they lived was frequently ransacked by the Gestapo.

In February 1945 Victor and Eva were told that the Jews' House was to be evacuated, although neither of their names appeared on the list of those to be deported. However, just before the evacuation was due to take place, Dresden was bombed. Victor Klemperer tore the Star of David off his coat and fled into the countryside where he was given shelter by a former domestic servant. After the war he and his wife returned to Dresden and he was restored to the status of Professor at the University of Dresden. Eva died in 1951 but Victor married again. He died in 1959 but it was not until the 1990s and after the fall of the Berlin Wall and the end of the communist East Germany that his second wife published the diaries.

In May 1942 when it was clear that all Jews in Germany were threatened by deportation, Klemperer wrote in his diary:

> But I shall go on writing, this is my heroism. I intend to bear witness, precise witness.

Turning points

September 1939

The advent of war in September 1939 was another crucial turning point in Nazi racial policy. Over the next four years the circumstance emerged in which the central point of Hitler's ideology – the removal of Jews from Germany and the destruction of the supposed power of International Jewry – could take place. The successful conquest of Poland in 1939 and then much of western Europe in 1940 brought millions more Jews under direct Nazi rule. The concentration of Jews in specified areas began early in the war. On 30 October 1939 Himmler ordered the deportation of Jews from the parts of Poland now incorporated into the Reich to the General Government (German-occupied Poland), which was administered by Hans Frank. In January 1940 Jews were used for slave labour and confined to ghettos in the previously Polish towns of Lodz, Warsaw, Lublin, Radom and Lvov.

Summer 1940

From the start of the war to the end of 1940, the Final Solution to the Jewish Question in the minds of most leading Nazis was to be a territorial one. By the summer of 1940, Richard Heydrich was suggesting that the three and a quarter million Jews under German control should be moved to a suitable territory. The response of the Jewish section of the Foreign Office was to suggest Madagascar. Hitler was openly enthusiastic about such a scheme and mentioned it to the Italian leader Benito Mussolini in June 1940. Such a plan was, in reality, a plan of annihilation; it was clear that Madagascar could not sustain the Jewish population of Europe and that most would perish during transportation or in the following months due to lack of food. The weakness of the plan was that it relied on the defeat of the British and on German control of the high seas.

June 1941

The invasion of the Soviet Union in June 1941 further increased the number of Jews under Nazi control. The invasion of Russia had raised the possibility of relocating Europe's Jews to the other side of the Urals, but, again, the plan relied on military victory. Far from being a stage on the route to the Holocaust, the invasion of Russia was an important reason for its implementation. Nazi propaganda relentlessly insisted that war with Russia was a 'racial war', but this focus was intended to convince an increasingly anxious public of the justification for the invasion. It should be remembered that Hitler's driving ambitions throughout his career were the destruction of communism and the conquest of *Lebensraum* (living space) in the East. The destruction of the Jews was a consequence of this policy. As in Poland two years before, the conquest of Russia brought contact with Orthodox Jews condemned as sub-human by racist extremists within the SS. In June, as Nazi troops swept across the western Soviet Union, SS *Einsatzgruppen* were authorised by Hitler to exterminate Jews in Russia. Eight months later 700,000 Jews had been murdered.

> **Definition**
>
> *Einsatzgruppen*
>
> Special groups of soldiers whose job it was to shoot Jews and hunt out partisans.

Autumn 1941

But even in September 1941 the Nazi regime was undecided about the fate of Europe's Jews. Shooting Jews, which had been the preferred option up to this point, was not a realistic option for the millions more Jews of German-dominated Europe because it was messy. Deporting Jews east beyond the Urals would have to wait until after the expected victory over the Soviet Union. Up to September 1941, Hitler dithered about the fate of the Jews, seeing them as potential pawns/hostages in any future dealings with the USA. The important turning point seems to have been in mid-September when Hitler changed his attitude for two main reasons:

- In August 1941 Stalin had ordered the deportation to Siberia of 600,000 ethnic Germans whose families had lived in the Volga region for generations. A further 400,000 were to follow.
- Hitler's fury at Stalin's order was matched by his response to Roosevelt's order on 11 September 1941 that the US navy should shoot on sight at any German warships considered as threatening.

Deportations

As summer turned to autumn on the eastern front the German advance slowed, and Hitler realised he could not wait until 1942 to deal with the Jewish Question. Conditions in the east, however, led to pressure for action. After its conquest, part of Poland was divided into regions known as *Gau*. All the *Gauleiter* were anxious to remove the Jews from their territories. However, as one *Gauleiter* deported the Jews of his *Gau* to the east, so another found his *Gau* with a greater number of Jews.

- By late 1941 the pressure came from *Gauleiter* in the west, including Goebbels, that they be allowed to deport their Jews. This initiative in turn triggered demands from *Gauleiter* in the east, such as Arthur Greiser of the Warthegau, for permission to take more radical action, i.e. extermination.

- On 16 September Hitler and Himmler met for lunch to discuss deportations. In mid-September the order was given for the deportations to the east; so, for example, on 18 September Arthur Greiser received a letter from Himmler outlining the deportations of Jews from Bohemia and Moravia to the Warthegau. This measure would be followed by deportations further eastwards at a later date.

This was, according to Ian Kershaw in *Nemesis* (published in 2000) 'the trigger to a crucial phase in the gradual emergence of a comprehensive programme for genocide'. Kershaw argues that the decision to deport to the east brought the Final Solution a massive step further.

However, Hitler's agreement to deportation of the Jews to the east was not tantamount to a decision for the Final Solution. What it did was lead to new initiatives from numerous local and regional Nazi leaders. In some areas in Poland, the order to deport eastwards led to local initiatives; for example, in October in Lublin, the Police Chief Globocnik ordered the construction of gassing facilities at a camp at Belzec for killing Jews incapable of work. In Lodz Jews were being shot and gassed in vans in the same month. In December 1941 gas vans began their work of killing 100,000 Jews of the Warthegau at Chelmno. Central policy was partly made in response to events taking place on the ground:

- In October the Gestapo chief, Heinrich Müller, published Himmler's order that no Jew could now emigrate from the Reich.

- On 21 November and in response to Goebbels's prompting, the Führer demanded an 'aggressive policy' to rid Berlin of Jews. Goebbels-inspired propaganda stirred up anti-Jewish hatred; for example, an article in *Das Reich* entitled 'The Jews are Guilty' explicitly spoke about the prophecy of the 'annihilation of the Jewish race in Europe'.

- In late November invitations were issued for a conference to discuss the Jewish Question to be held at Wannsee. Hinrich Lohse, the Commissioner for Ostland who had ordered the gassing of Jews in October concluded that by November 'the Jewish Question has probably been clarified by verbal discussions'. However, confusion persisted into November as 5,000 German Jews were shot in Lithuania while in Lodz the Germans were worrying about the sanitary conditions in the ghetto.

December 1941

The final turning point was the declaration of war against the USA on 11 December 1941. This, in Hitler's mind, had brought about the war mentioned as part of his 'prophetic speech' to the Reichstag of 30 January 1939. On 12 December he addressed a gathering of *Reichsleiter* and *Gauleiter* evoking his 'prophecy'. On 18 December Hitler told Himmler that the Jews were to be 'exterminated as partisans'. As Russian Jews were already being shot this could only mean the authorisation for the extermination of all European Jews. This meeting was critical in resolving any further doubt.

The ruthless enforcement of the Final Solution from January 1942 and the huge logistic effort required to sustain it as Germany began to lose the war suggests that by then a decisive clarification policy had been made.

Wannsee Conference

The next key stepping stone on the road to the Final Solution was the Wannsee Conference of 20 January 1942. The conference was chaired by Reinhard Heydrich, who attempted to coordinate the various arms of the Nazi government into an agreement about the steps that were to be taken next. At Wannsee the State Secretary of the Government General, Josef Bühler, asked that his area should have its Jews 'removed' as quickly as possible. By the spring of 1942 work began on the construction of the extermination centres of Sobibor, Belzec and Treblinka. By this point it is clear that a systematic programme for the annihilation of Europe's Jews had been formed. In the next few months German Jews were deported to the ghettos in the east and then on to the death camps of Belzec, Treblinka, Sobibor, Majdanek and Auschwitz.

Extermination

As the network of concentration camps spread, there were those within the SS such as Oswald Pohl who wished to exploit fully the labour resource at hand. Pohl was in charge of the development of the WVHA, which was the economic administration section of the SS. By 1942, he had control of 20 concentration and 165 labour camps. He envisaged a role for the camps akin to the **gulag** in the Soviet Union. Similarly, those with the responsibility for the administration of the territories in the east, such as *Gauleiter* Wilhelm Kube, argued that the export of labour to the fatherland had left them with a labour shortage of their own which could only be filled by the Jews. A compromise was for the SS to employ Jewish labour in and around the concentration camps – but to work them to death. German industry systematically exploited Jewish labour throughout the war; for example, IG Farben used labour at the huge Monowitz-Buna complex near Auschwitz. But the main industry was that of death. The figures for the transportation and systematic annihilation of Europe's Jewish population are vast. At the largest extermination camp, Auschwitz, over a million were murdered. At Treblinka, which was also in Poland, 800,000 were murdered; at Sobibor 300,000 died. What is clear is that even as late as July 1944 when resources were hard pressed, Adolf Eichmann clearly had priority to use the railways to transport Jews to their death, in this case from Hungary. The pursuit of the Final Solution clarifies the relationship between ideological considerations and the demands of the economy for labour and materials. There is little doubt that conquest in search for the latter was the means by which Hitler's *Weltanschauung* (world view) could be realised. By the time Auschwitz was liberated by Soviet troops in January 1945 approximately 6 million Jews had been murdered.

SKILLS BUILDER

1 There has been a lot of information to take in. From 1939 to late 1941, there is a radicalisation of anti-Semitic action. With a work partner, identify five reasons for that radicalisation.

2 What do you think is the most significant turning point on the road to the Final Solution? Explain your answer fully.

Biography

Adolf Eichmann

Eichmann was head of the innocuously named Department IV B2 of the RSHA, which was the chief administrative office of the SS. Department IV was the state police (the Gestapo), and the sub-section IV B2 was devoted to Jewish affairs.

Definition

Gulag

The vast Soviet prison system that was mainly located in Siberia. Prisoners were used as slave labour although many died because of the brutality of the system.

SKILLS BUILDER

Using information from this unit and from Unit 8, answer the following question:

'The Final Solution was mainly the product of short-term rather than long-term factors.'

To what extent do you agree with this judgement?

Here is a tip: it is best to use the start of the war in 1939 as the cut-off point between long-term and short-term factors.

The Final Solution: conclusion

In his diaries in March 1942, Goebbels described a 'fairly barbaric procedure' taking place in the east. He had been important, as had Heydrich, in the process of radicalisation of anti-Semitic policy. In the fulfilment of the Final Solution, complicity was huge, from the army to a civil service as willing as ever to 'work towards the Führer'. Hitler's role was in authorising more than directing but also decisive and indispensable. Part of the pressure for 'a solution' came from below; for example, Hans Frank, the *Gauleiter* of the General Government, was increasingly concerned that his area of the Nazi Empire was being used by Heydrich as a dumping ground for Jews. The Final Solution was the worst example of how thousands had become trapped in 'working towards the Führer', even if it meant selling their soul. In his conclusion to *The Third Reich: A New History* (published in 2000), Michael Burleigh wrote that the Nazi leaders:

> embodied the negation of everything worthwhile about being human; their followers demeaned and shamed themselves.

Unit summary

What have you learned in this unit?

Throughout most of the Second World War, morale held up well on the German Home Front. However, it was dented by military reverses, the prospect of defeat and bombing. But the Home Front did not collapse as in the First World War. Opposition was limited despite the realisation from 1943 onwards that Germany was heading for defeat. The opposition that did exist was divided, lacked leadership and was ruthlessly suppressed. Those who were in a position to form effective opposition to the Nazis failed to act decisively until late in the war. The war economy was not fully mobilised until 1942. Reforms introduced by Albert Speer added greater efficiency, but the war economy was hampered by lack of labour and raw materials throughout. The Final Solution was the result of numerous agencies working towards a Führer who had at the very heart of his world view a desire to see the removal of Jews from Germany and the destruction of International Jewry. The process of radicalisation, which sped up in the context of wartime, led to ever more murderous initiatives from above and below.

What skills have you used in this unit?

You have come to a number of decisions that have clarified your understanding of many issues. You have prioritised the importance of factors and you have made judgements that you have had to justify.

Exam style question

This is the sort of question you will find appearing on the examination paper as a Section A question:

'Systematic extermination emerged as the Final Solution to the Jewish Question as a result of the chaotic nature of the Nazi state.'

How far do you agree with this opinion?

SKILLS BUILDER

1 **Discussion point**

In groups, discuss the following question:

'Why was there so little opposition to the Nazi state in Germany during the Second World War?'

2 **Hitler's role**

Having studied how the Nazi state operates and the events in the evolution of the Final Solution, how would you summarise Hitler's role and that of his leading lieutenants including Himmler, Heydrich, Goebbels and Göring?

3 **Research**

Of Europe's approximately 11 million Jews in 1939, 6 million were murdered as part of the Final Solution. Many people's lives were touched by the events. Here are the names of just five of them:

- Anne Frank
- Petr Ginz
- Primo Levi
- Raoul Wallenberg.

In order to understand the Final Solution, you should try to research as much as you can about these individuals, their lives and their deaths.

Exam zone

Relax and prepare

Hot tips: what other students have said

From AS to A2 level

- Start reading around the topics studied in class as early as possible. Reading helped me understand how historians present their arguments and use evidence. There is plenty of material about Germany in the first half of the twentieth century to read.

- A2 level History seems like a big step up at first, with more demands made on independent reading and more complex source passages to cope with. However by the end of the first term I felt as if my written work had improved considerably.

- I do try to find out information from websites. It is sometimes hard to tell which websites might be useful to look at but I have become better at ensuring I know who has produced the site so that I can evaluate its material. Many universities have useful websites.

- The more practise source-based questions I attempted, the more confident I became and quite quickly I picked up the necessary style and technique required for success.

- Don't get flustered or panic. Ask your teacher if you are not sure. History teachers aren't that scary!

What I wish I had known at the start of the year

- I used the Student Book a lot during the revision period to learn the key facts. I really wished that I had used it from the beginning of the course in order to consolidate my class notes.

- I wish that I had taken more time reading and noting other material such as the photocopied handouts issued by my teacher. Reading around the subject and undertaking independent research would have made my understanding more complete and made the whole topic more interesting.

- It helps if you annotate your notes and reading material as you go. This makes your reading more active and therefore more useful.

- A level History is not just about learning the relevant material but also developing the skills to use it effectively. I wished that I had spent more time throughout the year practising source questions to improve my style and technique.

- I wish I had paid more attention to the advice and comments made by my teacher on the written work I had done. This would have helped me to improve my marks throughout the year.

How to revise

- I started my revision by buying a new folder and some dividers. I put all my revision work into this folder and used the dividers to separate the different topics. I really took pride in my revision notes and made them as thorough and effective as I could.

- Before I started the revision process, I found it helpful to plan out my history revision. I used the Edexcel specification given to me by my teacher as a guideline of which topics to revise and I ticked off each one as I covered it.

- I found it useful to revise in short, sharp bursts. I would set myself a target of revising one particular topic in an hour and a half. I would spend one hour taking revision notes and then half an hour testing myself with a short practise question or a facts test.

- Planning answers to key questions is helpful because it saves time later.

- I found it useful to always include some practise work in my revision. If I could get that work to my teacher to mark, all the better, but just attempting questions and setting time limits helped me improve my technique.

- Sometimes I found it helpful to revise with a friend. We might spend 45 minutes revising by ourselves and then half an hour testing each other. Often we were able to sort out any problems between us and it was reassuring to see that someone else had the same worries and pressures at that time.

Refresh your memory: revision checklist

The following provides a useful list for checking the information you need to revise for your exam.

Unit 1: What were the main issues in the Second Reich, 1900–14?

- The constitution of the Second Reich.
- The relative powers of the Kaiser, Chancellor and *Reichstag*, and how their relationships might be illustrated.
- Social and political divisions in the Second Reich at the beginning of the twentieth century.
- The economic and social changes of the years 1900–14 and the impact of these changes on politics and political parties.

Unit 2: Controversy: to what extent was Germany responsible for the outbreak of the First World War in 1914?

- German foreign policy c.1900–14.
- The controversy surrounding Germany's 'war guilt'.

Unit 3: What was the impact of the First World War on Germany, 1914–18?

- The social and economic effects of the struggle on Germany.
- The changing political climate from the *Burgfrieden* of 1914 to the mounting opposition to war in 1917–18.

- The impact of the conflict on the domestic situation; particularly the dramatic changes of 1918.

Unit 4: What were the problems faced by the Weimar Republic, 1919–23?

- The Weimar constitution and its supporters and opponents.
- Social, economic and political problems of 1919–23.
- The beginnings of relative stabilisation achieved in 1923.

Unit 5: How stable were the 'Stresemann Years' of the Weimar Republic, 1924–29?

- Economic, social and cultural developments 1924–29.
- The roles and significance of Stresemann and Hindenburg.
- The domestic impact of international relations.

Unit 6: What are the reasons for the rise of the Nazi Party, 1920–33?

- The birth and development of the Nazi Party before 1928.
- The reasons for its transformation between 1928 and 1930.
- The social, economic and political developments between 1930 and 1933 which led to Hitler's appointment as Chancellor in January 1933.
- The growth and consolidation of dictatorship in the first six months of 1933.

Unit 7: Controversy: how popular was the Nazi regime in the years 1933–39?

- The degree of consent the Nazi regime enjoyed.
- The extent to which consent was dependent on terror and repression.

Unit 8: Controversy: how effectively did the Nazi state operate from 1933 to 1939?

- The Nazi State was considered a chaotic 'polycracy'.
- The role of the Fuhrer.
- Cumulative radicalisation.

*Unit 9: What was life like in wartime
Germany, 1939–45?*

- The morale of the populace.
- The efficiency or otherwise of war production.
- Repression of dissent and opposition.
- The evolution of the 'Final Solution'.

This revision checklist is very knowledge-based.
Don't forget that in Section B of the examination
your skills in handling sources will also be tested.

Result

You have spent a lot of time working on plans and
constructing answers to the Section A and Section
B questions. So you now have a pretty good idea
about how to plan an answer and write a response
to the question of the examination paper. But what
are the examiners looking for? And what marks
will you get?

About the exam

As part of your A2 Level History course you are
required to carry out an in-depth study; in this
instance **From Kaiser to Führer: Germany
1900–45**. You will be required to gain a firm
understanding of the chronology of the topic and
of the key issues, problems and debates associated
with it. You will also be required to explore the
nature of challenges and conflict both within the
period and relating to the societies and political
systems studied, and will do this by working with
secondary sources that provide differing views
about historical controversies.

At the end of your A2 course you will take a
written exam and you will need to answer two
questions. The sources will be supplied with the
paper.

- In Section A you will need to reach a
  substantiated judgement on an historical issue
  or problem. You will have a choice of two
  questions, and this question will be worth
  30 marks.

- In Section B you will need to compare source
  material to explore an issue of historical debate,
  reaching a substantiated judgement using your
  own knowledge. There will be a choice of two
  questions and this question will be worth 40 marks.

The exam will last two hours. Make sure you plan
your time carefully and allow enough time to
answer both questions thoroughly.

Section A

These essay questions, from which you will choose
one to answer, will have an analytical focus that
will require you to reach a substantiated judgement
on an historical issue or problem. For example,
questions are likely to be worded with the
instruction 'how far/to what extent . . .' and to be
followed by either a statement or an interpretation
that you are asked to weigh up.

Section B

In this section you will be provided with five or six
secondary sources that total about 350–400 words.
You will then have to answer one question from a
choice of two. Each question will ask you to discuss
two or three of the sources while exploring an
issue of historical debate, and to reach a
substantiated judgement based on the sources and
your own knowledge.

Questions are likely to be worded with the
instruction 'How far do you agree with the view
that . . .' You will also be instructed to 'Explain your
answer using the sources and your own knowledge
of the issues related to this controversy'.

Section A

What will you have to do, and what marks will you
get for doing it?

This question tests your ability to recall, select and
deploy information and your ability to understand
key concepts and features. There are 30 marks
available for this section. You will be working at
one of five levels. Try to get as high up in the
levels as you can.

Level 1

1–6 marks

- **You are able to** produce a series of simple
  statements.

Knowledge will be generalised with few examples.
The answer will not be made relevant to the question.

Level 2

7–12 marks

- **You are able to** produce answers with some development using examples.

The range of examples is likely to be limited. There may be some attempt to link the material to the question but it will not be made explicit.

Level 3

13–18 marks

- **You are able to** produce an answer that shows an understanding of the question and what it is getting at.

The answer will, however, drift into irrelevance at times or be based on material which although developed in places is limited in its range.

Level 4

19–24 marks

- **You are able to** produce an analytical answer that shows a clear understanding of the focus of the question.

The answer is drawing out key points with detailed knowledge used to develop an argument. There may still be some drifting from the specific question or a lack of balance with some aspects dealt with briefly but the answer shows some attempt to evaluate the evidence used in the argument.

Level 5

25–30 marks

- **You are able to** produce a sustained analytical answer.

The answer is a well-structured argument that discusses the evidence used to support/reject/modify the statement in the question. The answer evaluates the evidence for the argument.

Now try this question

'The weaknesses of the Weimar Constitution explain the failures of the Weimar Republic in the period 1929 to 1933.'

How far do you agree with this judgement?

GUIDANCE NOTES

Remember that in order to weigh up a statement or interpretation you need to look at the following:

- Explain the statement/interpretation.
- Outline the evidence that could be used to support the statement/interpretation and discuss its validity.
- Outline the evidence that could be used to reject/modify the statement/interpretation and comment on its validity.
- Come to a developed, reasoned judgement that presents your own argument.

The best answers will show that they have thought seriously about the issue/problem and have a well-supported, reasoned argument of their own in relation to the question they have been asked.

This argument will be SUSTAINED i.e. be present from the introduction to the conclusion. Therefore special care is needed when you write your introduction.

The argument will be based on sustained CRITICAL EVALUATION of the evidence. This will require you to discuss the value of the evidence rather than just list the evidence itself.

Now use the marking criteria to assess your response.

How did you do?

What could you have done to achieve higher marks?

The examiners will not be nit-picking their way through your answer, ticking things off as they go. Rather, they will be looking to see which levels best fit your response, and you should do the same when assessing your own responses.

Section B

What will you have to do, and what marks will you get for doing it?

This section tests your ability to recall, select and deploy information and to understand key concepts and features. This objective carries 16 marks. You are also being tested for your ability to analyse and evaluate differing interpretations in relation to their historical context. This objective carries 24 marks. Thus, Section B has a total of 40 marks. You will be working at one of five levels. Try to get as high up in the levels as you can. The examiners will be marking your answer twice: once for knowledge and a second time for source evaluation.

This is what the examiners will be looking for as they mark the ways in which you have selected and used your knowledge to answer the question:

Level 1
1–3 marks
- **You are able to** produce a series of simple statements.

Knowledge will be generalised with few examples. The answer will not be made relevant to the question. Links to the sources will be few or indirect.

Level 2
4–6 marks
- **You are able to** produce answers with some development using examples.

The range of examples is likely to be limited and this may be linked to the sources. There may be some attempt to link the material to the question but it will not be made explicit.

Level 3
7–10 marks
- **You are able to** produce an answer that shows an understanding of the question and what it is getting at.

There will be some links between own knowledge and the sources. The answer will, however, drift into irrelevance at times or be based on material which although developed in places is limited in its range.

Level 4
11–13 marks
- **You are able to** produce an analytical answer that shows a clear understanding of the focus of the question.

The answer will draw out key points with detailed knowledge used to support analysis of the sources. There may still be some drifting from the specific question or a lack of balance, with some aspects dealt with briefly, but the answer shows some attempt to evaluate the evidence used in the argument.

Level 5
14–16 marks
- **You are able to** produce a sustained analytical answer.

The answer is a well-structured argument that discusses the evidence used to support/reject/modify the statement in the question. The answer evaluates the evidence for the argument.

This is what the examiners will be looking for as they mark your source evaluation skills:

Level 1
1–4 marks
- **You are able to** understand the sources at face value and use them to identify points.

There will be no integration of the sources with each other or with own knowledge – they will be treated singly and separately when a conclusion is reached.

Level 2
5–9 marks
- **You are able to** understand the sources and can use them to develop points relevant to the question.

The answer will link together some of the material from the sources. It will reach a judgement based on limited support from the sources.

Level 3
10–14 marks
- **You are able to** interpret the evidence from the sources drawing out key points from the evidence in the sources.

The answer will develop points that both support and challenge the interpretation under discussion and shows an awareness of the nature of the debate that the interpretation relates to.

The answer may well be unbalanced with not all aspects covered but there is a clear attempt to reach a reasoned answer supported by information and argument from the sources.

Level 4

15–19 marks

- **You are able to** interpret the sources with confidence, showing an understanding of the basis of the arguments offered in the sources.

The answer will relate the interpretations offered by the sources to their wider context by using own knowledge to discuss the arguments presented. Judgements will be reached that integrate the sources and own knowledge to support a well-developed and sustained argument.

Level 5

20–24 marks

- **You are able to** produce a sustained evaluation of the sources to present a fully-reasoned argument.

The interpretations offered by the sources are discussed and evaluated with the validity of the interpretation assessed by reference to own knowledge. Sources and own knowledge are effectively integrated to address the full demands of the question.

Don't forget to take care with your English. The quality of your communication can be used by the examiner to decide which mark to give you within a level. Quality of communication is about more than spelling. It is about whether your answer is well-structured, with paragraphs and clear sentences.

Now try this question

Use Sources 1, 2 and 3 and your own knowledge.

'The outbreak of war in August 1914 was the ultimately the result of decisions made by the German military.'

How far do you agree with this opinion? Explain your answer, using the evidence of Sources 1, 2 and 3 and your own knowledge of the issues related to this controversy.

Source 1

Given these indications that the war would not be localised, there were ample opportunities for Germany to back down. Yet the initial British peace keeping initiatives were given only the most insincere support by Germany. The Germans pressed on, urging the Austrians to make haste, and after 26 July openly rejecting diplomatic alternatives. Only at the eleventh hour did they begin to lose their nerve; the Kaiser first, on 28 July, and then Bethmann who, after hearing of Grey's warning of the 29th to the Germany ambassador [in London] frantically sought the Austrians to apply the brakes. Berchtold tried to respond; but it was the German military which ultimately secured, by a combination of persuasion and defiance, the mobilisation orders, the ultimata and declarations of war which unleashed the conflict.

From *The Pity of War* by Niall Ferguson, published in 1998

Source 2

Thus to the general necessity inherent in the Schlieffen Plan for the violation of Belgian neutrality and offensive action as soon as possible after mobilisation, the attack on Liege required even more immediate action, since it was scheduled to take place on the third day of mobilisation with such troops as were immediately available. It was, therefore, as Molkte was to argue in a long meeting with Bethmann on the evening of 31 July 1914, essential to launch the attack in the west the moment Russia proclaimed mobilisation, so as to carry out the onslaught on France before Russian mobilisation was complete and before fighting began on the eastern front. And to launch the attack in the west, it was equally essential to capture Liege within three days. The attack on Belgium had therefore to be launched almost immediately after the proclamation of mobilisation and there was no margin for any delay between mobilisation and the start of hostilities. The Liege operation had been kept a deep secret, and it looks as though the Kaiser himself had not been told about it and that Bethmann only grasped its implications on 31 July. While the other powers could order mobilisation and wait what to do next, in the case of Germany mobilisation inevitably meant war.

From *The Origins of the First World War* by James Joll, published in 1984

Source 3

Above all, it is time once and for all to discard Lloyd George's wornout phrase that Europe 'slithered' into war in 1914. Great powers throughout history have rarely, if ever, 'slithered' into major wars; rather, they undertake this most difficult of human endeavours only after carefully weighing the advantages and disadvantages. In this sense and only in this sense can one speak of a 'calculated risk' in 1914.

From 'Industry, Empire and the First World War' by Holder H. Herwig in *Modern Germany Reconsidered, 1870–1945*, ed. Gordon Martel, published in 1992.

GUIDANCE NOTES

These questions can be quite challenging to answer because they require you to integrate the sources with your own knowledge whilst discussing and making a reasoned judgement on an interpretation. Key features of a good answer will include the following:

- A discussion of the issues raised by the sources that shows a clear understanding of the arguments they present.

- An integration of sources with own knowledge. Own knowledge will be used to test the validity of the views expressed in the sources.

- Relevant discussion of all aspects of the controversy raised in the question.

- A developed, reasoned judgement that presents your own argument in relation to the question.

As with answers in Section A the best answer will contain arguments that are SUSTAINED and include CRITICAL EVALUATION of the interpretation offered in the question.

Now use the marking criteria to assess your response.

How did you do?

What could you have done to achieve higher marks?

The examiners will not be nit-picking their way through your answer, ticking things off as they go.

Rather, they will be looking to see which levels best for your response, and you should do the same when assessing your own responses.

How will I time my responses?

You have two hours to answer two questions. Both Section A and Section B give you a choice of questions.

Take some time, about five minutes, to read the paper carefully and think about your choice of questions.

The Section A question carries 30 marks and the Section B carries 40. You should therefore aim to spend more time on the Section B question, about one hour and ten minutes, compared with about 50 minutes for Section A. Remember that this includes reading and planning time.

Always conclude each answer with your overall judgement so that your answer reads as a coherent response as a whole. This is important even if you find you have not got enough time to cover all aspects in the detail you wanted to.

You have now had a lot of practice in planning, writing and assessing your responses to the sort of questions you can expect to find on the examination paper. You are well-prepared and you should be able to tackle the examination with confidence.

Good luck!

Bibliography

General texts

Blackbourn, David, *The Blackwell Classic Histories of Europe History of Germany 1780–1918 The Long Nineteenth Century*, 2003

Craig, Gordon, *Germany 1866–1945*, 1978

Pre-1918

Chickering, Roger, *Imperial Germany and the Great War, 1914–1918*, 2004

Clark, Dr Christopher, *Kaiser Wilhelm (Profiles In Power)*, 2000

Ferguson, Niall, *The Pity of War*, 1998

Henig, Ruth, *The Origins of the First World War*, 1993

Joll, James, *The Origins of the First World War*, 1984

Martel, Gordon, *The Origins of the First World War*, 2003

Mommsen, Wolfgang J., *Imperial Germany, 1867–1918: Politics, Culture and Society in an Authoritarian State*, 1995

Wilson, Keith (editor), *Decisions for War*, 1995

Post-1914

Burleigh, Michael, *The Third Reich: A New History*, 2000

Evans, Richard, *The Coming of the Third Reich*, 2003

Evans, Richard, *The Third Reich in Power*, 2005

Evans, Richard, *The Third Reich at War: How the Nazis Led Germany from Conquest to Disaster*, 2008

Kershaw, Ian, *The Nazi Dictatorship: Problems and Perspectives of Interpretation*, 1985

Kershaw, Ian, *Hitler, 1889–1936: Hubris*, 1998

Kershaw, Ian, *Hitler, 1936–1945: Nemesis*, 2000

Kershaw, Ian, *The 'Hitler Myth': Image and Reality in the Third Reich*, 2001

Kolb, Eberhard, *The Weimar Republic*, 1992

Noakes, John and Pridham, Geoffrey, *Nazism 1919–1945, Volume One: The Rise to Power 1919–1934*, 1998

Noakes, John and Pridham, Geoffrey, *Nazism 1919–1945, Volume Two: State, Economy and Society 1933–1939*, 1998

Noakes, John and Pridham, Geoffrey, *Nazism 1919–1945, Volume Four: The German Home Front in World War II*, 1998

Weitz, Eric, *Weimar Germany: Promise and Tragedy*, 2009

Glossary

Anti-Semites People who stood on a platform that was anti-Jewish. Anti-Semitism at this moment in German history was popular at court and among some sections of German society. It was further stirred up in 1900 by the publication of Englishman Houston Stewart Chamberlain's book *The Foundations of the Nineteenth Century*, which described history as a struggle for supremacy between the German and Jewish races.

Anti-Socialist Laws Introduced in 1878. The laws banned socialist groups, meetings and publications. They were upheld by police surveillance and powers given to local authorities.

Attrition One side winning a war by wearing down the other side.

Axis A military alliance consisting of Germany, Italy and Japan.

Bilateral relations Negotiation agreements between two countries.

Bocage An area of pasture and woodland. It is typified by small fields, narrow side-roads and lanes with high banks and thick hedgerows either side.

Bohemian lifestyle A way of living that does not conform to normal patterns.

Burgfrieden Refers to a castle that is under siege when the defenders put all differences aside in the name of survival.

Carthaginian peace A peace settlement that is particularly harsh and designed to maintain the inferiority of the loser. It is named after Rome's defeat of Carthage in 202 BC and the subsequent humiliating settlement.

Coalition government Formed when no single party has an overall majority of seats in parliament. The parties have to negotiate with others to gain an overall majority and then share the responsibility of government.

Comintern An international communist organisation founded in Moscow in 1919 and dominated by the Soviet Union. It was also known as the Third International.

Conscripted To be compulsorily enlisted to work or fight for the government.

Constitution The set of rules by which a country is run. It is, at least in theory, supposed to reflect the values and traditions of that country. Sometimes a constitution is written; sometimes it is a collection of accepted traditions that are not written down.

Convoy system A system of grouping merchant ships carrying goods and providing warships to accompany them for protection.

Cumulative radicalisation In this context, the way in which state policy gradually became ever more extreme.

Diktat The Treaty of Versailles being dictated to Germany without negotiation.

Doppelverdiener 'Second earners' in English.

Dreikaiserbund The League of the three Emperors.

Edelweiss Pirates A diverse group that emerged on the outbreak of war. They were essentially dissenters who rejected the regimentation of the Hitler Youth. There was no national movement; the Pirates were based on local groups from the Navajos of Cologne to the Kittelbach Pirates of Oberhausen.

Einsatzgruppen Special groups of soldiers whose job it was to shoot Jews and hunt out partisans.

Entente French for 'understanding'. The term is used here because the agreements between Britain, France and Russia were more understandings than formal alliances.

Ersatz German for substitute.

Federal state A state that is made up of individual states that have control over certain aspects of internal affairs but are also part of a central state.

First past the post When the candidate in an election with the most votes wins the seat even if he or she has not got a majority of the votes cast.

Führerprinzip Established the complete authority of the leader, Hitler.

Fulfilment   Germany's policy of fulfilling the terms of the Versailles treaty so that the terms could be shown to be unjust and unworkable.

Gauleiter   Leaders of *Gaue* or districts.

Gestapo   The secret police force created in 1933.

Gleichschaltung   The coordination – the bringing into line – of different elements of German life.

Gulag   The vast Soviet prison system that was mainly located in Siberia. Prisoners were used as slave labour although many died because of the brutality of the system.

Habsburgs   The royal family of Austria-Hungary, one of the most important royal families in Europe.

Historiographical revolution   Turning points in the writing of history when new ideas are put forward that change how people think. These ideas can constitute a revolution in the writing of history.

Hottentot   The slang name used to describe the Khoikhoi peoples of southern Africa. It is now considered to be an offensive term to use.

Hyperinflation   Occurs when the amount of paper money in an economy increases and pulls prices up to the point where the spiral of printing money and price rises goes out of control.

Imperial flag   The black, red and white tricolour.

Industrial Revolution   Involved the transition to factory based manufacturing and was the most significant economic change of the nineteenth century.

Intentionalist historians   Historians who stress the importance of the intentions of individuals such as Hitler.

International Jewry   The idea of anti-Semites such as Hitler that there was a worldwide conspiracy of Jews who wished to take over the world and destroy the Aryan people.

Irredentist   The lands containing Italian speakers that many in Italy argued should belong to Italy.

Kreisleiter   The administrative rank below the *Gauleiter*, equivalent to rural council.

Kulturkampf   An attack on the Catholic Church from 1871 to 1878. It included the abolition of religious orders and the expulsion of the Jesuits.

Legislative power   The power to make laws.

Milliard   A thousand million, so 132 milliard gold marks is equivalent to 132,000,000,000, for example.

Mittelstand   The lower middle class.

Monocratic state   A state that is governed by one person.

Nazi movement   Not just the leadership and political party, the NSDAP, but the SA, SS and all other organisations including those representing young people and women.

Omnipotent   All powerful.

Ottoman Empire   The Turkish based empire that lasted from the thirteenth century to the twentieth century and, in its prime, controlled the Balkans region of Europe, the Middle East and North Europe.

Paganism   In this context, the belief in ancient non-Christian gods.

Parliamentary sovereignty   Parliament is the supreme legal body as defined by the constitution.

Passive resistance   The refusal to work or collaborate with the French and Belgian forces of occupation.

Place in the sun   A term used to describe the desire to have the same number of colonies as Britain and France.

Pogrom   An organised violent attack on an ethnic minority.

Polarisation   When politics on the left and right becomes more extreme.

Political nation   Refers to all of the political parties together.

Polonaise   A slow dance that consisted of a procession. It is not surprising that it became the nickname for the food queue.

Polycratic   When a system is multi-centred and power is decentralised.

Promulgate   To issue or to pass into the public domain.

Putsch   A takeover of power.

Reichsleitung   Reich leaders with specific responsibilities, such as the NSDAP's treasurer.

Reichswehr   The name given to the German armed forces from 1921 to 1935.

Revanche   The idea that one day France would be able to gain revenge for the events of the early 1870s. Although it did not remain the political priority for the next 40 years, *revanche* still had the power to stir French emotions.

SA   Stands for *Sturmabteilung* or storm troopers. They were the Nazi street fighters.

Scorched earth policy   The destruction by a retreating army of everything that might be used by an advancing army, such as food and raw materials.

Second Reich   Reich is German for the word state. The First Reich was the Holy Roman Empire. The Second Reich was established in 1871 and lasted until 1918.

Second Revolution   The implementation of a National Socialist agenda as outlined in the Twenty-Five Points programme of 1920.

Sphere of influence   An area in which one nation has control over another or others.

Stab in the back   The idea that Germany's armed forces had been undermined by politicians and others in Germany who wanted peace in late 1918.

Structuralist historians   Historians who place a greater emphasis on structures such as the structures of the state when explaining what has happened in the past.

Synthesis   Coming together of ideas.

Third Reich   Reich means 'state'. The First Reich referred to the Holy Roman Empire, the Second Reich to the period from 1871 to 1918, and the Third Reich to the period from 1933 to 1945.

Total war   The mobilisation of all resources within a nation, human and otherwise, for the war effort.

Volksgemeinschaft   The ideal of a national community based on racial identity. All those of Aryan background would belong; all non-Aryans would not.

Wehrmacht   Replaced *Reichswehr* as the name of Germany's armed forces from 16 October 1935.

Wilson's Fourteen Points   Revolved around the idea of self-determination for all nationalities and a 'just peace'.

Wolf's Lair   Hitler's military headquarters near what was Rastenburg in East Prussia. He spent a considerable amount of time there between June 1941 and November 1944.

Index

Page references in *italics* indicate illustrations.